The General Model of Working Capital Management

Rodrigo Zeidan

The General Model of Working Capital Management

palgrave
macmillan

Rodrigo Zeidan
NYU Shanghai
Shanghai, China

Fundação Dom Cabral
Nova Lima, Brazil

ISBN 978-981-19-3333-2 ISBN 978-981-19-3334-9 (eBook)
https://doi.org/10.1007/978-981-19-3334-9

This Palgrave Macmillan imprint is published by the registered company Springer Nature Singapore Pte Ltd.
The registered company address is: 152 Beach Road, #21-01/04 Gateway East, Singapore 189721, Singapore

Acknowledgments

This book wouldn't exist without a global pandemic and the upheaval it created. Without the energy to continue the myriad projects I was working on when the world came to a halt, I chose to focus on a single project and put all my energy into it. If you don't like the results you are holding in your hands (or seeing on your tablet), feel free to blame it on covid. Gladly, I had plenty of support during these challenging times, including that of Melissa Nogueira, who had to put up with my disappearance acts to focus on the manuscript. Bruce Crooker and Denby Liu have helped me retain my sanity; our weekly correspondence, now totaling more than 300,000 words, is one of the highlights of my week.

Joanna Waley-Cohen, Jeff Lehmann, Svetlana Fedoseeva, Marti Subrahmanyam, Paul Wachtel, and many others have taught me how to be a better teacher and researcher. Thomas Lindner is a co-author on a currently unpublished manuscript but generously allowed me to use our material in the book.

Finally, this work is dedicated to Michel Fleuriet, the most carioca of all French, a dear friend, co-author, and mentor who left us too soon.

Contents

List of Figures

List of Tables

1

Introduction

The book in your hands (or, most likely, your electronic device) is not the first or the last extensive study on working capital management, trade credit, and supply chain finance. There are dozens, if not hundreds, of such tomes around. However, this book is different. It is not distinct because academics must claim that their work is extraordinary to justify their hard work, but different because it is built on a unique combination of theory and practice that integrates otherwise disparate management areas. Or at least, that is what I hope.

For instance, the leading case study of the book involves a large listed company in which an intervention that I supervised helped generate over U$1 billion for shareholders. That is a bold claim, but the study was published in one of the top scientific finance journals globally, the Journal of Corporate Finance. In that article, there are four distinct methodologies to show, as much as something in social sciences can be demonstrated, that the working capital management project for MRV worked as intended, freeing over U$1 billion of working capital overinvestment.

The MRV case integrates distinct areas of knowledge. Working capital management is usually viewed as an accounting and finance subject. But inventory management and other parts of supply chain finance are related to operations and supply chain management (OSCM), or industrial engineering. Aspects of working capital are also tied to game theory and negotiations. Some areas of trade credit hark back to retail management, while

R. Zeidan, *The General Model of Working Capital Management*,
https://doi.org/10.1007/978-981-19-3334-9_1

essential strategic issues correspond to topics in business ethics and corporate social responsibility.

I aim to harmonize all these different approaches to working capital management into a coherent framework. It all starts with finance, though. Here, working capital management is bonded with cash flow management. Payments terms matter because capital is scarce. Inventory efficiency carries weight because there are significant opportunity costs to excessive inputs and unused raw material. Of course, cash flow management covers much more than trade credit and changes in working capital, but cash flow projections require a deep understanding of the financial cycle.

The major innovation of the book, in my opinion, is the treatment of working capital as a dynamic process. Unlike most textbooks, which build on first principles, in this book, trade credit, and working capital management are easier understood by analyzing already operating companies. Here, trade credit emerges from recurrent procurement, production, and sales processes; therefore, working capital becomes an investment similar to fixed assets. The implication is minimizing working capital metamorphoses into ongoing efforts; hence, usual metrics should be abandoned for company-specific managerial financial statements. Working capital dynamics also generate tension between cash-flow optimization and lending behavior. Firms with market power can extract resources from the supply chain, even achieving negative cash conversion cycles, or use their cash reserves or access to credit to lift cash flow restrictions for small suppliers or customers. Because firms may switch between these two types of behavior over time, there is no way to develop an unambiguous framework for working capital management. That poses a problem for a writer. After all, readers of technical books prefer univocal theories and models. Ambiguity can be frustrating. There is a famous (likely apocryphal) story in which American President Harry Truman exasperatedly requested: "Give me a one-handed economist. All my economists say 'on the one hand...', then 'but on the other..." Here, working capital management is a two-handed discipline. There are explicit concepts and models with context-independent conclusions, but working capital strategies are company-specific. Small and medium-sized companies are usually credit-constrained, and for many, payment terms management would be about freeing as much cash as possible. For other companies, trade credit can be used strategically for increasing market share or achieving higher profit margins.

Writing a textbook, which is not my first one, requires conscious decisions about the turns as the research road keeps forking in front of you. In the end, I chose long written explanations over dry algebra and myriad real-life case studies over made-up end-of-chapter exercises. Of course, there is still a fair bit of math in the book, but hopefully, the equations do not get in the way of understanding the material.

Many readers may wish to skip parts of the book. That is fine, as the manuscript was written in multiple levels, with some chapters light on math and others filled with equations. Thus, I also elected not to weed out the repetition of the central arguments regarding working capital management, which are sprinkled throughout the book.

There are many other critical choices. Maybe the essential one is about precision versus customization. Take the excellent books "Working capital management: strategies and techniques" by Hrishikes Bhattacharya and "Working Capital Management: Application and Cases" by James Sagner. Both authors painstakingly related the concepts of working capital management to financial statements. For instance, Bhattacharya and Sagner describe the relationship between cost accounting and working capital, omitted here. I choose to develop a comprehensive framework to allow managers to build their own working capital monitoring tools without relying solely on official financial statements.

Another departure from most other works is the many case studies regarding small and medium-sized companies in emerging markets, based upon two decades of executive education and consulting in Latin America, Africa, Europe, and Asia. Of course, I also include several studies of multinational corporations, such as Apple, Tesco, and H&M. Still, one big blind spot in the scientific literature regarding trade credit is that most empirical works on working capital use data from listed companies. However, most credit-constrained companies are small and medium-sized companies; working capital management is vital to their survival.

In addition, I take another unusual approach: the book is written for practitioners and students simultaneously. Usually, textbooks are geared towards academics, while popular versions of scientists' research are aimed towards laypersons. That is not the case here. I aim to write an accessible book for anybody interested in administering working capital and provide the formulas and details necessary for students to learn about the subject. The key for that framework is to divide the material into chapters with managerial lessons and formal modeling. Readers can skip some chapters without loss of generality. Also of note is that instructors can pick and choose chapters to complement other material in finance and management courses, such as Corporate Finance, Multinational Financial Management, International Finance, Corporate Social Responsibility, Operations Management, Supply-Chains, and more.

Another central theme throughout the book is that working capital management is connected to cash-flow management. After all, supply chain finance matters more to companies that need access to credit for some reason. Still, cash-flow management is more than optimizing trade credit, and not every aspect of short-term asset management is included in the book.

Finally, no finance textbook today would be complete without treatment of one of the biggest challenges to humankind: climate change. I have been lucky to have worked on significant projects on sustainable finance. I have helped develop a sustainability credit score system for a multinational bank (published as an academic study in the Journal of Business Ethics in 2015), and worked with NGOs and the Center for Sustainable Business at NYU Stern to develop new accounting methodologies. Supply chains have a prominent role to play in decarbonizing the economy. Trade credit policies (and regulations) can help us get to a less unsustainable future.

I hope you enjoy the book. It results from over a decade of research and consulting on the subject. It is certainly not the last word on the subject, but maybe it will be a helpful one.

2

Why the General Model of Working Capital Management? The U$1 Billion Question

"Nothing beats cold, hard cash." Working capital management is about cash-flow management. Companies that optimize their cash conversion cycle are looking to spend as little as possible to grow their operations. Working capital inefficiencies are meaningless for many companies, as access to credit and plentiful cash reserves allows executives to focus their attention elsewhere. However, most companies in the world are credit-constrained in some manner. Of the hundreds of millions of businesses globally, a few thousand may have enough cash reserves and access to credit to ignore the inefficient allocation of capital in the production process.

Working capital management combines finance, supply-chain logistics, operations management with some contract law, and human resources. Like many critical.

Even large companies can benefit from improved operations. We motivate the rest of the book by describing the basics of the case study on MRV, a large listed company. Changes in working capital management have liberated over U$1 billion trapped in disorganized operations. These savings could go directly to shareholders, increasing dividends by over U$100 million per year for decades, or managers could choose to invest the proceeds in the company's growth. For other companies, improving the management of the company's cash conversion cycle is the only way to keep the business afloat. Of course, few entities may have more than a billion dollars that could be freed by the lessons delineated throughout this work. Still, few managers

R. Zeidan, *The General Model of Working Capital Management*,
https://doi.org/10.1007/978-981-19-3334-9_2

wouldn't benefit from better efforts in reducing their companies' financial cycle. Without further ado, let's summarize the intervention at MRV.

2.1 MRV and the Billion-Dollar Gains

The case study of MRV is based on an intervention designed and implemented by Rafael Albuquerque, a finance executive at the company. The intervention formed the basis of his EMBA final project at Fundacao Dom Cabral, which I supervised. Rafael not only designed the project but oversaw its implementation. The documentation of his work's impact forms the basis for Zeidan and Shapir (2017), which uses publicly available data from the financial statements of MRV, a listed company.

MRV is a real estate developer in Brazil that specializes in residential housing. It focuses on building housing for low-income families, buoyed by a government program called "My Home, My Life" (MCMV in Portuguese). In 2015, the company built 2.1 million square meters and delivered 40,000 homes. Before 2006, the company averaged 3,000 units per year, increasing to 25,000 in 2007–2010 and more than 38,000 per year. When the project was designed, companies in that industry shared two characteristics: strong revenue growth and long economic cycles. MRV is an ideal case study to illustrate the importance of sound working capital management strategies because it needs to generate more cash for its growing investment opportunities. The firm's business model, like its competitors, is based on long operating cycles, which produces large working capital requirements. More importantly, the MCMV business model leads to a relatively stable operating margin, an ideal situation to highlight changes in working capital management not hampered by higher costs or lower sales. Moreover, external validity can be established by comparing it with its peers, all listed companies with available financial information and the same constraints as MRV.

In the MCMV model, sales can only begin after the project is incorporated, and construction follows a certain percentage of sales. There is also a gap between sales and the transfer of contracts from companies to final consumers. The outstanding sales cycle is tied to the unique business model of MCMV. Projects related to MCMV have an economic cycle of roughly five years. Figure 2.1 describes the cycle, which goes from purchase to registration, sales, and construction.

There is a long period from sales to cash flow; Caixa, the Brazilian state-owned bank responsible for financing MCMV consumers, only disburse funds after measuring the evolution of the construction, the last step in the

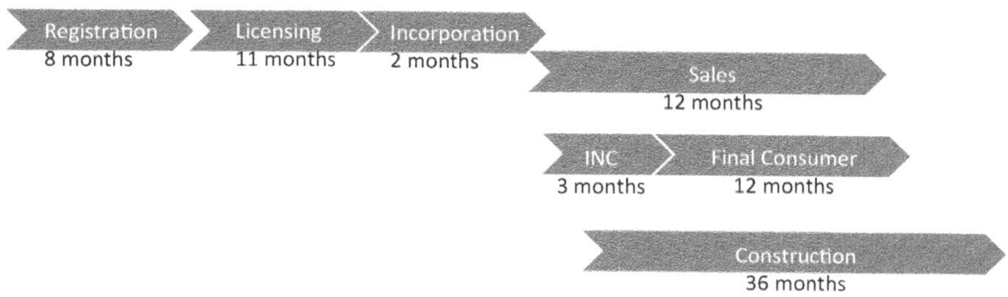

Fig. 2.1 MRV's economic cycle (*Source* Albuquerque (2014))

economic cycle. Securitizing receivables cannot shorten the outstanding sales cycle because of the regulated housing transfer to final consumers. This business model is related to how the government set up the subsidies for the MCMV program. Companies cannot change the model, but they can speed up the process, especially regarding registration and incorporation, sales, and contract registration with the financial institution.

The project's design happened in the early 2010s, and its implementation started in January 2013. The project had five phases: analysis of the company's data, benchmarking, simulation of possible gains, critical factors to reduce the CCC, and proposed actions. The project's final goal was straightforward: reduce the cash conversion cycle to a sustainable level. The faster the company could turn purchased land into apartments and the faster it could hand keys to customers, the quicker it could recoup its investments.

The cash conversion cycle is measured in days (in later chapters, there will be a formal definition for the concept). The components of the financial cycle are days sales outstanding (DSO), days inventory outstanding (DIO), and days payable outstanding (DPO). The interpretation of these components is as follows: DSO is the time it takes for a business to collect on sales; DIO is the period to turn inventories into final products. DPO is how long it takes for a company to pay its bills. For the first two, the shorter the period, the lower the amount of cash tied into the company's operations. For DPO, a more extended period is better, as it means that the company can hold on to its money for longer before settling its bills. The cash conversion cycle is:

$$\text{CCC} = \text{DSO} + \text{DPO} - \text{DIO}$$

Associated with this cycle is the company's total operating working capital, or the firm's amount to invest in supporting the lag between purchasing land and receiving the proceeds from selling the finished apartments.

Table 2.1 reports the data for the company in the years before the project began. The financial is particularly long, around 508 days in 2012. The values

Table 2.1 MRV's operating working capital, 2010/2012 (US$' 000)

	2010	2011	2012
DSO	389	419	440
DIO	227	244	280
DPO	134	174	212
CCC	482	489	508
OWC	1,994,655	2,689,540	2,647,035
Annual Revenue	1,510,475	2,007,530	1,901,905

Source Zeidan and Shapir (2017)

are converted at an exchange rate of BRL 2 per US$1, which is the average over 2010–2013.

Table 2.1 shows that the CCC increased during 2010–2012 from 482 to 508 days, although DPO increased sharply. There is a cyclical component of the behavior of the CCC; incorporating more units of subsidized housing, with its long economic cycle, can change the cycle over any short period.

How does MRV compare with its peers? Table 2.2 shows the CCC pattern for all listed MRV's competitors in the MCMV market. These companies have similar geographical dispersion, product portfolio composition, and history (all companies were listed in a three-year window, as shown in Fig. 2.2), among other characteristics.

As we can see from Table 2.2, every company, from medium-sized Even and Ez Tec to the most prominent companies such as PDG and Cyrela, had a long CCC, at least 362 days for the firm with the shortest CCC and up to 836 days for PDG. MRV's CCC (508 days) was below the market average (561 days). However, that was due to the longest DPO among its peers, 212 days. In fact, MRV's DIO (440 days) and DSO (280 days) were almost at the market average of 442 and 270 days, respectively.

Table 2.2 reports data for the CCC of MRV and its direct competitors, along with OWC, annual revenue, EBIT/Revenue, and Net Profits/Revenue.

The case of MRV was similar to those of other companies in the real estate and construction sectors for three reasons. First, all companies, including their direct competitors, follow similar economic cycles because of the business model imposed by the MCMV program. The requisites for sales and construction were identical. Thus the CCC varied across companies due to differences in the quality of inventory, how quickly each manages to turn over their stock, and each company's terms with suppliers. Second, companies grew at similar rates in the sample period. Finally, the quality of senior management in Brazilian companies was not very high then. The intervention at MRV was designed under the assumption that inefficiencies could be

Table 2.2 CCC and other financial measures, Brazilian companies, 2012 (US$' 000)

	MRV	Cyrela	Gafisa	Brookfield	PDG	Rodobens	Even	Ez Tec
DSO	440	386	354	485	644	386	339	506
DIO	280	251	240	359	382	157	177	329
DPO	212	198	142	202	190	181	66	88
CCC	508	439	452	642	836	362	450	747
OWC	2,647,035	3,383,908	1,736,856	2,406,621	5,000,311	476,505	293,110	647,127
Revenue	1,901,905	2,813,500	1,402,550	1,368,250	2,183,150	480,454	237,745	316,200
EBIT/Revenue	15%	16%	4%	-5%	−42%	16%	15%	39%
Profits/Revenue	13%	13%	−2%	−12%	−50%	11%	13%	42%

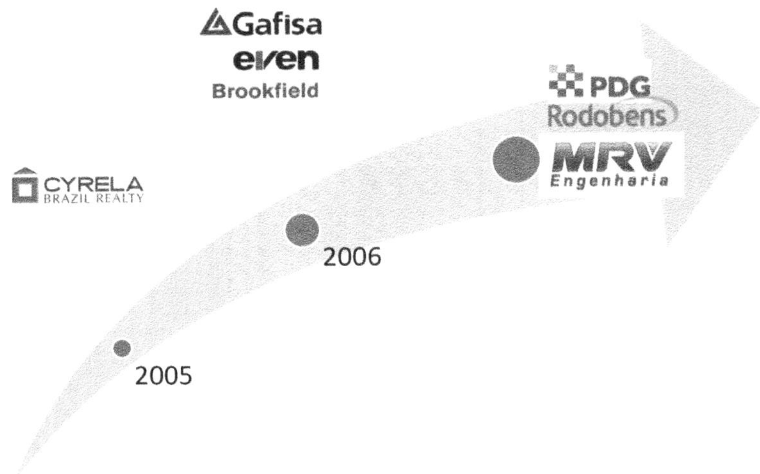

Fig. 2.2 IPO wave of real estate developers in Brazil (*Source* Albuquerque (2014))

improved upon that would bring down the company's financial cycle and thus reduce their working capital investment, freeing up capital for other purposes.

The main issue in establishing the parameters of CCC improvement policies is how to integrate operations and financials to avoid compromising profitability. As we will describe later, there are two competing effects: a longer CCC increases profitability if it allows companies to increase sales; however, the opportunity cost of investments in working capital affects the bottom line (Deloof, 2003). A successful CCC management program allows a firm to shorten its CCC without losing sales. In the present case, this means looking at the company's operations to unearth the possible sources of inefficiencies that affect DIO and DSO.

A thorough analysis of MRV operations identified five possible areas to improve its CCC: a reduction in average purchasing and land registration times, project design, financing, commercialization, and the registration of individual contracts. None of these processes involved building housing units. The next step was to develop possible interventions to reduce the average execution time for each area.

But what were its effects? Zeidan and Shapir (2017) estimate the causality between the intervention and the financial outcomes of the company in subsequent years and find a strong indication that the project was successful. Later, we will detail the intervention and how the finance department coordinated with other departments to implement the actions and monitor the results.

Table 2.3 presents the impact of the restructuring of MRV's operations

Table 2.3 CCC and Operating working capital (OWC) at MRV, 2010–2015 (US$' 000)

	2010	2011	2012	2013	2014	2015	2015*
DSO	389	419	440	371	339	313	440
DIO	227	244	280	233	212	203	280
DPO	134	174	212	176	172	165	212
CCC	482	489	508	428	379	351	508
OWC	1,994,655	2,689,540	2,647,035	2,269,468	2,175,112	2,289,024	3,314,553
Daily Revenue	4,139	5,500	5,211	5,302	5,735	6,525	6,525
Annual Revenue	1,510,475	2,007,530	1,901,905	1,935,305	2,093,093	2,381,519	2,381,519

Note 2015* represents the OWC that the company would have if it maintained the same CCC as in 2012
Source Zeidan and Shapir (2017)

on its financial results. The table compares the results derived from the company's financial statements and the scenario in which the financial cycle would be the same as before the intervention. In other words, for the results of 2015, we create a simple counterfactual in which the CCC would be at the same level as 2012 to contrast actual expenditure in working capital with that of a constant CCC.

Later chapters will describe how to calculate working capital investments and other variables from accounting data. But the most relevant indicator in Table 2.3 is the operating working capital, or the amount mobilized to maintain and grow the business. If the financial cycle were the same as before the intervention, the company would be investing U$3.31 billion in working capital. By 2015, the actual amount invested did not reach U$2.89 billion, savings of more than U$1 billion.

What is more, revenues increased by 25% from 2012 to 2015. One should expect working capital to rise in tandem, but the amount invested in the operations by MRV went down by 13.5%, or US$ 358 million. Even if DPO decreased, both DSO and DIO dropped sharply. DSO was 29% lower when the values from 2015 to 2012 were compared, and DIO was 27% smaller between these two years.

MRV dramatically improved its free cash flow, which is particularly important in a country with scarce and expensive capital. In the end, the company's operating working capital savings totaled US$ 1.02 billion. What are the main lessons from this case?

- Working capital management is cash flow management. Working capital management is not as crucial if a company has more cash than it needs or easy access to credit.
- Companies can enhance cash flow by improving operations and shortening their financial cycle.
- Such improvements must be perennial. If DSO, DPO, and DIO were to revert to pre-intervention values, the firm would reinvest their previous savings.
- One can't manage what is not measured. MRV did not track DSO, DPO, and DIO and thus were missing a key component in cash flow management.
- Accounting and managerial information serve different purposes. The implementation of changes at MRV was based on measures that are not directly reported in financial statements. Indicators must be calculated and adjusted to the realities of a business. There is no universal optimal working capital policy: for some companies, that might mean each business unit has full autonomy while headquarters centralize working capital policies for others.

References

Albuquerque R (2014). O caso MRV. EMBA FDC. Mimeo.

Deloof, M. (2003). Does working capital management affect profitability of Belgian firms? *Journal Business Finance Accounting, 30*, 573–588.

Zeidan, R., & Shapir, O. M. (2017). Cash conversion cycle and value-enhancing operations: Theory and evidence for a free lunch. *Journal of Corporate Finance, 45*, 203–219.

3

The General Dynamic Model of Trade Credit

"Revenue is ego, profit is fantasy; what matters is cold, hard cash." Owners of small and medium-sized companies would do well to remember that. In many, if not all countries, most managers face credit constraints limiting their ability to increase production, negotiate lower costs, or be flexible in closing sales. Profit maximization is the cornerstone of the neoclassical theory of the firm, but there is no equivalent general theory on maximizing cash generation. In this book, we generalize working capital management for companies to optimize cash generation over time. We depart from previous presentations of the material on assuming that firms are perennial sellers with built-in capital or other types of investments. Cash conversion cycle management is often neglected and particularly relevant for credit-constrained companies. Yet it also impacts large corporations; should companies extend credit to their supply-chain or extract value through lengthening payment terms to suppliers and shortening periods to customers? The dynamic approach creates a roadmap for increasing shareholder value by optimizing a company's cash-conversion cycle. Importantly, this approach uses readily available accounting data.

Usually, it is challenging to relate working capital management to product market competition because companies do not optimize a single output in the relationship between financial and operations management. Working capital investments are necessary to turn inputs into outputs, and companies, sometimes credit constrained, optimize their ability to turn inputs into cash. Profits and cash converge in the long run, but market power enhances

R. Zeidan, *The General Model of Working Capital Management*, https://doi.org/10.1007/978-981-19-3334-9_3

the possibility of survival by cushioning shocks to cash flows. It is relatively common for companies to have solid business models but shut down due to cash constraints at some point in their life cycle (Bernanke, 1981; Dickinson, 2011). Financing from the supply chain (trade credit) is usually viewed as an expensive but essential alternative source of funds for financially constrained firms (Biais & Gollier, 1997; Carbó-Valverde et al., 2016; Cuñat, 2006; Nilsen, 1994; Petersen & Rajan, 1997). In many instances, it also acts as a substitute to bank credit (Huang et al., 2011; Nilsen, 2002), especially for small and medium enterprises (SMEs), as well as a risk-sharing mechanism throughout the supply chain (Acharya et al., 2014; Cuñat, 2006; Yang & Birge, 2018).

The ability to generate cash by managing payment terms is even more critical in developing countries. While the current savings glut depresses real interest rates in rich countries, SMEs face at least some binding credit restrictions. Evidence shows that companies lack the skills to maximize the terms of payments. In other words, companies with poor working capital management experience operational inefficiencies and leave plenty of money at the table (Zeidan & Shapir, 2017).

3.1 The Basics of the Financial Cycle

Trade credit optimization is about achieving a predictably short, or as short as possible given a company's business, financial cycle. The financial cycle is the time it takes for a company to recoup the money spent on producing and selling goods and services. The easiest way to visualize this cycle is by contrasting it to the economic process. In the latter, a company purchases inputs, transforms them into final goods and services, and sells them to its customers.

At first, let's concentrate on the simplest case, an industrial company that purchases mainly raw materials, transforming and selling them.

The economic cycle starts when the company places an order for inputs. However, that usually does not mean a cash outflow, as suppliers typically extend credit to other companies in the supply chain. The time it takes for a purchasing order to be paid is defined as Days payable outstanding. Internally, inputs are processed and become final goods; this period is the Days inventory outstanding. Finally, companies sell their final goods (sometimes before finishing them), but there is no immediate cash inflow unless customers pay immediately in kind. The period between sales and getting the money is the Days sales outstanding.

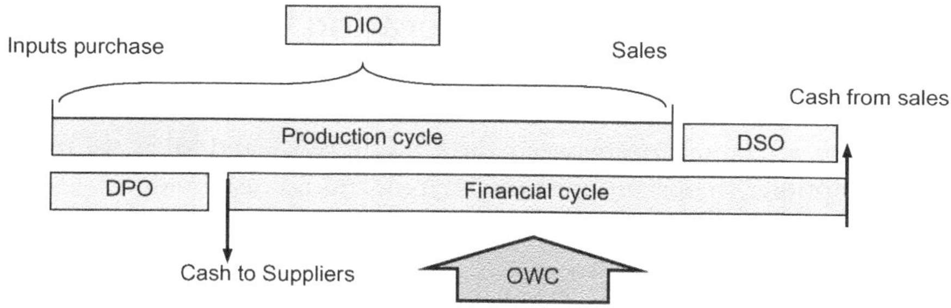

Fig. 3.1 Economic (production) and financial cycles

Figure 3.1 describes the difference between the economic and financial cycles.

Figure 3.1 also illustrates a crucial element for trade credit analysis: operating working capital (OWC) or working capital requirements (WCR). These concepts are straightforward: companies must have enough financial resources to fund this process because they usually produce first and then sell their products.

The financial cycle is tied to continuous operations, in which the company must, time and again, produce and sell its goods.

The financial or cash-to-cash cycle (CCC or C2C) is just the sum of DIO, DSO, and DPO. Thus, if a company must pay its suppliers after 28 days, it takes 21 days for raw inputs to be transformed into final goods and services, and consumers pay for their purchases after 14 days, the CCC is 21 + 14 − 28 or seven days. Of course, this simple calculation is based on several assumptions: all consumers pay precisely after 14 days, there is no delay, the company purchases all required inputs simultaneously, and all its suppliers allow the firm to pay for inputs after 28 days. But the central assumption, and the crux of the current approach towards optimizing trade credit, is that it is easier to manage the financial cycle when DSO and DPO share the same denominator.

The intuition behind it is straightforward. If a company is going to sell a product for U$100, it must be put that aside as operating working capital. In other words, the operating working capital is primarily a function of how long it takes for a company to recoup its operational investment. Of course, companies aim to sell products for more than it costs to produce them. Nevertheless, assuming a constant operating margin and ignoring margins, at first, has one significant benefit: it is much easier to extract information about the financial cycle from accounting data and interpret it.

3.2 Building Dynamics: Operating Working Capital and Working Capital Requirements

To establish a relationship between the CCC, OWC, and sales, we rely on two assumptions: a constant operating margin and no cash holdings. Usually, the cash conversion cycle or cash-to-cash cycle is defined as:

$$CCC = DIO + DSO - DPO$$

where *DIO* is days of inventory outstanding or average inventory divided by the costs of goods and services sold (*COGS*); *DSO* is days of sales outstanding or average accounts receivables divided by daily revenue; and *DPO* is days payable outstanding, which is average accounts payable divided by *COGS*. If the operating margin (*revenue* – *COGS*) is constant, we can rewrite *DIO* and *DPO* without loss of generality, as

$$DIO = \frac{Inventories}{Daily\ Revenue} \text{and } DPO = \frac{Accounts\ Payable}{Daily\ Revenue}$$

We can then rewrite the CCC as

$$CCC = DIO + DSO - DPO = \frac{Inventories + Receivables - Accounts\ Payable}{Daily\ Revenue}$$

If we define OWC as the capital tied up in operations (inventories + receivables – accounts payable), then

$$CCC = \frac{OWC}{Daily\ Revenue * 365} = \frac{OWC}{Annual\ Revenue}$$

The firm that best fits the equation above is a mature single-product company. The ideal company would constantly purchase inputs, transform them into final products, and sell them, with a constant operating margin and predictable deadlines for suppliers and consumers.

Variations in OWC come from changes in the CCC or increased sales and a combined effect that occurs only if both variables change simultaneously (assuming daily revenue * 365 as annual revenue):

$$\Delta OWC = CCC * \Delta Revenue + \Delta CCC * Revenue + \Delta CCC * \Delta Revenue$$

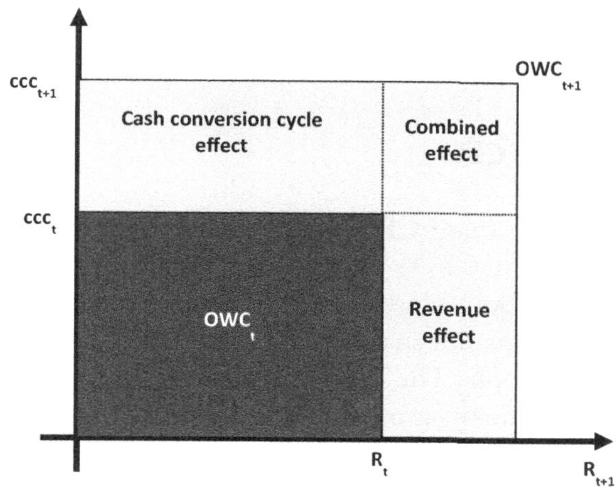

Fig. 3.2 Graphical representation of the linear relationship between the CCC and OWC

That is similar to the concept of working capital productivity (BCG, 2004), which measures the ratio of the CCC to sales rather than the cost of goods sold. The result is a direct relationship between the CCC (days), OWC, and sales. Figure 3.2 illustrates it.

Allowing only the CCC or sales (revenue) to change, we have two transmission mechanisms from investment to profits: the revenue and CCC effects. In Fig. 3.2, the revenue effect is value-creating. The CCC effect is value-destroying. The combined effect destroys or creates value depending on the profit margin and working capital investments opportunity cost.

Given the constant operating margin hypothesis, profits are a linear function of the increase in sales. If π is profits, P price, c average $COGS$, and Q the number of goods and services sold:

$$\pi = (P - c) * Q$$

If the CCC is constant and positive, then cash flow and profits move in tandem, and working capital investments are:

$$\Delta OWC = CCC * \Delta Revenue = CCC * (P - c) * \Delta Q$$

Optimizing OWC means minimizing the CCC conditional on its effects on operating margins and actual sales. Minimizing the CCC means fewer investments for the same amount of profits, thereby maximizing shareholder value if there are no impacts on sales (e.g., lost sales due to decreasing the period for consumers to pay for their purchases). The revenue effect is a classic indicator of capital budgeting. Firms budget working capital investments in line with expectations of increased sales.

3.2.1 The Crying CEO

The story behind the crying CEO happened in Rio Grande do Sul, Brazil, during an event called CEO's forum. The event's set-up required that I initiate a discussion about working capital management and let the CEOs of medium-sized companies share their experience about overcoming challenges related to the topic. The event started with a presentation about how working capital investments grow in tandem with revenue. This relationship is illustrated in Table 3.1 below, which displays the initial process of working capital investment in columns 1–4, how it grows with higher sales in columns 5–8, and the effects of lengthier terms of payment in columns 9–12.

Investment in working capital emerges in the following way. First, let's assume that a company is about to start operating. Second, it has perfectly predictable sales of U$1000 per day, every day, in perpetuity. Third, managers decide to extend credit to consumers, who must pay their orders after 30 days. Finally, there is no risk or uncertainty; consumers settle their debts without delay.

In columns 1–4, we can see that the company sells U$1000 worth of goods on the first day but does not receive a penny. This amount is accounted for as receivables, without cash inflows just yet. On the second day, the same happens. The receivables balance totals U$2000, but there is still no cash inflow. After 30 days, the receivables' balance is at U$30,000, and finally, the company gets the first batch of U$1000 payments. From then on, the working capital dynamics are set like clockwork. Every day, the company sells U$1000 worth of goods and receives U$1000 from earlier consumers, while the receivables balance remains constant, at U$30,000. Notably, the receivables balance is, in this instance, the total working capital investment by the company. In turn, this invested working capital is akin to purchasing machinery or other capital expenditure. As long as the patterns of sales and payment terms to consumers remain the same, the receivables balance doesn't change. The few differences between working capital and regular capital investments relate to depreciation and volatility. In this example, working capital investment does not depreciate and can be earned in full 30 days after the company ceases operations.

Working capital grows through the revenue and cash-conversion-cycle effects. What happens if sales double overnight or the sales director allows customers to pay after 45 days? To see that, assume that the director

Table 3.1 Cash flow process with different levels of daily revenue and DSO

Daily revenue			1000	Daily revenue			2000	Daily revenue			2000
DSO			30 days	DSO			30 days	DSO			45 days
Day	Revenue	Receivables	Cash	Day	Revenue	Receivables	Cash	Day	Revenue	Receivables	Cash
1	1000	1000	0	1	2000	2000	0	1	2000	2000	0
2	1000	2000	0	2	2000	4000	0	2	2000	4000	0
3	1000	3000	0	3	2000	6000	0	3	2000	6000	0
4	1000	4000	0	4	2000	8000	0	4	2000	8000	0
5	1000	5000	0	5	2000	10,000	0	5	2000	10,000	0
29	1000	29,000	0	29	2000	58,000	0	29	2000	58,000	0
30	1000	30,000	0	30	2000	60,000	0	30	2000	60,000	0
31	1000	30,000	1000	31	2000	60,000	2000	31	2000	62,000	0
45	1000	30,000	1000	45	2000	60,000	2000	45	2000	90,000	2000
46	1000	30,000	1000	46	2000	60,000	2000	46	2000	90,000	2000
47	1000	30,000	1000	47	2000	60,000	2000	47	2000	90,000	2000
58	1000	30,000	1000	58	2000	60,000	2000	58	2000	90,000	2000
59	1000	30,000	1000	59	2000	60,000	2000	59	2000	90,000	2000
60	1000	30,000	1000	60	2000	60,000	2000	60	2000	90,000	2000

announces that the company is now expected to sell U$2000 daily. During the following 30 days, receivables increase daily, stabilizing at U$60,000, and cash-flow jumps from U$1000 to U$2000. While explaining the process and how to meet the additional U$30,000 in working capital, one of the CEOs started laughing under his breath at first, then hitting a crescendo, finally doing it so hard he started crying. Eventually, he composed himself and addressed the whole room.

First, he provided some context, mentioning that he did not finish primary school. Initially producing cheap underwear to compete against Chinese imports, the firm wasn't created with a business plan behind it. Instead, the company started in the same way many micro-enterprises do, in a garage with the founders working out how to manufacture their goods competently. Thus, their trajectory was similar to successful privately-owned businesses in emerging markets, with growth financed mainly from retained profits. The crying CEO was there to educate himself to make his business more resilient. And why did he start laughing uncontrollably?

He explained that it was because, for the first time, he understood why his company was on the verge of bankruptcy during its first period of rapid sales growth. The company was doing well, with revenue growing in double digits every quarter since its launching. But one day, a few weeks before Christmas, he found that the firm did not have enough money to pay its bills before the end of the month. Like that, the CEO had an existential decision: to declare bankruptcy or go, hat in hand, to ask for a loan from their bank.

That night, the CEO recalled going to bed firmly decided to declare bankruptcy the next day. "Why not just go to your bank?" asked one of his colleagues. The CEO answered that he didn't know why he would be going to the bank to ask for a loan. "If I borrow and then can't repay it, the company will go under, but I wouldn't have enough assets to cover my debts to employees and suppliers." He argued that by preemptively closing down his operations, he could sell off assets to meet his obligations with his employees and suppliers. He remembered demurring about the possibility of starting a new business if there were enough money left.

He viewed borrowing money as a dangerous path, which could lead him to permanent ruin. Still, the CEO negotiated a credit line to survive the following few weeks. He recalled worrying about the debt constantly. Early morning or late at night, his main concern was paying off the debt as quickly as possible. The credit line worked, and the company did not take long to amortize the entire debt, getting them off the books in a few weeks.

Why did the CEO cry during that executive education lecture? Because until then, he had never understood why his company almost went bankrupt.

He finally got why the firm was cash strapped; it was growing too fast, and the suppliers' bills were coming quickly. As the higher production turned to sales, which turned to cash, the company promptly settled its obligations with suppliers and the bank. The CEO also mentioned that it is likely that the company lost some substantial profitable opportunities, as it was unwilling to take on new debt.

3.3 Working Capital and Firm Value: A Simple Framework

We can separate working capital investments into two types:

- OWC investment (ΔOWC) that leads to higher sales is profitable as long as the operating margin is constant and higher than the firm's cost of capital.
- ΔOWC that prompts a higher CCC, *ceteris paribus*, destroys an amount of value equal to the present value of ΔOWC, of at least (where *EV* is enterprise value):

$$\Delta EV = -\frac{\Delta OWC}{wacc}$$

This equation reconciles many previous empirical results on the inefficiency of working capital investments. In particular, it may drive the results in Kieschnick et al. (2013). They find that firms overinvest in working capital and that an incremental dollar invested in net OWC is worth less than an incremental dollar held in cash. In other words:

Hypothesis 1: Any investment in OWC (inventories, accounts payable, accounts receivables) that does not generate sales or a higher operating margin destroys a firm's enterprise value by at least $\Delta EV = -\Delta OWC - \frac{\Delta OWC * g}{wacc}$ given a constant growth rate *g* for revenue; alternatively,

Hypothesis 1.1: Any permanent reduction in the CCC that does not affect the operating margin or volume of sales will create shareholder value by, at least:

$$\Delta EV = |\Delta CCC * Revenue| + \left|\frac{\Delta CCC * Revenue * g}{wacc}\right|$$

Assuming that a firm's opportunity cost is its *WACC*, any investment in working capital that does not generate sales or improve the operating margin results in capital tied up in operations that yield no return. The present value of such an investment should be discounted at the cost of capital; this would be the sum of an infinite series, which equals the initial investment, ΔOWC, that would grow at the same rate as the growth in revenue, *g*. This hypothesis is trivial at first; however, unlike other types of investments, it does not depreciate at any rate. It can only be recovered by streamlining operations, which yields this amount back into cash holdings, or *n* days after the company ceases its operations, where *n* is DSO.

Although it is formally identical to its original formulation, the alternative hypothesis has different implications. Without changes in the operating margin or sales dynamics, a permanent reduction in the CCC frees up cash equal to $\Delta OWC = \Delta CCC * Revenues$ in the first period. More importantly, it also diminishes the need for future investments in working capital as sales grow. Here, we assume a constant growth in sales, *g*, to simplify the exposition.

Mismanaging DIO, DSO, and DPO results in the greater allocation of cash, which increases the cost of capital but generates no marginal return. We can reconcile other empirical results with the present framework as follows:

Financially constrained firms have trouble with rapidly increasing sales (e.g., Bierman & Smidt, 2012).

Shortening the CCC improves firms' profitability, especially for financially constrained firms such as SMEs (Carpenter & Petersen, 2002). Managing inventories, accounts payables, and accounts receivables can sharply improve the return on working capital investments if a firm can do this without losing sales. That also explains why investments in DSO are more profitable than those in DIO, as in Kieschnick et al. (2013). On the one hand, DSO investments should result in higher sales, and it is easy to assume that the investment would have a more significant revenue effect than the CCC effect. On the other hand, investments in DIO are not directly linked to higher sales, and they should influence the CCC effect first. For example, optimal inventory policies usually relate to fluctuations in the price of raw materials (Berling & Martínez-de-Albéniz, 2011). Mapping the effect that increases OWC significantly changes the relationship between working capital and profitability. In particular, cash-starved firms should raise cash internally by shortening the CCC.

The combined effect highlights a pressing issue for rapidly growing firms because rapid growth often results in the mismanagement of the CCC, compounding the liquidity issues resulting from increasing revenue.

Hambrick and Crozier (1985) first illustrated this issue, and subsequent studies have highlighted the relevance of cash management for rapidly growing firms and SMEs (Beck & Demirguc-Kunt, 2006). Moreover, most companies in emerging markets do not use the key performance indicators of the CCC and thus lack a cash culture (KPMG, 2010).

It presents a compelling argument for the U-shaped curve reported for privatized companies (Ben-Nasr, 2016). Financially constrained companies invest little in working capital and thus have lower growth and value, while firms that invest too much suffer from the value-destroying CCC effect.

One can easily see why working capital investments might destroy value: without ex-ante assumptions, such investments might increase sales (value-enhancing); nevertheless, they can also increase the CCC (value destroying). Since most companies do not monitor or manage their CCC, overinvestment in working capital is frequent because of the inefficiencies related to the CCC; any working capital investment that results in a higher CCC without operating margin effects destroys value. In this respect, the present framework reconciles most of the results in the empirical literature.

Working capital investments generate value as long as companies sell more without higher costs and lost sales. Although the CCC and sales are usually correlated, if companies can shorten the CCC without losing sales, they can improve the return on working capital investments. The academic literature has been shown this indirectly throughout the years. Still, there has been no comprehensive dynamic working capital management framework to tie down all empirical results about these issues. For instance, Kieschnick et al. (2013) and Almeida and Eid (2014) find that any positive changes in the CCC yield significantly less value from extra investments in working capital on average than an additional cash investment. Unless companies manage their CCC correctly, increasing working capital at the beginning of a fiscal year should reduce company value for any value above the revenue effect.

Better working capital management can improve credit-constrained and unconstrained cash flows, even if cash generation improvements are more relevant for the former. The inefficient allocation of working capital investments is pervasive in emerging markets, and progress can unlock significant growth opportunities.

3.4 Operating Working Capital: The Central Concept in Working Capital Management

This subsection expands on operating working capital, central to working capital management throughout the book.

It is common to see working capital defined as current assets minus current liabilities, but such a definition conflates operating and non-operating accounting variables in a single concept. Here, the operating working capital refers to the balance of cyclical accounts linked to a company's operations: OWC = Cyclic Assets − Cyclic Liabilities.

By defining OWC in this manner, we highlight the true nature of working management: liquidity and not solvency. Solvency is about long-term commitments, while liquidity is related to short-term obligations. As it stands, the usual definition of OWC as the difference between current assets and liabilities is not about liquidity, as it is often assumed, but about solvency. In other words, if a significant crisis requires a company to pay its short-term debt, will current assets be enough to cover it? However, short-term liabilities assets are not redeemable if firms continue to operate. As long as companies maintain their production level at similar payment terms, accounts payable is never reduced; short-term production-related debt is rolled over. Accounts payable are eliminated when companies face bankruptcy but not before.

As we are going to see, OWC is akin to capital expenditures. Financing considerations are also similar: companies do not need to sell assets quickly unless they face bankruptcy. The same holds for non-seasonable OWC (we treat seasonality, such as a spike in sales for retail companies during Christmas in Sect. 6.1).

Accounting classification often does not allow for a clear identification of cyclical asset and liability accounts. Moreover, OWC is sensitive to changes in firms' economic environment. Thus, changes in supplier credit, inventory decisions, and input purchases change in the short term, the company's OWC. Still, OWC primarily depends on the nature and level of business activities.

$$\begin{aligned}\textbf{OWC} = &\ \textbf{Cyclic operating requirements (cyclical assets)} \\ &- \textbf{Cyclic operating resources (cyclical liabilities)}\end{aligned}$$

Remember that:

Cyclical assets (held for less than 12 months (in principle) and required for production or sale, or both) include the following:

- Customers (accounts receivable)
- Stocks
- Prepaid expenses

Cyclic Liabilities (linked to negotiation with consumers and suppliers in recurring operations) include:

- Providers
- Salaries and Charges Payable
- Tax obligations related to current operations
- Advances from Customers.

Thus, in principle, we can calculate the current OWC as:

OWC = Accounts receivable + Inventories + Prepaid expenses − Suppliers − Salaries and charges payable − Tax liabilities related to current operations − Advances from Customers.

Companies have a perennial need for investment to finance their operations. In most companies, cash outflows occur before inflows. Production transforms raw materials and components into final products or, for service companies, the firm's structure must be set up before services are delivered.

In some rare cases, the OWC can be a negative number. In these cases, cash outflows occur after cash inflows. Thus, cyclical liabilities are larger than cyclical assets, turning excess liabilities into sources of funds for the company.

Financial cycles tend to be positive numbers because of DIO. In a broad sense, the physical production cycle comprises three main phases: receiving raw materials, transforming raw materials into final products, and storing final products. Raw materials are usually purchased through credit given by suppliers, increasing accounts payable. To ensure a continuous production flow, a factory maintains inputs in stock. Costs incurred in a factory follow the physical movement of raw materials as they are received, stored, and transformed into final products.

An important note is that the credits offered by suppliers (and for customers) are not technically loans; supply contracts do not involve charging interest. When giving credit to a company, a bank enters into a loan agreement. When it grants a payment term to its customers, a company offers trade credit.

In economic terms, one could argue that there is no significant distinction between the two, as credit from suppliers may be granted with implicit interest rates embedded in them. In some of the models described later in the book, trade credit and bank loans are interchangeable for companies.

However, we should remember that trade credit is directly tied to a firm's operations. Issues with suppliers may impact the quality of inputs, delay the production process, or change investment decisions. The fewer potential suppliers are or, the more the company uses their products, the larger the distinction between trade and bank credit.

3.5 An Initial Step-By-Step Guide to Estimating Operating Working Capital

The expenses towards raw materials, labor, and fixed production costs go into the finished goods inventories. The credit extended to customers generates receivables. The payment term for raw materials results from negotiation with suppliers: increasing (decreasing) the credit period increases (decreases) accounts payable.

The central idea about our dynamic approach is that operating working capital is perennial, and working capital investments emerge from the production cycle. Let's illustrate it with an example. A company consumes inputs at a rate of U$10,000 per day, with an average payment term of 30 days. Assuming that the first daily purchase of raw material occurs today, its purchasing pattern can be represented in Table 3.2 below.

If the company purchases U$10,000 daily, there are no actual disbursements in the first 30 days. Accounts payable increases daily until the 30th day, reaching U$300,000. After that, the company pays U$10,000 to suppliers, and accounts payable goes up by the same amount each day. Accounts payable remains at U$300,000 while the company produces goods and services that require daily input purchases of U$10,000. This relationship between the

Table 3.2 Accounts payable and working capital dynamics

Day	Input purchases	Expenses	Accounts payable
1	10,000	0	10,000
2	10,000	0	20,000
3	10,000	0	30,000
10	10,000	0	100,000
20	10,000	0	200,000
30	10,000	10,000	300,000
31	10,000	10,000	300,000
32	10,000	10,000	300,000
60	10,000	10,000	300,000
360	10,000	10,000	300,000
N	10,000	10,000	300,000

production process and the Balance Sheet accounts gives rise to the concept of cyclical indicators in the present dynamic model. These accounts are cyclic precisely because they result from the recurring production process.

It is also essential to observe that by establishing the cyclical accounts, we can quickly abandon the notion of assets as something a company owns and liabilities as something that the company owes. Cyclical assets represent the use of funding, which comes from the liabilities (or equity) part of balance sheets. The distinction between considering assets as ownership and borrowed funds is subtle, but its implication is profound. It would be natural for an entity to maximize its value regarding asset ownership. After all, the image of wealthy people is usually related to them owning yachts, mansions, secluded islands, and more. However, if we consider that borrowed funds generate assets, we expect the opposite behavior. If managers must compensate somebody (debt and shareholders) for each asset in the balance sheet, they should be judicious about asset growth. Managers' goal becomes to use funds efficiently, and assets that don't generate enough income to remunerate debt and shareholders should be scuttled. It is not that asset growth is to be avoided, but that managers should be careful about allowing the assets part of the Balance Sheet to grow. That turns the idea of Balance Sheet variation on its head. The best type of company would be the one that generates the most return with the fewest possible assets. That is true regardless of the nature of a firm's assets. Organizations should not keep extra cash lying around if they have no expected use for it. Mergers that do not increase productivity, directly or indirectly, shouldn't be pursued. Finally, efficiency trumps size for fixed and cyclical assets alike.

Cyclical uses of funds comprise all operating costs incurred but not yet used or sold, such as inventories and all sales that have not yet been paid. They contain funds containing all charges incurred in the operational process that have not yet been paid (e.g., suppliers' bills, wages, social insurance, and other taxes) and the value of products that have not yet been delivered.

For the dynamics of working capital management, the same dynamic process works for receivables, like in Table 3.3.

In this case, the firm's bank accounts are only credited a month after the initial sales. The daily sales of U$20,000 lead to receivables totaling U$600,000, which will only be collected when the organization ceases operations.

There is also an imperfect correlation between a company's operations and its accounting cash flow implications. Take, for example, the "wages payable" account. Assuming that the company's fiscal year ends a few days before the

Table 3.3 Receivables and working capital dynamics

Day	Sales	Receipts	Receivables
1	20,000	0	20,000
2	20,000	0	40,000
3	20,000	0	60,000
10	20,000	0	200,000
20	20,000	0	400,000
30	20,000	20,000	600,000
31	20,000	20,000	600,000
32	20,000	20,000	600,000
60	20,000	20,000	600,000
360	20,000	20,000	600,000
N	20,000	20,000	600,000

date the salaries are paid, there is a lag between the payment date of wages and the date it is considered an expense for that year.

For illustrating these points, let's assume a company, L.Euler, that has two activities, the sale of goods and service provision contracts in the civil construction area. Given the multi-purpose nature of the firm, we can use it to analyze the central concepts in working capital management for both manufacturing firms and service companies.

The goal is to estimate the financial cycle and the operating working capital for L.Euler. We assess these variables for three years, from 2021 to 2023. We use as little information as possible to show that analyzing a firm's working capital dynamics is possible without access to detailed proprietary data.

The assets part of L.Euler's balance sheet is in Table 3.4 (remember that we are not interested in accounting precision).

Table 3.4 L.Euler's assets, 2021–2023, U$'000

	2021	2022	2023
Assets	38,500	45,000	57,000
Current assets	7500	8000	13,000
Cash and cash equivalents	1100	1700	3200
Accounts Receivable	3000	3000	4000
Inventory	1000	1000	2000
Advance to suppliers	2000	1800	3500
Others	400	500	300
Non-Current Assets	31,000	37,000	44,000
Fixed assets	1000	3500	8000
Investment	2000	1000	1000
Others	8000	10,000	11,000
Goodwill	20,000	22,500	24,000

For L.Euler, inventory remained constant from 2021 to 2022, at U$1 million, rising to U$2 million in 2023, either due to higher sales or DIO changes. Receivables also remained stable until 2023, rising to U$3.2 million. L.Euler's liabilities and equity are in Table 3.5.

Accounts payable increased from U$3.2 million in 2021 to U$5 million in 2022 and U$5.5 million in 2023. Unless sales are growing significantly, an increase in accounts payable probably means that the average payment term has increased.

We can rearrange the accounting variables from the balance sheet into cyclical and non-cyclical current assets, as shown in Table 3.6. However, this

Table 3.5 L.Euler's liabilities and equity, 2021–2023, U$'000

	2021	2022	2023
Liabilities and Stockholder's equity	**38,500**	**45,000**	**57,000**
Current Liabilities	**11,500**	**14,000**	**20,000**
Debt maturing within one year	4500	6000	11,000
Suppliers	3200	4000	4500
Wages and other accrued liabilities	1800	2000	2100
Accrued taxes	1000	1500	1100
Others	1000	500	0
Non-current liabilities	**14,000**	**17,000**	**21,000**
Provisions	2000	2000	2200
Long-term debt	12,000	15,000	18,800
Equity	**13,000**	**14,000**	**16,000**
Equity capital	6000	6000	6000
Retained earnings	7000	8000	10,000

Table 3.6 L.Euler's cyclical and non-cyclical assets, 2021–2023, U$'000

	2021	2022	2023
Assets	**38,500**	**45,000**	**57,000**
Non-cyclical assets	**1500**	**2200**	**3500**
Cash and cash equivalents	1100	1700	3200
Others	400	500	300
Cyclical assets	**6000**	**5800**	**9500**
Accounts Receivable	3000	3000	4000
Inventory	1000	1000	2000
Advance to suppliers	2000	1800	3500
Non-Current Assets	**31,000**	**37,000**	**44,000**
Fixed assets	1000	3500	8000
Investment	2000	1000	1000
Others	8000	10,000	11,000
Goodwill	20,000	22,500	24,000

Table 3.7 L.Euler's income statement, 2021–2023, U$'000

	2021	2022	2023
Net revenue	**40,000**	**41,800**	**50,500**
Cost of sales	−26,000	−30,000	−38,000
Gross profit	**14,000**	**11,800**	**12,500**
Selling, general and admin expenses	−5000	−6000	−6500
Other expenses	−300	−500	−600
EBIT (Operating Income)	**8700**	**5300**	**5400**
Gain (losses) on foreign currency	0	0	0
Interest expenses	−1350	−1600	−1650
Income before tax	**7350**	**3700**	**3750**
Income taxes	−2500	−800	−1400
Net profit	**4850**	**2900**	**2350**

is not mandatory, as we can easily extract the cyclical accounts from regular balance sheets without straying too far from accounting standards.

Notably, other current assets have been classified as non-cyclical assets in this example. However, that might not be the case for every company. If "others" refers to recurring operational assets, its values should go into the cyclical assets category.

Finally, we show L.Euler's income statement in Table 3.7.

Remember that we calculate DIO as the ratio between inventory and net revenue and not cost of sales, as is usual in other books:

$$DIO = \frac{Inventory}{Daily\ Revenue}$$

Here, we also assume 360 days in a year. The 360 days convention is used because there are many instances of calculating the financial cycle from quarterly data throughout the book. Since we assume that months have 30 days and quarters 90 days, it follows that 360 days is preferable to 365 days in the present case. Hence, L.Euler's daily revenue for 2021 is U$111,111.11, which results in DIO for 2021 being nine days (from 1,000,000/111,111.11). Repeating the process for the other years, DIO for 2022 and 2023 are 8.6 and 14.3 days, respectively. That means the economic cycle became shorter from 2021 to 2022 and increased in 2023.

DPO and DSO are calculated similarly:

$$DPO = \frac{Accounts\ Payable(Suppliers + wages + taxes)}{Daily\ Revenue}$$

$$DSO = \frac{Receivables(Accounts\,receivable + advance\,to\,suppliers)}{Daily\ Revenue}$$

Thus, DPO is 54, 64.59, and 54.89 days, and DSO, 45, 41.34, and 53.47 days. The cash-conversion cycle is merely the sum of its components:

$$CCC = DIO + DSO - DPO$$

From that, L.Euler's financial cycle is 0 in 2021, −14.64 days in 2022, and 12.83 days in 2023. Finally, the company's operating working capital is given by:

$$CCC = \frac{OWC}{Daily\ Revenue * 360} = \frac{OWC}{Annual\ Revenue}$$

Therefore, L.Euler's operating working capital was zero in 2021, a negative number, U$1.7 million, in 2022, and returns to a positive number, U$1.8 million, in 2023.

Table 3.8 summarizes the components of the financial cycle, the cash conversion cycle, and the operating working capital for the 2021–2023 period.

Operating working capital goes through two transitions in the 2021–2023 period. First, as the cash-conversion cycle turns negative from 2021 to 2022, operational cash flow increases by U$1.7 million even as sales go up by 4.5%. However, that cash flow must be returned as working capital investments in the following year. The change in operating working capital is U$3.5 million, as revenue skyrocketed by over 20%.

We have not yet seen what has been driving the changes in the financial cycle and operating working capital, as the focus has been on extracting the indicators from accounting data. The L.Euler example includes the company

Table 3.8 L.Euler's financial cycle components (in days) and operating working capital (U$'000), 2021–2023

	2021	2022	2023
Days inventory outstanding (DIO)	9.0	8.6	14.3
Days payable outstanding (DPO)	54.0	64.59	54.89
Days sales outstanding (DSO)	45.0	41.34	53.47
Cash-conversion cycle (CCC)	0.0	−14.64	12.83
Operating working capital (OWC)	0	−1700	1800
Annual Sales	40,000	41,800	50,500

selling goods and services because that may explain the two cash flow transitions. For instance, let's assume that the company sells its services before producing them, while its manufacturing unit has a long economic cycle. Furthermore, let's assume that the services division has blossomed in 2022, while the manufacturing division led in 2023. That could explain the changes in the evolution of L.Euler's operating working capital in the 2021–2023 period.

Therein lies one of the shortcomings of consolidated financial statements: they do not usually provide enough information for managers to understand the dynamics of the different company's divisions. In addition, we may have underestimated the financial cycle indicators by including variables that bear no relation to the firm's current operations or excluding some that do.

For instance, the account "others" from current assets was inserted in the calculation of DSO, but the "others" from liabilities have not. That choice highlights how managerial reports should differ from accounting financial statements. To have included "others" in the current assets, we must have some information that the numbers are related to the recurring nature of the production process. In the present example, we assumed that "others" referred to tax credits generated by the services division. However, the indicator in current liabilities was labeled as a non-cyclical account because we assumed it was related to dividends that would be paid to shareholders, which is not an operational decision.

Summing up, this section has described each step in building the financial cycle indicators from the fundamental balance sheet and income statements reports. For multi-product firms, there are limits to the usefulness of consolidated indicators. Still, the basics of determining the financial cycle indicators translate to more complicated scenarios. It is also the foundation for customized benchmarks for improving a firm's working capital management.

3.5.1 An Example of Financial Cycle and OWC Indicators

The company's business model, the sector in which it operates, and its ability to negotiate with customers and suppliers explain the financial cycle. For example, supermarkets with high bargaining power try to squeeze their suppliers to extend payment terms while getting their products to rotate quickly on the shelf. Service companies that require high entry levels, or upfront payments, manage to have negative OWC, as do some companies in the retail sector. Given this step-by-step guide, can you build the financial cycle and OWC indicators for three companies, which data follows in Table 3.9 below?

Data (which were slightly modified) are for three large listed multinational companies: Cisco Systems Inc. (ticker: CSCO), Costco Wholesale Corp. (COST), and Exxon Mobil Corp. (XOM). Cisco is a more services-oriented company, Costco is a retail giant, and Exxon is one of the largest oil companies in the world. Cisco designs, manufactures, and sells networking products and services related to the communications and information technology industry. Costco operates retail supermarkets open for members who join and renew their membership annually. Exxon explores, develops, and distributes oil, gas, and petroleum products.

Following the step-by-step guide, including the assumptions that other current assets impact DSO, but other current liabilities do not influence DPO, the financial cycle indicators for the three companies are in Table 3.10.

One wouldn't need, in principle, to calculate the financial cycle indicators to guess which company referred to which data. Exxon is one of the largest companies in the world. Hence the total assets being over U$300 billion are a dead giveaway that the second set of indicators refers to that company.

However, it shouldn't be difficult to see that the last set of financial cycle indicators refers to Costco. Supermarkets must keep the cash-conversion cycle as short as possible, and Costco's financial cycle is negative for every year in the 2019–2021 period. Remarkably, Costco's DIO, DSO, and DPO change very little during the global covid pandemic. Days payable outstanding increase by over 10% from 2019 to 2020 (from 35 days to 38.4 days), but the changes in DIO and DSO are minimal. More importantly, Costco experienced a surge in sales in 2020 and 2021, with revenue growing from U$150 billion in 2019 to U$167 billion in 2020 and U$196 billion in 2021. However, working capital decreased from 2019 to 2020 and remained constant from 2020 to 2021. That has important implications for Costco's management. During covid, remote workplaces flourished, and the increase in food consumption inside people's homes led to a spike in demand for Costco's products. But unlike most companies, Costco did not require additional investments to meet the extra demand. We can see from Table 3.10 that Costco's DPO is higher than the sum of DIO and DPO. Thus, for the company, an increase in demand, as long as the stores can accommodate it, is almost as simple as ordering more products from suppliers. There is no cash flow risk from doing so. The only danger is commercial, larger orders that do not translate into more sales.

While Costco has a negative cash-conversion cycle due to its business model (low margin and high turnover), Cisco and Exxon have positive but

Table 3.9 Selected financial statement indicators for three large companies, 2019–2021, U$ billion

	A			B			C		
	2021	2020	2019	2021	2020	2019	2021	2020	2019
Cash & short term investments	24.5	29.4	33.4	4.4	3.1	3.0	12.2	13.3	9.4
Total accounts receivable	10.1	10.5	10.6	20.6	27.0	24.7	1.8	1.6	1.5
Inventories	1.6	1.3	1.4	18.9	18.5	19.0	14.2	12.2	11.4
Other	2.9	2.3	2.4	1.1	1.5	1.3	1.3	1.0	1.1
Total current assets	39.1	43.6	47.8	44.9	50.1	48.0	29.5	28.1	23.5
Total non-current assets	58.4	51.3	50.0	287.9	312.5	298.2	29.8	27.4	21.9
Total assets	97.5	94.9	97.8	332.8	362.6	346.2	59.3	55.6	45.4
	–	–	–	–	–	–	–	–	–
ST Debt & current portion LT debt	2.8	3.3	10.2	21.6	21.8	17.3	1.1	0.4	1.7
Accounts payable	2.4	2.2	2.1	15.5	22.7	19.1	16.3	14.2	11.7
Accrued payroll	3.8	3.1	3.2	2.0	2.0	2.0	4.1	3.6	3.2
Other current liabilities	17.2	16.6	16.2	17.2	17.5	18.8	8.0	6.7	6.7
Total current liabilities	26.3	25.3	31.7	56.4	64.0	57.1	29.4	24.8	23.2
Total non current liabilities	30.0	31.6	32.5	112.3	99.7	90.5	11.7	12.0	6.6
Total liabilities	56.2	56.9	64.2	168.6	163.7	147.7	41.2	36.9	29.8
Total shareholders' equity	41.3	37.9	33.6	164.1	198.9	198.5	18.1	18.7	15.6

	A			B			C		
	2021	2020	2019	2021	2020	2019	2021	2020	2019
	–	–	–	–	–	–	–	–	–
Sales/Revenue	49.8	49.3	51.9	178.2	256.0	279.2	195.9	166.8	152.7
Cost of goods sold (COGS) incl. D&A	18.1	17.8	18.7	146.0	201.0	212.2	170.7	144.8	132.9
EBITDA	15.5	15.9	16.4	16.6	30.8	39.6	9.4	7.9	6.3
EBIT	13.6	14.1	14.5	(4.1)	11.9	21.5	7.3	6.1	4.8
Pretax income	13.3	14.0	14.6	(28.9)	20.1	31.0	6.7	5.4	4.8
Days inventory outstanding (DIO)									
Days payable outstanding (DPO)									
Days sales outstanding (DSO)									
Cash-conversion cycle (CCC)									
Operating working capital (OWC)									

Source Companies' financial statements

Table 3.10 Financial cycle and OWC for Cisco, Exxon, and Costco, 2019–2021

	Cisco			Exxon			Costco		
	2021	2020	2019	2021	2020	2019	2021	2020	2019
Days inventory outstanding (DIO)	11.3	9.4	9.6	38.1	26.1	24.4	26.1	26.4	26.9
Days payable outstanding (DPO)	44.7	39.0	36.6	35.4	34.7	27.2	37.4	38.4	35.0
Days sales outstanding (DSO)	94.1	94.0	89.9	43.8	40.0	33.5	5.7	5.6	6.2
Cash-conversion cycle (CCC)	60.7	64.4	62.9	46.5	31.3	30.8	(5.6)	(6.4)	(1.9)
Operating working capital (OWC)	8.4	8.8	9.1	23.0	22.3	23.9	(3.0)	(3.0)	(0.8)

Source Companies' financial statements

not unduly long financial cycles. Cisco is also a remarkable example of resilience amidst a global pandemic. The company's DSO is around three months, most likely the result of long-term maintenance contracts that pay the company at specific intervals. DSO increased by four days, from 90 to 94 days, from 2019 to 2020, and remained at the same level in 2021. While the pandemic might have disrupted many facets of the business, it did not affect much the average payment terms of Cisco's clients.

Of the three companies in Table 3.10, Exxon showed the most significant changes in how fast it turned its products into bank deposits, but only in the comparison between 2020 and 2021. In 2019 and 2020, the company's financial cycle was approximately one month, increasing to 45 days in 2021, from a sharp increase in DIO. Even if Exxon is a capital-intensive company, which means it is used to mobilizing vast amounts of resources to extract and refine oil, a sharp increase in CCC leads to higher working capital needs. In the case of Exxon, that did not happen in 2021. The company's operating working capital increased from U$22.3 billion to U$23 billion from 2020 to 2021. How can the financial cycle increase by almost 50% and the operating working capital increase just by approximately 4%? Sales crashed. Exxon's revenue declined by 30% in the same period. Thus, the financial cycle and the revenue effect were countervailing forces in 2021.

The three examples of these large companies show how the accounting reports, when interpreted correctly, illustrate the business realities, including the effects of economic crises.

3.6 Ideal vs. Accounting Processes and Their Implications

The economic and financial cycles are potentially stable and easy to track. If a company's payment terms are 30 days, that should be its DPO. Similarly, if customers have 25 days to pay after placing orders, that should be a firm's DSO. However, the reality is never that simple. Figure 3.3 describes a stable repeated operation process that is perfectly predictable.

However, even in the absence of economic shocks, there is no reason to expect the components of the financial cycle to be stable over time. Take the production process, for instance. A table DIO would indicate that the organization can reproduce its production process and take the same time to sell its wares month in and month out, which is rarely the case. A stable DSO suggests that consumers pay for their orders a certain number of days without fault. Of course, these scenarios are not realistic.

In real life, DIO, DPO, and DSO change constantly. Accounting measures are limited if managers don't understand what drives these changes. For instance, a sales team member negotiating extended terms with a customer and another client delaying payment for an order placed a few weeks ago will impact DSO similarly. However, while the former may bring benefits, such as customer loyalty or a higher operating margin, the latter will require that the firm repurposes its cash reserves to deal with the delay.

Throughout the book, sometimes we will make inferences about companies' working capital management from publicly available data, but such analyses come with significant caveats. Ideally, accounting data would map company operations changes, but one shouldn't expect that to happen even for single-product companies. There are many kinds of users of accounting reports: regulators, managers, shareholders, banks, and others. Accounting reports are intricate, given how important it is for regulators to access reliable

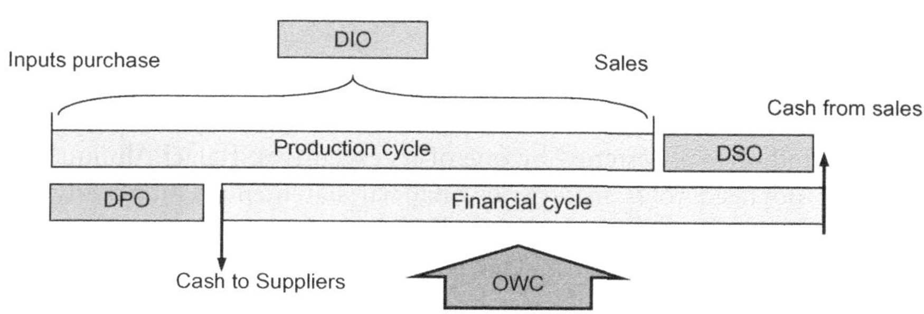

Fig. 3.3 Economic (production) and financial cycles

information. A firm's financial reports must be a good representation of its business deals, but there is no single way to fill out accounting statements. Companies have significant discretion in filling out paperwork; it would be impossible to design a reporting method that would work perfectly for all businesses, from small to large companies, from single-product industrial firms to multi-service multinational conglomerates.

In some countries, it is a common saying that "we can only trust two data points from a financial statement: the name of the company and how much is their current account balance, which must match information from the firm's banks. Everything else is up for grabs." Of course, accounting information is usually reported in good faith. However, it is not straightforward to use financial reports to improve managerial decision-making. This section will highlight the tradeoffs in redefining operation working capital as a sales function and assuming a constant operating margin. Later, issues such as separating fixed inventories from the continuous flow of inputs will illustrate the myriad ways to extract actionable data from accounting reports.

Given that accounting data have shortcomings, what should managers do?

- Build internal systems where the information that feeds accounting reports generates managerial indicators.
- Adjust published financial reports to the business reality, to the best of one's abilities.

Bellisario and Pavlov (2018), in their analysis of performance management practices in lean manufacturing organizations, explicitly address the tension between accounting and operational realities. They find that performance management (PM) practices employed in lean manufacturing organizations (LMOs), but that can be generalized to other companies, are more relevant if they are located closest to front-line actions and explicitly address operational realities. They argue for a limit in the primacy of accounting-driven controls, suggesting that operational rules may be more effective than top-down accounting-based PM practices.

The MRV example in Chapter 2 is an example of adjusting public reports to improve managerial decision-making. Even if the intervention generated over U$1 billion was designed by one of its executives, Rafael Albuquerque, there was no need to transform its financial statements significantly. The intervention's goal was to reduce MRV's financial cycle, but there were no formal targets. Hence, there was no reason for precise estimates of MRV's DIO, DPO, and DSO; calculating the indicators from published accounting statements served Rafael's purpose (and had the additional benefit of allowing for a straightforward benchmarking of MRV's competitors). Internally, some adjustments were made to account for land purchased years before the project started. However, nothing much was done to the managerial reports other than that.

One can't manage what one can't measure. And wrong measurements result in lousy management. If some accounting details bear no relation to a firm's actual operations, the computation of the financial cycle should reflect that.

3.6.1 Should Safety Stocks Be Part of the Operating Working Capital Calculations?

Safety stocks are buffers of inventory held to protect firms against stock-outs from issues such as demand exceeding sales forecast and supply chain disruption resulting in long lead times. Safety stocks also include parts and equipment to maintain companies' most crucial machinery.

Stock-outs are situations in which products can't be supplied for sale, deliveries after purchase are unreasonably held up, or components aren't available during manufacturing (Roughan, 2020). Stock-outs reduce customer satisfaction and efficiency. Of course, holding inventory costs money, both directly and in terms of opportunity costs.

Holding excess inventory may result in wastage losses, but our main concern is: should safety stocks be part of the operating working capital? And the answer is: it depends. The current general approach for working capital management requires that changes in the operation process impact the company's cash flows. And safety stocks may or may not vary with the operation process. For instance, if company A establishes that its safety buffer of raw materials is 10% of the expected sales for the quarter, the safety stock should be accounted for the operating working capital. However, if Fig. 3.4 below represents firm B's inventory cycle, then the safety stock is part of just the initial working capital investment. But as we can see in the figure, the safety stock does not vary with demand; thus, it should not be part of operating working capital budgeting.

A good rule of thumb is that if the safety stock is part of the economic cycle, it should be accounted for as working capital; if not, it is more akin to a fixed asset. If specific inventory must be at a manufacturing plant because of safety issues or other types of regulation, it is not part of its operating working capital. Critical stock is usually invariant to sales or payment terms.

Before, we have seen that initial working capital investments share some characteristics with tangible assets: both types are fixed, long-term assets that are liquidated when the company ceases operations. In the case of safety

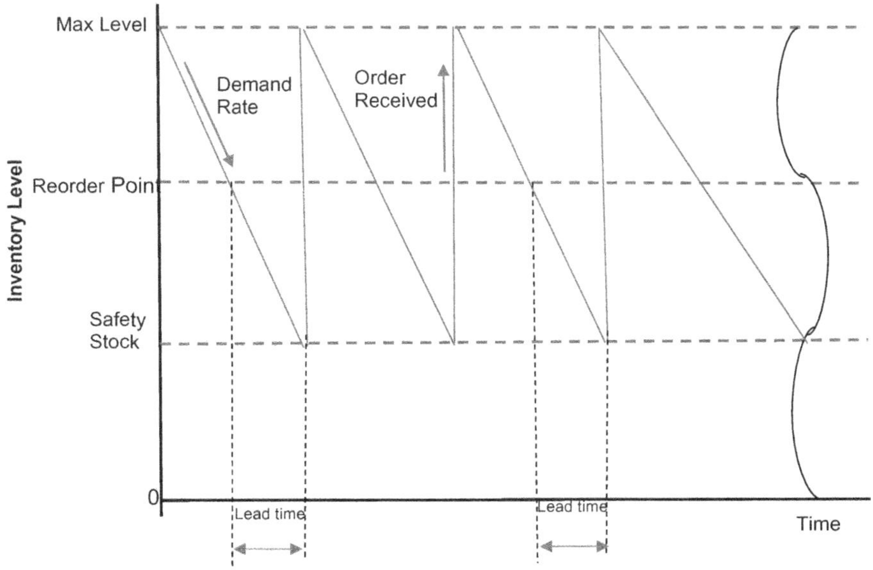

Fig. 3.4 Inventory restocking process (*Source* Roughan [2020])

stocks that are invariant to the rest of the firm operations, they can be separated from the rest of the cash-conversion cycle. Firms may create unique financial statements that distinguish between cyclical and non-cyclical inventory for managerial purposes. Regardless, when analyzing financial data from listed companies, we should remember that not all variation in inventory accounts is related to the production process.

3.6.2 Lean Accounting Management Practices

Some lean management terms can be just buzzwords so consultants can repackage managerial best practices. However, others are useful for executives to shake up business as usual in search of productivity gains. Finally, some terms may be both, easily abused in some instances but helpful guidance in others. One such example is lean thinking and the related concept of simplified management accounting practices (SMAP, per Fullerton et al., 2014).

As the authors put it, lean thinking creates significant changes in an organization's business practices. Hence, if the goal is to be flexible and adaptable, firms should develop accounting reports tailored to their new reality. Another way to put it is that the efforts to eliminate waste and inefficiencies on the shop floor should be extended to accounting practices (Fullerton et al., 2014).

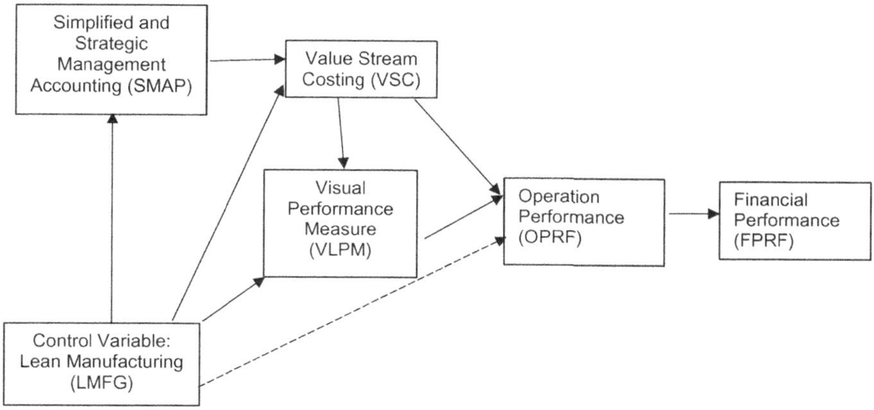

Fig. 3.5 Relationship between lean accounting and manufacturing (*Source* Fullerton et al. [2014])

They develop hypotheses based on the processes of a lean manufacturing firm, as illustrated in Fig. 3.5.

Their claims state that simplified and strategically aligned management accounting practices and visual performance measures increase value in companies implementing lean manufacturing strategies.

Because lean manufacturing operations are refocused from a task or product to a value stream, operations personnel should seek the relevant information to manage bottlenecks and capacity to maintain smooth production flow. That would also provide capacity information so value stream managers could better understand the costs pertinent to expansion and production decisions, such as whether to take on special orders or in-source rather than out-source.

Fullerton et al. (2014) also argue that visual performance measurement information would be an integral part of SMAPs. Most accounting reports allocate costs to products, but in this instance, aggregation of costs would be associated with value streams.

The authors test their hypothesis by surveying 265 managers from American companies on six primary constructs: extent of lean manufacturing, simplified and strategically aligned MAP, visual performance measures, VSC, operations performance, and financial performance. They find that the extent of lean manufacturing is positively related to operations performance, but there is no indication that operations performance increases because firms rely more on VSC. Finally, they conclude that when accounting personnel get on board and implement lean MAP, operations managers and shop-floor employees tasked with making manufacturing decisions are provided with simpler, more concise, and relevant information. That, in turn, enhances operations performance.

Summing up, companies shouldn't necessarily rely on official accounting reports that must be deposited with government authorities. Customized managerial accounting statements can generate immense value for firms of all sizes, from the smallest mom-and-pop shop to the largest multinational corporation.

3.7 Long-Term Dynamics, Life-Cycle, and Working Capital Policies

Working capital policies should change as firms mature. Sales growth plateau after some time, and firms should pay more dividends as the business matures.

Figure 3.6 below illustrates a company's life-cycle with no significant structural changes. The company is founded on an idea taken to market, develops its products and services until there is a solid business model, becomes profitable and mature, and winds down operations, returning funds to shareholders.

This figure, created by Aswath Damodaran, a colleague at NYU, also describes the dimensions that drive firm value. Damodaran regularly uses the figure to inform his approach to the valuation of companies that may not be in the same life-cycle stage. Thus, the valuation of a relatively young firm is based more on a narrative surrounding the business model than financial indicators, which are more helpful in finding the value range of mature firms.

The usefulness of analyzing companies through a life-cycle lens is due to the relation between the primary transitions (e.g., from idea to the development of the products/services and from mature to the end, to name a couple) and working capital policies. It should be noted that there are no specific measures that the company has moved from one state to the subsequent one. Companies don't develop through generic and similar paths. Internal departments may be stuck in one stage for any firm while others behave as if the organization has moved on. In addition, managers may try as hard as possible to bypass a step or avoid at all costs the end-stage.

Damodaran (2021) also distinguishes between tech and non-tech firms' life cycles. In Fig. 3.7, the life cycle of tech firms is shorter, and they can climb the growth ladder faster.

For non-tech companies, the scaling up of the business should consume vast amounts of working capital if the cash conversion cycle is a positive

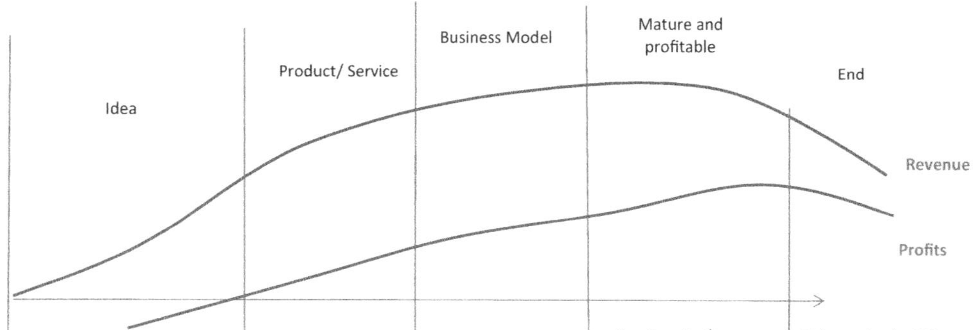

	Idea	Product/ Service	Business Model	Mature and profitable	End
Main Questions	Is there a Market? Is it big? Can the company survive?	Do people use it? Do they like it?	Do people pay? Is there a growth path?	Can it make $ even with high competition?	Fair asset value? How to return return $ to shareholders?
Metrics	Market size, Access to capital	No of users (EV/ users)	Satisfaction index, EV / Revenue	Profits+growth (PE, EV/EBIT)	C-flow, EV/ EBITDA, Leverage
Narrative x Numbers	Basically narrative	Narrative > numbers	Mix numbers narrative	Operational margin & ROIC	Mostly numbers
Value drivers	Market size, *market share* and target-margin.	Revenue growth	Revenue growth reinvestment needs	Numbers > narrative	Dividends and leverage
Dangers	Macro *delusion*, herd behavior.	Wrong value drivers	Growth illusion	Ignore disruption	Wrong value to assets.

Fig. 3.6 Companies' life-cycle (*Source* Damodaran [2021])

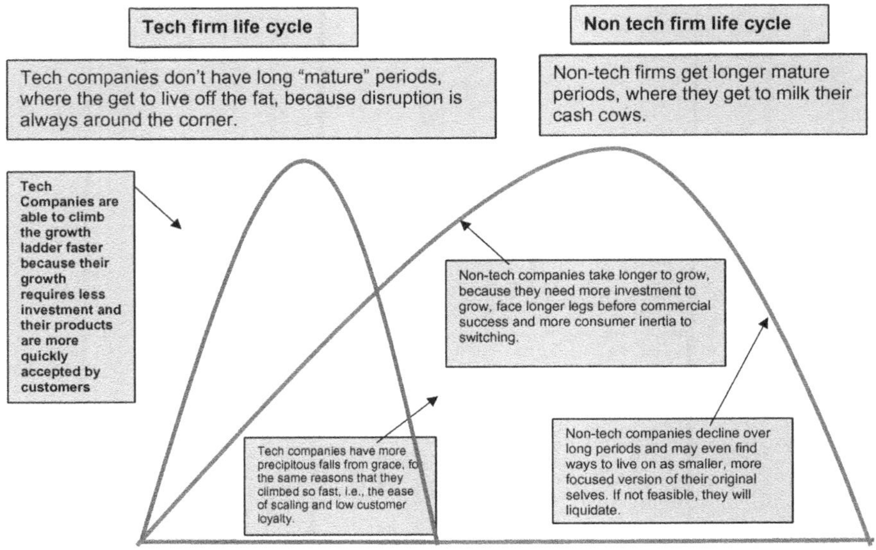

Fig. 3.7 Tech and non-tech firms' life cycles (*Source* Damodaran [2021]. https://aswathdamodaran.blogspot.com/2021/12/managing-across-corporate-life-cycle.html)

number. In contrast, mature companies are usually cash-generation entities. Profits, in the figure, refer to the gross and operating margins. For the first transition, from an idea to the development of the product/service, the primary indicator is the gross margin. For most new companies, the initial batches are loss leaders, and we assume that the product development phase starts when there is an indication that sales revenue can at least cover variable costs.

At this phase, the main questions are regarding the fit of the products and services with consumers. The transition to the subsequent stage is the maturing of the company's business model. There is a final push for growth in the business mode phase, but that does not come solely from new capital expenditures; there are already reinvestment needs from previous rounds of investments. In this phase, cash inflows top cash outflows, a sign that the company sees returns from past investments.

In the following stage, the firm is solidly generating more income than it needs to maintain its productive capacity. As the business environment hardens, shareholders must decide if they will extract value or search for a way to avoid the following stage. Usually, suitable investments opportunities dwindle, and the main drivers of shareholder value become the operating margin and the return of invested capital. In many small companies, the fear of the final stage trumps almost anything else, and managers become trapped in a rat's race to avoid sales decline, burning shareholder value.

In Fig. 3.7, the final stage is represented as a relatively smooth process in which sales gently decline over time, as managers return cash to shareholders. Of course, an end to a company's operations can come swiftly and without warning. In that case, having returned resources to shareholders would be even more crucial than in the instance in which managers expect sales to decline slowly over time. Of course, for many individuals, their family-owned small business is their primary source of income. Thus, a family may look for making a firm last as long as possible. Still, the central dilemma of a company at the end-stage remains: should managers extract as much value as possible from a dwindling business or reinvest what may be the last cash flow of a dying business to extend a company's life?

The life-cycle figure allows us to pinpoint the significant transitions a business goes through as it matures. As a firm evolves, so do its working capital requirements. The life-cycle approach also allows us to identify the primary external risks to a company's cash flow as the organization matures.

3.7.1 Which Working Capital Strategies Matter During Firms' Life Cycles?

Working capital management is not essential to a firm, depending on its standing. For mature companies, limiting x-inefficiency is much more critical than for organizations still developing their business model. Figure 3.6 divides a firm's life-cycle into five stages: idea, product/service, business model, mature and profitable, and the end.

There are unlimited types of working capital management. The most common type is the invest as you go strategy, in which companies organically use retained profits or other sources of funds to allow the business to expand. However, companies that aim to grow exponentially will not rely on internally generated cash flow. Many of the recent tech unicorns tapped into capital markets to develop the required capital to expand quickly.

The financial cycle is not particularly relevant for organizations developing their ideas, with one caveat. As the goal of startups is to ensure that they have viable products or services, efforts should go into designing them. However, viability is not just a cost-related issue. When entrepreneurs discuss subsistence, they usually refer to producing and selling something at a profit.

Take the standard business canvas model (Osterwalder & Pigneur, 2010). The main dimensions refer to infrastructure, value proposition, customers, and finance. Regarding the latter, a firm's finances are broadly divided into cost structure, if the business is cost-driven or value-driven, economies of scale and scope, and revenue streams.

Working capital management is not prominently featured in the standard business canvas model. But businesses cannot survive without generating enough cash flow to pay off debts and return value to shareholders.

Extended payment terms may turn otherwise viable business models into losing propositions. For instance, supplying wares to supermarkets that retain part of the sales as marketing fees to be repaid a year later may exacerbate the funding restrictions of a new company. Amazon has notably informed shareholders that it had no intention to pay dividends to use any cash generated by its operation to fund its remarkable expansion. Firms can write up their business models to postpone profitability to grab market share. They may even sell their products below cost. Stories about ambitious start-ups burning cash are familiar. For such types, solid working capital management allows managers to focus on what matters most: growth. One example of appropriate trade credit policies for startups willing to sell below cost is to require upfront payments from customers. Clients won't usually mind paying upfront for unduly cheap goods and services if the deal is good enough.

Another example from Amazon is their Prime service. The company launched Prime subscription in February of 2005, offering unlimited 2-day delivery on over 1 million in-stock items (or, as they announced it, "all-you-can-eat express shipping"). Initially, the price was $79 a year (Hatch, 2020). Amazon was likely subsidizing its clients to ensure their loyalty. But to prevent the company's coffers from bleeding dry, payment was made upfront. Setting up payment terms with suppliers and terms to customers should be a crucial step in a business plan development. Yet working capital management is not as meaningful for startups in the subsequent stages.

Figure 3.8 below brings Jeff Bezos' letter to Amazon's clients announcing Prime (Wohlsen, 2015).

The letter marks Amazon's transition to the product/service stage in its life cycle. Interestingly, even after 15 years, it is unclear if Prime would be a viable business model if it were not embedded into Amazon's ecosystem. Even though signing new customers brings immediate resources to the company, it may be that the average customer ends up costing the company due to the free shipping and unlimited access to other products from the company. However, Prime likely generates immense value to Amazon, making it harder for customers to switch to other companies. As Wohlsen (2015) puts it, Prime is a "finely tuned engine that drives the consumption of physical and digital goods in a seemingly unstoppable cycle optimized for the 21st-century economy."

amazon.com. Prime

Dear Customers,

I am very excited to announce Amazon Prime, our first ever membership program, which provides "all-you-can-eat" express shipping. It's simple: for a flat annual membership fee, you get unlimited two-day shipping for free on over a million in-stock items. Members also get overnight shipping for only $3.99 per item—order as late as 6:30PM ET.

Amazon Prime takes the effort out of ordering: no minimum purchase and no consolidating orders. Two-day shipping becomes an every day experience rather than an occasional indulgence.

We are offering Amazon Prime membership at the introductory price of $79 per year, which includes sharing the benefits with up to four family members in your household.

Considering that we normally charge $9.48 for two-day shipping on a single book and $16.48 for overnight, many of our customers will find the program very rewarding. It works across books, DVDs, music, electronics, kitchen, tools, health, personal care, etc, etc.

We expect Amazon Prime to be expensive for Amazon.com in the short term. In the long term, we hope to earn even more of your business, which will make it good for us too. We hope you enjoy our latest innovation.

You can sign up for membership with 1-Click.

Sincerely,

Jeff Bezos
Founder & CEO

Fig. 3.8 Jeff Bezos' letter to Amazon's clients

In the product/service maturation stage, firms should start to optimize their cash conversion cycle. They scale their production and build the processes needed to position themselves in their markets. Companies establish relationships with banks, suppliers, and customers as the products are developed. There are limits to working capital strategies in the product development stage. Managers should not sign long-term contracts that could bring more favorable terms with suppliers and offer extremely advantageous credit lines to customers. However, companies should expect a reduction in the financial cycle's volatility during this phase. Managerial effort should not focus on working capital management in the product development phase, but it cannot be disregarded entirely. After all, companies in that step of the life cycle are still likely to be burning cash, and any process that limits money outflow should be welcomed.

In the business model stage, managers should have a significant focus on working capital management. Reinvestments become an intrinsic part of the business in this step. The business should be stable enough that long-term relationships can bring down costs and allow companies to optimize payment terms. Managers can set up predictable receivables and accounts payable procedures without subsidizing customers. Given that growth is still a significant concern reducing the cash-conversion cycle should be managers' goal in the business model stage of companies' life cycle.

Companies are usually not strapped for cash in the mature and profitable stage. In that stage, managers should consider the tradeoffs with extended payment terms. Firms don't need to minimize their financial cycle anymore, so managers have the option of acting as lenders to small companies in their supply chain. In addition, executives usually have more resources, financial and managerial, to set up working capital optimization strategies.

> "Would you be comfortable with raking in profits while sales remain steady for years?" is a question I regularly ask ultimate owners of medium-sized corporations. The answer is almost always a resounding "No!" with myriad qualifications: "my company has grown 20% a year for 20 years, and the business would not survive stagnant sales"; "lack of growth would hand market-share to competitors"; "there are many investment opportunities in the markets where the firm operates; the only reason we are not investing more is that I don't want to borrow funds."

Many business owners equate a lack of revenue growth with a crisis, internal or external. However, many of the most valuable companies globally are mature, profitable companies that won't mind sailing through stormy markets by setting up anchor, reducing investments, working to keep revenues stable, and raking in profits.

Counterintuitively, many business owners find that the most challenging stage of working capital management is when their companies are reliably profitable. MRV's case of extracting over U$1 billion in x-inefficiency fits the transition from a solid business model to a mature and profitable company. MRV was still multiplying its sales alongside the "Minha Casa Minha Vida" market. However, executives knew that the program was unlikely to continue growing at its earlier pace. They were preparing the company for slower growth and a shift towards cash flow generation. Thus, minimizing the company's financial cycle was a catalyst for MRV's stage as a mature and profitable organization.

Finally, working capital ceases to be relevant for companies ending their operations. In the last stage, the managers' goal is to return value to shareholders. As revenue declines, the total operation working capital contracts. That frees resources that can fund special dividends. Figure 3.9 illustrates that process.

In the figure, assuming that the financial cycle remains constant, sales decline reduces operating working capital from OWC_t to OWC_{t+1}. In other words, the working capital investment required at the beginning of a company's history is finally freed up as the firm approaches the end of its operations.

To sum up, the importance of working capital management changes over a company's life cycle. It matters most when capital is required to accelerate growth and when x-inefficiency reduces capital efficiency. Optimizing the cash-conversion cycle is a constant process of hitting moving targets; when firms meet their financial cycle targets for the year, it is time to prepare to change gears for next year.

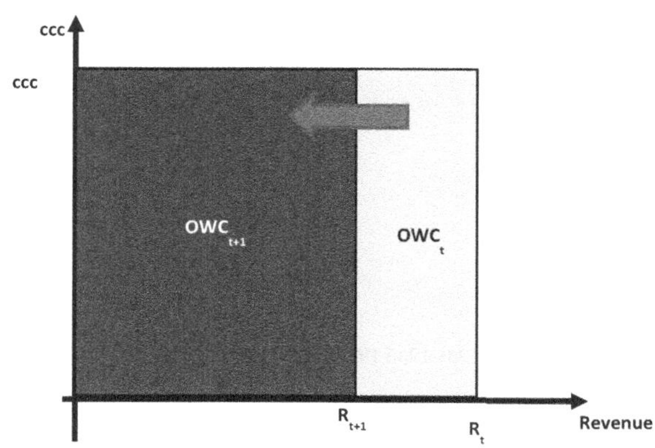

Fig. 3.9 Changes in operating working capital as sales decline

3.7.2 Mature Liquidity Management and Limiting x-Inefficiency: The Apple Wall

In one dimension, Apple is not different from most mom and pop shops worldwide: cash-flow crises have cut deep and left deep-marred scars that inform behavior years or decades after.

Apple famously did not pay dividends during Steve Jobs' second tenure as CEO. Less known is Apple's aggressiveness regarding payment terms to customers and suppliers, something that did not change even after the company was swimming in cash.

Jobs' first tenure with the company he co-founded was cut short partly because his ambitions were more extensive than the cash flow generated by the company at the time. From 1980, when the company became public, until 1997, when Jobs returned to Apple, its best year, in terms of income, was 1992, when income before extraordinary items (Fig. 3.10) stood at U$530 million.

The financial constraints followed Jobs into his other endeavors, and it was not until the middle of his second tenure that Apple turned into a cash-generation machine. Apple's income crossed the U$1 billion threshold in 2005, tripled to U$3.5 billion by 2007, and almost quadrupled to U$14 billion by 2010 (Fig. 3.11). In the second half of the 2010s, Apple's income before extraordinary items averaged over U$50 billion per year.

In the mid-2000s, Steve Jobs, for the first time in his career, was unencumbered by cash-flow restrictions. Yet, while Apple's success opened the

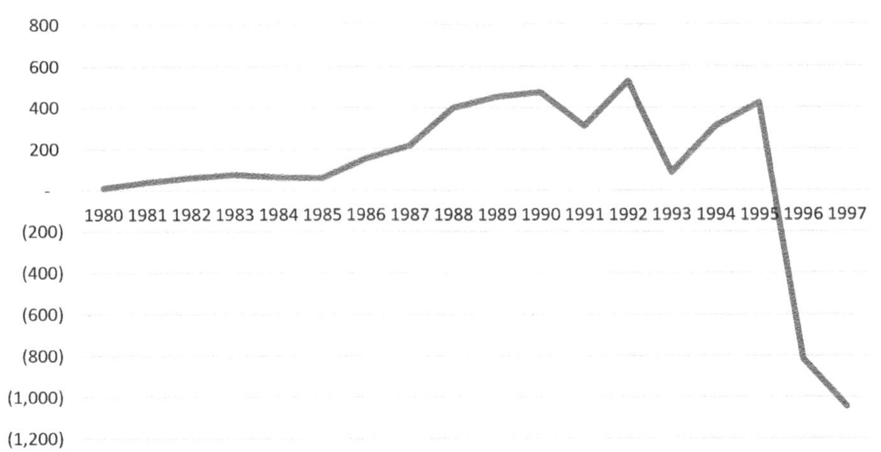

Fig. 3.10 Apple's income before extraordinary items, 1980–1997, U$ million (*Source* Apple's financial statements)

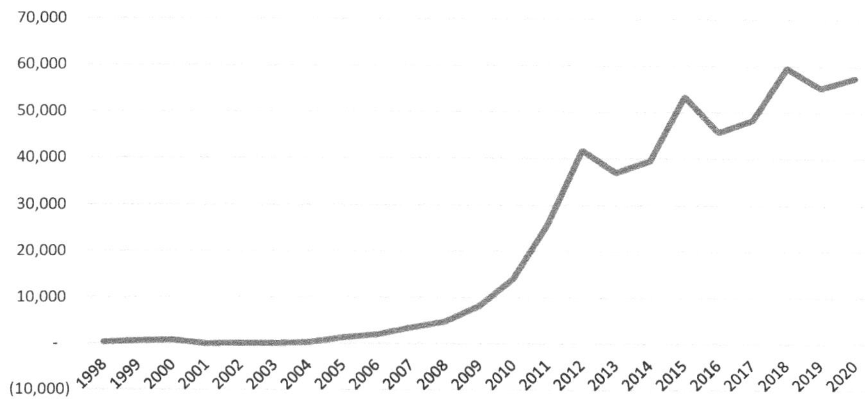

Fig. 3.11 Apple's income before extraordinary items, 1998–2020, U$ million (*Source* Apple's financial statements)

possibilities of funding the ideas of the product development team, the lean times had made a mark. Jobs made two momentous decisions: Apple would not pay dividends as long as he was CEO, and it would build a wall between the operations and the financial management departments. These decisions would ensure that Apple always has enough cash to fund projects, from the simplest to the most outrageous.

While Jobs' reluctance to pay dividends made the most news, it was arguably more challenging to build a wall between finance and operations than announce to shareholders that the company would delay returning money to them.

Successful companies tend to grow complacent; as profits grow, the drive for maximum efficiency wanes. Without the pressure to generate every last dollar, managers tend to extend credit to customers or search for cost savings by paying suppliers early. It is well understood that shareholders are uncomfortable when companies hold on to too much cash, as it is tempting for managers to embark on vanity projects. Less known is the impact of excess money on payment terms.

Firms tend to lose x-efficiency as their market power increases. Organizations with a firm financial footing may act as lenders of last resort to supply-chains or absorb macroeconomic shocks in their balance sheet. And those are some of the most benign by-products of companies finding themselves in a sound financial position.

X-efficiency refers to how a company can achieve maximum outputs from its inputs. Managers in larger and more profitable companies don't have the same incentives to be as efficient as their peers in smaller companies. Organizations are forced to survive efficiently in more competitive markets or amidst crises.

In 2010, Steve Jobs defended his decision to keep shareholders' hands of Apple's growing cash pile by arguing that hoarding cash allowed bold moves. He claimed that it was better to save the money for bold risks, like acquisitions, than to spend it on stock buybacks or cash dividends. (Madway & Oreskovic, 2010). In that year's shareholder's meeting, Jobs claimed that "We're a large enough business now, that to really move the needle, we've got to be thinking pretty bold, pretty large. And who knows what's around the next corner. When we think about big, bold things, we know that if we needed to acquire something, a piece of the puzzle, to make something big and bold a reality, we could write a check for it." (Madway & Oreskovic, 2010). Still, then or now, nobody believed that Apple's strategy consisted of spending a significant portion of their cash holdings to acquire other companies. Steve Jobs likely wanted to ensure that he would never be in a position of being hampered by a lack of funds for Apple's projects.

Also likely is that drive for accumulating cash helped Apple develop its primary strategy to keep cash inflows as high as possible: the wall that separated money management from operations and sales.

Regardless of the billions of dollars that the company was raking in during the 2010s, procurement and sales departments could not change payment terms. If anything, as the company grew, it made payment terms for suppliers and customers worse.

In 2018, in one of my executive education classes, the cellphone and IT retailer owner told other CEOs and me that she would love to carry Apple's products but could not afford them. One of the reasons was that the payment terms were too stringent, with the company having to pay for the phones and other products before receiving them.

In 2021, Apple changed its terms to suppliers, resulting in affected companies publicly decrying the company. Titcomb (2021) reported that Apple had made complex demands to suppliers, changing how it handles products for sale in the online and physical Apple Store. Before according to Owen (2021), terms could be negotiated between suppliers and distribution companies, but the new terms were set by Apple and turned out to be not negotiable. Moreover, suppliers who disagreed with the new terms risked their placement on Apple's shelves. Among the changes, Apple would pay suppliers in 60 days instead of 45 days. That would not be too bad, resulting in the suppliers' DSO going up by 15 days.

However, the most significant change transferred sales and cash-flow uncertainty from Apple to its suppliers. Suppliers had to accept a "consignment model," being paid only once an item was sold (Owen, 2021). The effect on suppliers is a new source of cash-flow volatility. The previous model was the standard practice of Apple ordering products from suppliers, getting an invoice, and paying a specific time later (usually, 45 days). Apple would then sell the products, paying customers directly or debit and credit card companies. Apple revamped the standard retail model to eliminate cash-flow volatility due to sales uncertainty.

By establishing a consignment model, unsold inventory is not Apple's problem. For suppliers, it means not only economic but also financial risk. For suppliers, the economic cycle changes are represented in Fig. 3.12.

The best way to represent the consignment model is to show how it changes both DIO and DSO. Before, suppliers would purchase input, produces final products, and sell them to Apple. The economic cycle would end when orders from Apple stores arrived. The consignment model now makes the end of the economic cycle uncertain. Suppliers would have to produce and ship their goods, and their products would be considered sold only when Apple informed them that customers bought their wares.

For suppliers, this change was meaningful because it created a new source of uncertainty: working capital would have to be tied up until Apple

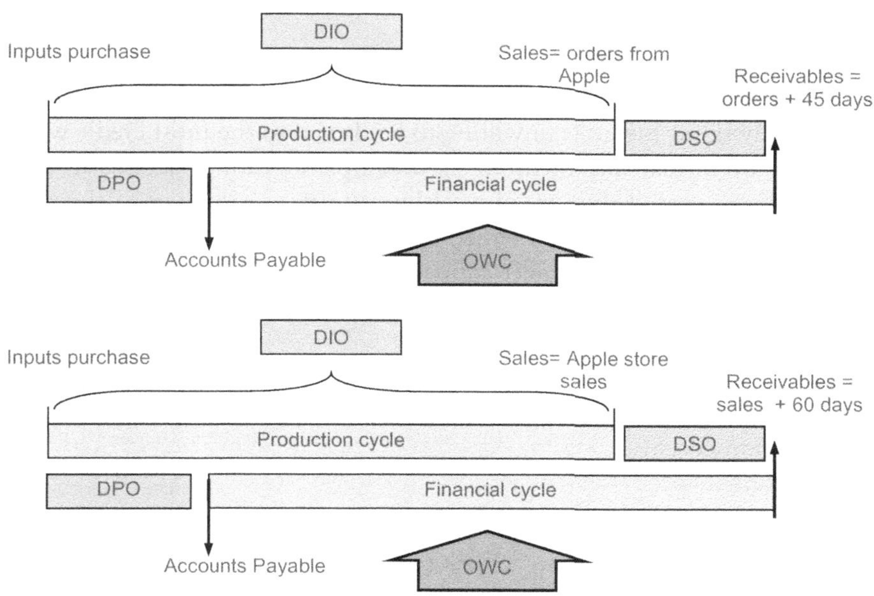

Fig. 3.12 Apple retail: from standard to consignment model

informed them that their products sold. Thus, suppliers could expect to receive payment for these sales after 60 days.

The change to the consignment model is akin to Apple extracting cash-flow from suppliers, alongside the outsourcing of sales' risk to its partners. Yet, Apple is a money generation machine, ending 2020 with over U$90 billion in cash and cash equivalents. Still, the clear demarcation between cash management and operations means that the company's managers behave as Apple were a cash-hungry company. Even amidst a global pandemic, if that squeezes the supply chain, so be it.

Since Steve Jobs died, the company has reversed its decision not to pay dividends or buy back shares. In the 2015–2020 period, Apple has repurchased around U$70 billion of its stocks per year. Nevertheless, Steve Jobs' legacy of always ensuring a steady cash flow stream still lives on.

3.7.3 Illiquidity Events

Viable companies may go bust due to cash-flow shocks that result in the inability to meet short-term obligations. For large and mature companies in rich countries, that possibility is remote, as they have access to bridge financing.

Bridge finance is a form of temporary financing that a company can use to cover short-term needs for funds until they can secure either long-term funds or more structured loans.

There is one exception to the ability of large companies to access credit markets: financial crises. During periods of economic turmoil, frozen credit markets may result in banks unwilling to lend even to the most credit-worthy firms. However, small and medium-sized companies cannot necessarily count on credit lines, even if they are in wealthy countries in the best of times.

Here, an illiquidity event is defined by a situation in which a company does not have enough funds to meet immediate obligations. More importantly, illiquid events matter even if they don't lead to bankruptcies, for the following non-exhaustive reasons:

- Managerial costs related to procuring emergency financing;
- Transaction costs;
- Reputational costs;
- Effects on short and long-term borrowing rates;

Sometimes, an illiquid event can be resolved by such actions as delaying payment to a supplier for a small fine. Nevertheless, illiquidity events can be traumatic and affect a firm years after. For instance, if a firm misses an interest payment because of an illiquidity event, managers may find it difficult or more expensive to borrow in the future.

One of the reasons for the lack of comprehensive working capital models is that some companies may find illiquidity events less problematic than others. For instance, organizations with significant cash reserves can easily absorb financial cycle shocks. The same is true for companies that expect their production and sales to decrease. As corporations downsize, they monetize previous working capital investments.

It is assumed that minimizing working capital requirements generates value throughout the book because capital is usually scarce, and shareholders prefer to use idle money rather than let it sit on companies' books unmolested. Verily, that may not be the case for every company. Still, as we will see, many of the more liquid companies globally, including Apple, Inbev, and Johnson & Johnson, maintain solid working capital strategies, even if they can much more easily access capital markets than a small company in a developing country.

It is also important to note that companies may trigger illiquidity events in their supply chain due to network relationships. A large conglomerate that goes bankrupt may trigger the failure of many of its suppliers. Even a large company that changes its payment terms unexpectedly can generate a supply chain crisis. Yet, large corporations can also act as buffers, absorbing shocks from financial crises by keeping suppliers and customers afloat amidst economic turmoil.

3.7.4 Arbitraging in Future Markets: Margin Calls and the Perilous Competitive Advantages of SOEs

A colleague who works for a Chinese state-owned company (SOE) described his main task as implementing the following strategy: "we use our inventory in different provinces to arbitrage prices using derivatives exchanges around the country."

Its operational strategy relies on its ability to short-sell commodities such as corn and wheat across China. The goal is to close price differentials in Chinese provinces, using future contracts from the Dalian futures exchange to hedge their positions as needed. For example, suppose wheat prices in a specific region are extraordinarily high. In that case, the company will sell inventory from its silos close to it, buying (longing, to use the correct jargon) futures contracts to lock in the profits.

For our purposes, the relevant part of their strategy is the reliance on bank credit to cover the possibility of margin calls.

Margin requirements are the ultimate expression of working capital requirements in futures markets. Future contracts are settled daily. To take a position in futures contracts, agents must post margins. For instance, for the December 2025 corn futures contracts in the Chicago Mercantile Exchange, the margin requirements for a position in one contract were US$ 875 as of early 2022. Each contract is for 5000 bushels. A trader's margin account is credited or debited as future prices change. If the balance on a margin account falls below a certain threshold, the trader must top up the margin account to the initial margin. In the past, the broker would call the trader to warn about the need for additional funds, which is the origin of the term margin call.

The strategy of the Chinese SOE is as close to arbitrage, or a riskless trade, as most companies can get to in real life. However, one risk remains, the liquidity risk from margin calls. The canonical cases for that are Metallgesellschaft (best described by Edwards & Canter, 1995) and Aracruz (Zeidan & Rodrigues, 2013).

Both companies failed to cover the losses of derivatives contracts that were supposed to insure their operational exposure. The only reason that Metallgesellschaft did not go bankrupt was because of a massive U$1.9 billion rescue operation by 150 German and international banks (Edwards & Canter, 1995).

Metallgesellschaft was using its derivatives position to hedge against oil price fluctuations. The company had entered contracts to supply approximately 160 million gasoline and heating oil barrels for ten years at fixed-priced. Interestingly, the company started to lose money on its financial positions because oil prices collapsed, which made its fixed-priced contracts much more profitable. However, as oil prices collapsed, they triggered margin calls on Metallgesellschaft's positions. The company did not have the funds to honor its positions (Edwards & Canter, 1995).

Regarding the Chinese SOE, it has a competitive advantage in closing price differentials in China due to its network of silos and distribution centers. However, the part of its strategy that relies on future contracts brings a liquidity risk from unexpected margin calls. Of course, margin calls don't matter very much for most companies, as it is unusual for financial executives to take prominent positions in futures contracts. My colleagues' argument that the organization's strategy was a pure arbitrage operation was surprising. He argued that there was no risk as the firm had an open credit line with its bank (another state-owned institution). Therein lies the danger, and managers should be wary of things that look too good to be true. In typical times, the

SOE could enter as many contracts as it wanted without fear of repercussion from margin calls. However, any crisis that would lead to banks freezing loans to market participants could jeopardize the company's future. Financial crises are rare events, but liquidity management that relies too heavily on bank credit is dangerous. In China, capital markets were shaken several times during the 2010s. Even though the People's Bank of China and other regulators successfully prevented bank lending from freezing up completely, companies should be prepared for such scenarios. It is one thing to enter futures contracts understanding that they pose a liquidity risk from the company's reliance on bank credit, but another to claim that there is no risk whatsoever.

Indeed, managers from Metallgesellschaft and Aracruz believed that their profitable companies were immune to market fluctuations, as these were large companies with credit lines with many banks. But extreme events happen, and misunderstanding the sources of risks may lead even the most profitable companies to ruin. No executive has ever had an unproductive meeting with the goal of answering these elementary questions: what can go wrong, and under which conditions we would not have enough money to honor our obligations?

3.8 In-Kind Finance: The Burkart and Ellingsen Model

This subsection summarizes the trade credit model by Burkart and Ellingsen (2004), in some parts using their words. The model formalizes some essential observations, which complements the lessons gained from previous sections. Specifically, the model explains why trade credit has short maturity, why trade credit is more prevalent in less developed credit markets, and why accounts payable of large unrated firms are more countercyclical than those of small firms.

At the core of the model is the conventional idea that moral hazard at the investment stage gives rise to the credit rationing of poor entrepreneurs. The model is based on a competitive input market, and two crucial assumptions: inputs are less easily diverted than cash is, and input transactions are more easily observed by suppliers (who take part in them) than by banks.

First, let's consider a risk-neutral entrepreneur who has observable wealth, $\omega > 0$, and has the opportunity to invest in a project, which transforms an input into an output. Let q denote the amount of purchased input, which is observable to the input supplier but not to outside parties, such as the bank. The input quantity into the project is the investment and is denoted by I. The investment I is not verifiable to outsiders. The entrepreneur is a price taker in both the input and the output markets. The revenue, pQ, is assumed to be verifiable.

Given an interest rate r_B and input prices normalized to 1, the entrepreneur's first-best investment level, $I^*(r_B)$, is:

$$pQ'(I^*) = 1 + r_B$$

For the model to be interesting, the entrepreneur is wealth constrained and cannot fund the investment internally, i.e., $\omega < I^*(r_B)$. There are two potential sources of funding, bank credit and trade credit.

Crucially, the model is based on the possibility that entrepreneurs may get external funding without any intention of repaying it. They can divert cash by borrowing money and using it to pay immediate dividends, for instance, instead of investing the funds in the projects, as they are supposed to do. In other words, entrepreneurs may divert credit by using part of the available resources to generate nonverifiable private benefits. Because outside parties cannot observe input purchases and investments, banks do not know if the entrepreneurs use the borrowed funds for investment or diversion in the model's scope. Banks learn about it later, as both output and sales revenues are verifiable and can therefore be pledged to outside investors. Entrepreneurs enjoy project returns only after honoring all repayment obligations. However, diverted resources can be appreciated immediately and thoroughly and are only repaid if project returns are available. If all resources are diverted, nothing is repaid.

Diversion may happen because the two external funding sources differ in their exposure to moral hazard. For each unit of cash that entrepreneurs divert, they receive $\phi < 1$ units of private benefit while obtaining only $\beta\phi$ units of personal benefit for each unit of input diverted. Thus, the level of creditor vulnerability is directly related to ϕ.

The variable β (which rests in the interval between 0 and 1) measures input liquidity. When β is large, the input can be transformed into private benefits almost as quickly as cash. If β is small, the input cannot easily be diverted. For instance, an input can be illiquid if it is a piece of specific machinery or a performed service with no residual value.

The following step is to assume that diversion yields a marginal private benefit exceeding the average rate of return to first-best investment at an interest rate of zero:

$$\varnothing > \underset{-}{\varnothing} = \frac{pQ(I^*(0)) - I^*(0)}{I^*(0)}$$

Banks and suppliers offer credit in the form of overdraft facilities, L_b and L_s, respectively. Suppliers can more easily observe if entrepreneurs use the borrowed money to purchase inputs. The final sequence of events is thus:

- Banks and suppliers simultaneously make their contract offers.
- The entrepreneur visits the supplier, which must be done only once.
- The entrepreneur chooses among the contract offers.
- The entrepreneur chooses L_B, L_S, and q.
- The entrepreneur invests/diversion decision.
- The payoff realizes, and repayments are made.

The model also allows dividing entrepreneurs into cash-starved and wealthy. Formally, there is a critical wealth level $\widehat{\omega}(\varnothing, p) > 0$ such that entrepreneurs with less wealth than $\widehat{\omega}$ are credit-constrained and invest strictly less than I*(0). Entrepreneurs with more wealth than $\widehat{\omega}$ borrow less than their credit limit and invest I*(0).

3.8.1 Credit Rationing

One of the main results of the model is that trade credit eases credit rationing. How does that happen? Formally, for given parameters (ϕ, β, p) there are critical wealth levels $\widehat{\omega}_1$ and $\widehat{\omega}_2 > \widehat{\omega}_1$ such that: (i) entrepreneurs with wealth above and $\widehat{\omega}_2$ take no trade credit and invest $I \in [I*(rs), I*(0)]$; (ii) entrepreneurs with wealth in-between $\widehat{\omega}_1$ and $\widehat{\omega}_2^{\widehat{\omega}}$ take trade credit and invest $I^*(r_S)$; (iii) entrepreneurs with wealth below $\widehat{\omega}_1$ exhaust both bank and trade credit limits and invest less than I*(rS).

Entrepreneurs with wealth above $\widehat{\omega}_2$ are unaffected by the availability of trade credit because they can already invest I*(rS) or more. However, if trade credit were unavailable, all other entrepreneurs would have invested less than $I^*(r_S)$.

Also important is how parameter changes affect the two credit limits, $\overline{L}_B$ and $\overline{L}_S$. For entrepreneurs with wealth smaller than $\widehat{\omega}_1$ the equilibrium credit lines $\overline{L}_B$ and $\overline{L}_S$ is increasing in the output price (p) and the entrepreneur's wealth ($\widehat{\omega}$), and are decreasing in the creditor vulnerability (ϕ), in the input liquidity (β), and the trade credit interest rate (r_S).

Finally, trade credit utilization $\overline{L}_S$ is decreasing in the entrepreneur's wealth (ω) and increasing in creditor vulnerability (ϕ). Interestingly, increases in the output price (p) or in the trade credit interest rate (r_S) have an indeterminate effect on $\overline{L}_S$.

3.8.2 Credit Substitution and Credit Volume

Another significant result is about the conditions for credit substitution and credit volume. Credit-constrained entrepreneurs use as much trade credit as possible, so the process is better visualized by considering their investment behavior.

Credit substitution arises from changes in either ω or ϕ. The credit-constrained entrepreneurs exhaust the bank credit limit and invest I*(rS) independent of wealth and creditor vulnerability. However, following changes in either ω or ϕ, they continue to invest I*(r_S) and compensate the reduction (increase) in $\overline{L}_B$ by an increase (reduction) in $\overline{L}_S$.

This reasoning does not apply to variations in the output price or the trade credit interest rate because these parameters also affect I*(r_S). In that instance, there is a credit volume effect as well. For example, an increase in r_S leads to both a decrease in I*(r_S) and $\overline{L}_B$. The overall effect on trade credit utilization depends on which reduction is more extensive.

Burkhart and Ellingsen predict a sharp difference in trade credit dynamics depending on whether the borrower is rationed in the trade credit market or not. Bank credit and trade credit should typically move in opposite directions for entrepreneurs who are not constrained by their trade credit limits. Bank credit volumes and trade credit volumes move in the same direction for constrained entrepreneurs. For these entrepreneurs, bank credit is also procyclical. However, trade credit is procyclical for entrepreneurs who exhaust their trade credit limit; and countercyclical for others.

In a recession, all companies would face tighter bank credit limits; credit-constrained firms would also reduce trade credit, while unconstrained firms would borrow more from suppliers. As the authors point out (p. 578): "the only thing worse than having to increase trade credit borrowing is to be unable to do so."

The model also leads to two intuitive propositions: the ratio of trade credit to investment is nonincreasing in wealth (ω) and nondecreasing in creditor vulnerability (ϕ); and if entrepreneurs reach their trade credit limit, trade credit as a fraction of investment is decreasing in input liquidity, β. In other words, companies with better credit ratings will use more trade credit, but if they exhaust their credit limit, input liquidity is the main factor determining how much trade credit they will use.

3.8.3 Credit Limits from Banks and Entrepreneurs

The model is also helpful to explain why banks don't offer trade credit against the face value of all trade credit claims and under which conditions the entrepreneur will provide credit to customers.

Regarding banks' credit limits, there are two main reasons for that. The first is the possibility of diversion, as we have already seen. The second is that the entrepreneur may lend recklessly to customers. In other words, it is optimal for banks to keep entrepreneurs with some skin in the game.

As for the entrepreneur, a one-dollar receivable translates into 1 + s dollars. It also yields an additional bank loan of κ ($0 < \kappa < 1$). Even if entrepreneurs face tight credit limits, as long as a dollar of trade credit yields as high a return as a dollar of real investment, they will extend credit to consumers. Formally, trade credit to consumers is extended if and only if:

$$s \geq (1 - \kappa)(pQ^{'}(I) - 1$$

For instance, if κ is 80%, which the authors motivate because previous research has shown that many banks lend around 80% of accounts receivable, the interest rate on trade bills must exceed 20% of the return to real investment for the entrepreneur to be willing to offer credit to consumers. In addition, a business owner who can borrow at the rate r_S but whose suppliers do not ration is willing to offer trade credit if:

$$s \geq (1 - \kappa)r_S$$

Because receivables can be used as collateral, firms may be willing to extend trade credit at a lower rate than they pay. An extra dollar invested in receivables is not funded by an extra dollar of payables, as receivables create additional bank funding.

Finally, the model predicts that with few exceptions, high real trade credit interest rates are due to lack of competition among suppliers and that trade and bank credit have different maturities. As the authors write: "Intuitively, trade credit ceases to be useful in constraining diversion once illiquid input is transformed into liquid output. Therefore, sales revenues should be used to repay input suppliers as fast as possible, with new trade credit being granted only in connection with new input purchases." We will return to that intuition later, as it seems to go against the motivation of our approach, in which working capital investments are required to fund regular operations; trade credit arises from sales growth (or changes in the cash-to-cash cycle).

3.8.4 The Limits of Traditional Liquidity Ratios

There are four main types of traditional liquidity ratios:

- The current ratio (CR) is a simple measure of current assets to liabilities. It is purposed to inform whether the company has sufficient resources to cover its short-term debts (current liabilities).

$$Current\ Ratio = \frac{Current\ Assets}{Current\ Liabilities}$$

- The quick ratio (QR) compares a company's most liquid assets with its short-term obligations.

$$Quick\ Ratio = \frac{Cash + Cash\ equivalents + Accounts\ Receivable}{Current\ Liabilities}$$

- The operational cash flow ratio indicates if current liabilities can be covered by the cash flow generated by a firm's operations.

$$Operating\ cash\ flow\ ratio = \frac{Operating\ cash\ flow}{Current\ Liabilities}$$

- The cash ratio uses the companies' most liquid assets to short-term obligations. $Cash\ ratio = \frac{(Cash + Marketable\ securities)}{Current\ Liabilities}$

The standard view is that these types of ratios are tests of liquidity. The Corporate Finance Institute (2022) is explicit in sharing this belief: "In terms of how strict the tests of liquidity are, you can view the current ratio, quick ratio, and cash ratio as easy, medium, and hard."

However, these ratios are not proper liquidity ratios; they are solvency ratios. Let's assume that current assets are valued higher than current liabilities. What does that mean? Can the company use its short-term assets to pay off its obligations? Not at all. Accounts payable, for instance, are recurring accounts. The same is valid with inventories. When would an organization need to sell its stock to meet its short-term obligations? When it ceases operations. As accounts payable, inventories are recurring accounts. They are not assets but materials needed for a firm to operate.

The Corporate Finance Institute mentions that liquidity tests can be viewed as easy, medium, and hard. Hard against what? Here is the thing: these ratios are widespread not because they measure liquidity but due to their use by financial institutions. For banks, the knowledge about companies' abilities to pay off obligations is relevant information.

Firms usually must report these ratios to financial institutions to access loans. Banks may require that certain proportions are kept within specific intervals. But that is not because these ratios are liquidity measures; banks are interested in the firms' ability to meet their obligations if they fail. Thus, managers have the incentives to track and keep the ratios from going above particular values. However, there is not much reason to use the traditional liquidity ratios for decision-making. They are static measures of solvency and not liquidity.

References

Acharya, V., Drechsler, I., & Schnabl, P. (2014). A pyrrhic victory? Bank bailouts and sovereign credit risk. *The Journal of Finance, 69*(6), 2689–2739.

Almeida, J. R., & Eid, W., Jr. (2014). Access to finance, working capital management and company value: Evidences from Brazilian companies listed on BM&FBOVESPA. *Journal of Business Research, 67*(5), 924–934.

BCG. (2004). *Working capital productivity: The overlooked measure of business performance improvement*. https://www.bcg.com/documents/file14447.pdf

Beck, T., & Demirguc-Kunt, A. (2006). Small and medium-size enterprises: Access to finance as a growth constraint. *Journal of Banking & Finance, 30*(11), 2931–2943.

Bellisario, A., & Pavlov, A. (2018). Performance management practices in lean manufacturing organizations: A systematic review of research evidence. *Production Planning & Control, 29*(5), 367–385.

Ben-Nasr, H. (2016). State and foreign ownership and the value of working capital management. *Journal of Corporate Finance, 41*, 217–240.

Berling, P., & Martínez-de-Albéniz, V. (2011). Optimal inventory policies when purchase price and demand are stochastic. *Operations Research, 59*(1), 109–124.

Bernanke, B. S. (1981). Bankruptcy, liquidity, and recession. *The American Economic Review, 71*(2), 155–159.

Biais, B., & Gollier, C. (1997). Trade credit and credit rationing. *The Review of Financial Studies, 10*(4), 903–937.

Bierman, J. R., & Smidt, S. (2012). *The capital budgeting decision: Economic analysis of investment projects*. Routledge.

Burkart, M., & Ellingsen, T. (2004). In-kind finance: A theory of trade credit. *The American Economic Review, 94*(3), 569–590.

Carbó-valverde, S., Rodríguez-fernández, F., & Udell, G. F. (2016). Trade credit, the financial crisis, and SME access to finance. *Journal of Money, Credit and Banking, 48*(1), 113–143.

Carpenter, R. E., & Petersen, B. C. (2002). Is the growth of small firms constrained by internal finance? *Review of Economics and Statistics, 84*(2), 298–309.

Corporate Finance Institute, The. (2022). Liquidity ration. https://corporatefinanceinstitute.com/resources/knowledge/finance/liquidity-ratio/

Cuñat, V. (2006). Trade credit: Suppliers as debt collectors and insurance providers. *The Review of Financial Studies, 20*(2), 491–527.

Damodaran, A. (2021). Managing across the corporate life cycle: CEOs and stock prices! Aswathdamodaran.Blogspot.Com. https://aswathdamodaran.blogspot.com/2021/12/managing-across-corporate-life-cycle.html

Dickinson, V. (2011). Cash flow patterns as a proxy for firm life cycle. *The Accounting Review, 86*(6), 1969–1994.

Edwards, F. R., & Canter, M. S. (1995). The collapse of Metallgesellschaft: Unhedgeable risks, poor hedging strategy, or just bad luck? *The Journal of Futures Markets (1986–1998), 15*(3), 211.

Fullerton, R. R., Kennedy, F. A., & Widener, S. K. (2014). Lean manufacturing and firm performance: The incremental contribution of lean management accounting practices. *Journal of Operations Management, 32*(7–8), 414–428.

Hambrick, D. C., & Crozier, L. M. (1985). Stumblers and stars in the management of rapid growth. *Journal of Business Venturing, 1*(1), 31–45.

Hatch, G. (2020). Amazon prime: A timeline from 2005 to 2020, Pattern.com. https://pattern.com/blog/amazon-prime-a-timeline-from-2005-to-2020/

Huang, H., Shi, X., & Zhang, S. (2011). Counter-cyclical substitution between trade credit and bank credit. *Journal of Banking & Finance, 35*(8), 1859–1878.

Kieschnick, R., Laplante, M., & Moussawi, R. (2013). Working capital management and shareholders' wealth. *Review of Finance, 17*(5), 1827–1852.

KPMG. (2010). Cash matters—Cash and working capital management in China. https://www.kpmg.de/docs/CashMatters.pdf

Madway, G., & Oreskovic, A. (2010). Apple's jobs says cash hoard allows for bold moves. *Reuters*. https://www.reuters.com/article/us-apple-idUSTRE61N4EH20100226

Nilsen, J. H. (1994). *The impact of credit markets on monetary policy* (Ph.D. thesis).

Nilsen, J. H. (2002). Trade credit and the bank lending channel. *Journal of Money, Credit, and Banking, 34*(1), 226–253.

Osterwalder, A., & Pigneur, Y. (2010). *Business model generation: A handbook for visionaries, game changers, and challengers* (Vol. 1). John Wiley & Sons.

Owen, M. (2021). Apple store suppliers suffering through longer payment terms, consignment model. Appleinsider.com. https://appleinsider.com/articles/21/02/06/apple-store-suppliers-face-longer-payment-terms

Petersen, M. A., & Rajan, R. G. (1997). Trade credit: Theories and evidence. *The Review of Financial Studies, 10*(3), 661–691.

Roughan, G. (2020). Government support for businesses by country. *Unleashed*. https://www.unleashedsoftware.com/blog/COVID-19

Titcomb, J. (2021). Apple store suppliers squeezed by tougher payment terms. *The Telegraph*. https://www.telegraph.co.uk/technology/2021/02/06/apple-store-suppliers-squeezed-tougher-payment-terms/

Wohlsen, M. (2015). Amazon prime is one of the most bizarre good business ideas ever. Wired.com. https://www.wired.com/2015/02/amazon-prime-one-bizarre-good-business-ideas-ever/

Yang, S. A., & Birge, J. R. (2018). Trade credit, risk sharing, and inventory financing portfolios. *Management Science, 64*(8), 3667–3689.

Zeidan, R., & Rodrigues, B. (2013). The failure of risk management for nonfinancial companies in the context of the financial crisis: Lessons from Aracruz Celulose and hedging with derivatives. *Applied Financial Economics, 23*(3), 241–250.

Zeidan, R., & Shapir, O. M. (2017). Cash conversion cycle and value-enhancing operations: Theory and evidence for a free lunch. *Journal of Corporate Finance, 45*, 203–219.

4

Market Power and Working Capital Optimization

This chapter establishes a general relationship between trade credit and market power. Usually, companies use their market power to reduce costs or increase prices. In addition, they use their influence over market outcomes to deter entry, bundle products, collude, or refuse to enter into a deal.

The main tradeoffs that companies with market power face are extracting value and acting as banks through supply-chain finance. The latter gives corporations the option to increase sales or reduce costs, as funds are indirectly loaned to suppliers and customers. The former allows companies to reduce their own cash-conversion cycle, thus freeing cash and increasing the return of their working capital investments.

There is no general model that companies should follow in their choices of exercising or not their ability to extract or distribute funds throughout the supply chain. There are essential short and long-term considerations to be made. A company that behaves as the lender of last resort for its supply chain erects another barrier to entry that makes it less likely to lose its market power in the long run. However, corporations that borrow from the supply chain through forcibly reducing DSO and lengthening DPO don't need outside capital to finance some of their growth.

The intuition for the general nature of the relationship between market power and trade credit comes from behavior like that of Mondelez, which unilaterally instituted payment terms for 120 days (Parekh, 2013), squeezing suppliers in the name of "payment predictability."

R. Zeidan, *The General Model of Working Capital Management*, https://doi.org/10.1007/978-981-19-3334-9_4

However, corporations may choose to refrain from extracting every dollar from the supply chain due to supplier and customer relationships, the nature of the transacted good, and the characteristics of the banking relationships, among others. Still, in the absence of strategic considerations, companies should optimize payment terms in the same way they look to maximize profit. Firms may also optimize payment terms for part of the supply chain, with distinct rules for certain suppliers due to strategic relationships. Another way to frame this issue is that the value-extraction relationship between market power and payment terms dominates strategic supplier and customer relationships when large companies are credit-constrained.

There have been a few essential scientific articles about the relationship between CCC and market power. Works have focused on bargaining power (Fabbri & Menichini, 2010), collateral liquidation (Fabbri & Klapper, 2016), and the behavior of (de)centralized banks in concentrated markets (Canales & Nanda, 2012). Fabri and Klapper (2016) document that suppliers with weak bargaining power towards their customers are more likely to extend trade credit, sell a larger share of goods on credit, and offer a more extended payment period before imposing penalties. Dass et al. (2015) rely on a model with incomplete contracts and bargaining power to argue that trade credit can serve as a commitment device for making relationship-specific investments. The present version of our model cannot treat some specific characteristics of trade credit contracting (also in Giannetti et al., 2011). Still, through different means, we can show that trade credit is decreasing in market power (here, for both upstream and downstream companies).

4.1 Determinants of Working Capital

Generally, firms cannot predict all the relevant inputs for their working capital requirement (for instance, firms cannot perfectly forecast sales). Uncertainty and trends are decomposed in a deterministic part and a stochastic part (for instance, a trend in sales may be related to firms' life cycle; sales might decrease or increase if companies are expanding or contracting). Thus, sales or quantity demanded (Q) is represented as:

$$Q = Q_0 + N(\mu, \sigma).$$

Sales (Q) follows a random walk with a trend (any value, including zero) and standard deviation σ. Later, we assume that trends are not equal to zero. A similar logic holds for the price (P).

Overall, a firm must maintain the share of the working capital within the amount it procures to finance inputs and for the period taken to transform cash outflows for inputs into cash inflows from outputs. For simplicity, firms do not generate economic rents, which implies that the operating margin equals the cost of capital. Consequently, the price of a product equals input prices plus the cost of capital.

Other assumptions include that the firm uses an invariant technology and does not incur product loss. WCR is thus the average daily output multiplied by the number of days it takes for a firm to translate cash outflows for inputs into cash inflows from sales. The difference between WCR and OWC is straightforward—OWC is the realization of WCR ((WCR $=$ E(OWC)). For the moment, let's assume that firms do not maintain additional liquidity cushions. The equity sign acknowledges that the noise in the stochastic process is not known when the firm chooses the WCR.

$$\text{OWC} \sim \text{CCC} \cdot P \cdot Q$$

Components in this equation can be subdivided into deterministic and stochastic parts. The related CCC (as in Zeidan & Shapir, 2017, with an invariant operating margin) is given below:

$$\text{CCC} \sim \text{DSO} + \text{DIO} - \text{DPO} + N(\mu_1, \sigma_1)$$

While DIO is primarily determined internally, DSO and DPO are functions of interactions with other firms. The degree to which a firm can influence the difference between the two depends on its market power relative to suppliers and customers. Consequently, let's define market power as the firm's ability to push the difference between DSO and DPO to a negative number. Indeed, in the same way that contestability constrains monopolies in regular profit maximization practices, there are limits to how firms can exploit their market power. Still, the intuition is straightforward—if a focal company uses its market power to drive customers toward the faster payment of bills, it may experience a decline in the number of orders. For that purpose, the model includes an elasticity of demand (denoted as ν following Nadiri, 1969) concerning DSO. This elasticity is usually positive because customers prefer a higher DSO over a lower DSO; this is similar to selecting low- to high-priced goods and services. Consequently, market power is represented by $\nu_{\text{DSO},Q}$.

$$\nu_{\text{DSO},Q} = \frac{\text{dQ}}{\text{dDSO}} \cdot \frac{\text{DSO}}{Q}$$

This elasticity implies that, in a period following a reduction in the DSO, customers demand fewer units of the product provided by the focal firm (since the operating margin is invariant). That translates into:

$$\begin{aligned} Q_t &= Q_{t-1} \cdot \left(1 + \frac{\mathrm{DSO} \cdot \nu_{t-1}}{100}\right) + N(\mu, \sigma) \\ &= Q_{t-1} \cdot \left(1 + \frac{\mathrm{DSO}}{100} \cdot \left[\frac{\mathrm{dQ}}{\mathrm{dDSO}}\right]_{t-1} \cdot \frac{\mathrm{DSO}_t}{Q_{t-1}}\right) + N(\mu, \sigma) \end{aligned}$$

This equation reflects that a firm may extend different degrees of trade credit depending on its market power and the associated DSO-elasticity of demand. The higher a focal firm's market power, the weaker the DSO-elasticity is (the simplest way to interpret this is a lack of alternatives by customers). The weaker this elasticity, the more negative is the difference between DSO and DPO. Firms with more market power increase DSO such that there is a decrease in their demand for working capital and an increase in customers' demand for working capital. The firms follow this practice until the reduction in sales equals the decrease in working capital cost.

In the model, the firm wants to minimize the probability of insolvency. To keep the model simple, there is no function for overall profits, which would require a substantially more complex model and a relationship between payment terms and costs alongside the modeled relationship between these terms and sales. The limitation of this approach is the loss of some generality. The model does not capture some of the adverse effects of extending unfavorable terms to value chain participants. The model introduces an exogenous constraint that limits how a firm uses its market power to recover some generality. This constraint in the downstream market is set relative to a firm's market power in the upstream market. The variable limits the lower end of the DSO space according to the following relation:

$$\mathrm{DSO}_{\min,t} = \max\left\{\mathrm{DPO}_{t-1} \cdot \left(1 - \frac{\nu_{t-1}}{100}\right), 0\right\}$$

This equation implies the symmetry of market power between the upstream and downstream relationships in the supply chain. That is done for the model to have only one elasticity ($\nu_{\mathrm{DSO},Q}$) that connects market power to the CCC. Market power defines the minimum DSO value a firm may achieve for any given DPO value. Consequently, the minimum CCC a firm can achieve is the sum of $\mathrm{DSO}_{\min}$ and DIO. For simplicity, we set DIO to zero for simulations.

4.2 Transaction Costs

The model starts by introducing uncertainty in sales and price. The model can be extended to comply with a more realistic setting. Let's add borrowing and transaction costs. The cost of capital plays a role in working capital management, even for firms without borrowing constraints. The (opportunity) costs of working capital investment are increasing in the weighted average cost of capital (WACC). Adding the cost of capital also allows us to incorporate the economic impact of OWC (and thus WCR) volatility. Less predictable WCR prompts more considerable working capital costs. The financial cost of a chosen WCR over a period is represented by:

$$\mathrm{CF_{WC}} = \mathrm{WCR} \cdot \mathrm{WACC} = \mathrm{CCC} \cdot P \cdot Q \cdot \mathrm{WACC}$$

Trade credit transactions are usually more complex than simple cash payments, from paperwork to monitoring expenses and costs associated with defaults and delays. However, equity and other types of debt, which are the alternatives to trade credit, have their own sets of transaction costs. The extent of relative transaction costs is essential for the choice of trade credit to its alternatives. It also constrains the procedure for minimizing CCC.

The variable $\mathrm{TC_{WC}}$ represents the total transaction cost of borrowing money from commercial banks. There is a per-unit symmetric transaction cost τ to take out additional funding or reduce a credit line.

$\mathrm{TC}_{\mathrm{WC},t} = |\mathrm{CCC}_t \cdot P_t \cdot Q_t - \mathrm{CCC}_{t-1} \cdot P_{t-1} \cdot Q_{t-1}| \cdot \tau.$

Also, the WCR to minimize the probability of default depends on previous periods' characteristics, making the model inherently dynamic. Thus, the total financial effect of holding as well as raising working capital is:

$$\mathrm{CF}_{\mathrm{WC},t} = \mathrm{CCC}_t \cdot P_t \cdot Q_t \cdot \mathrm{WACC}_t + |\mathrm{CCC}_t \cdot P_t \cdot Q_t - \mathrm{CCC}_{t-1} \cdot P_{t-1} \cdot Q_{t-1}| \cdot \tau^{\cdot}$$

4.3 Simulations on Working Capital Changes

To understand how firms manage their working capital, a point estimate of WCR is not enough. Mistakes in setting WCR lower than OWC limit sales growth and may result in insolvency if firms can't borrow easily. Firms typically choose a liquidity buffer on top of their WCR to cushion themselves from unexpected shocks. Below are simulations that estimate the holdings needed for companies to operate unimpededly.

On average, firms need to raise cash or go insolvent every 20 years. Simulations are based on the amount of capital that limits insolvency to a probability of 5% per year. The initial set comprises 100 simulations of 1,000-time steps, thus assuming that companies plan to operate indefinitely.

4.3.1 Boundary Conditions

To avoid singularities and corner solutions, there are a few additional contingencies. Given that firms do not make working capital decisions in isolation, the model incorporates incentives to integrate the context of other managerial decisions with their own sets of objective functions.

In the model, firms' use of market power is a gradual process. Firms cannot (ab)use their market power (conceptualized as $\nu_{DSO,Q}$) immediately. The changes in DSO are delayed if firms exert market power. A parameter also captures firms' willingness to use their market power. The higher this coefficient, the faster firms transition from higher DSO values to lower DSO values to the extent to which their market power allows it. There are many reasons firms may not want to use all their market power or may refrain from using it immediately. One reason is that exerting pressure on their supply chain leads to a nonzero probability of shocks to sales (Q). Since customers may not repay the debt quickly, they may default or order from different suppliers. If customers become illiquid and delay payments, there will be a rise in the focal firm's WCR (and OWC). The mere act of using market power to reduce a company's OWC may contribute toward raising it. Other incentives to refrain from (ab)using market power comes from the non-modeled long-term contracting costs, input quality, effect on variable costs, relationship-specific investments, and anti-trust oversight, among others.

4.3.2 Parameters and Paths

The first set of simulations has a relatively simple set of parameters. The number of goods sold in the first iteration (Q_0) is set to 50, the same as P_0 (the price of one item). The trend is zero, and the standard deviation is 1 for both price and quantity. The cost of capital ($WACC_0$) is set to 10%, with a standard deviation of 0.1%. The initial DSO is 30, while the initial DPO is 20. Both DSO and DPO have a standard deviation of 0.1. Figure 4.1 illustrates how the working capital and the transaction cost to maintain the level of working capital change over time for the initial setting in which the firm uses its market power to lower DSO from 30 to 10 gradually over the 1,000-time steps (with DPO fixed at 20) under the parameters given above.

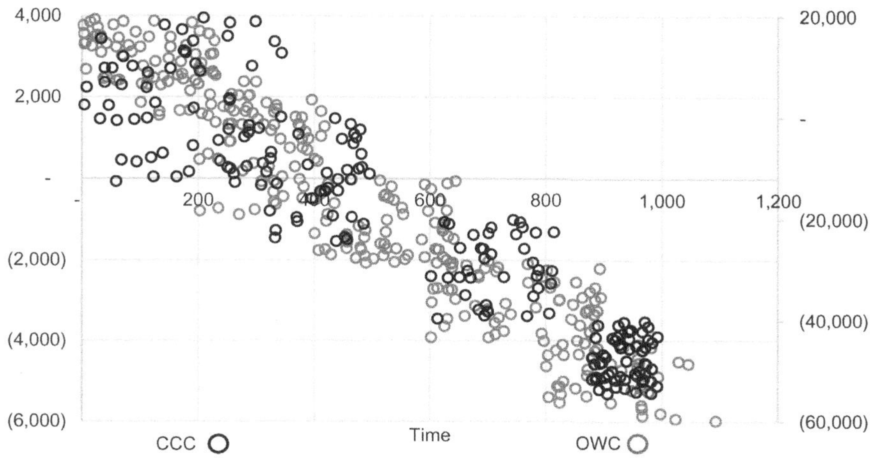

Fig. 4.1 Simulations (1,000) of OWC as firms use their market power (*Note* Cash flow impact, given transaction costs, of changes in the OWC in a simulation of 1,000 iterations. OWC changes as the firm uses its market power to reduce the CCC from +10 (DSO: 30, DPO: 20) to −10 (DSO: 10, DPO: 20))

Figure 4.1 shows how OWC (the realization of WCR) changes as the firm uses its market power to reduce the CCC from +10 (DSO: 30, DPO: 20) to −10 (DSO:10, DPO: 20) over 1,000 iterations. As indicated by the blue data points, interest payments, which start between 1,000 and 2,000, decline to zero and become negative (the firm earns interest from a negative cash conversion cycle) with a decline in the working capital. This process entails a positive cash flow of approximately 40,000 because of the reduction in OWC. The relatively large variation at the beginning and end of the plot is explained by the variation in P and Q (for the black data points) and the variation in WACC (for the blue data points), which is reinforced if the operating working capital is nonzero.

4.3.3 Simulating Firm Behavior

Firms do not actively manage (point estimate) their working capital every period as it would introduce substantial monitoring costs and insolvency risk. Therefore, we move our simulation by one level of abstraction to determine the amount of WCR firms must hold at the beginning of a simulation to obviate their need to take on additional capital over a certain period. We simulate 100 paths (each corresponding to 1,000 iterations shown in Fig. 4.1), assuming that companies want to keep the probability that realized

OWC is higher than WCR below 5%. We argue that this is a reasonable proxy for firms' strategy to maintain operations under uncertain OWC. Figure 4.2 shows how the working capital necessary to keep the probability of default below 5% increases with the standard deviation in revenue. In Fig. 4.2, the standard deviation of Q is allowed to vary between zero and one.

Proposition 1: The higher the uncertainty in Q, the higher a firm's WCR.

We intend to show the dependency of the WCR on the market power, as expressed by $\nu_{DSO,Q}$ (Fig. 3.2). Following the elasticity logic presented above, the minimum DSO a firm can achieve decreases with increasing market power ($\nu_{DSO,Q}$). For any initial setting of DSO relative to DPO, the CCC will move toward DSO_{min} minus DPO. As shown in Table 5.2, this transition is not instantaneous but spread out over the simulation iterations. Nevertheless, the average WCR decreases with the minimum in DSO. This relationship is shown in Fig. 4.3. Positive market power implies that focal firms can push DSO below DPO. An increase in market power increases the difference between DSO and DPO.

Consequently, the amount of capital necessary to avoid illiquidity is reduced. Owing to the noise in the variables that influence WCR, Fig. 4.3 only shows a general trend. The variance in WCR around the mean increases with market power because of the spread between DSO and DPO.

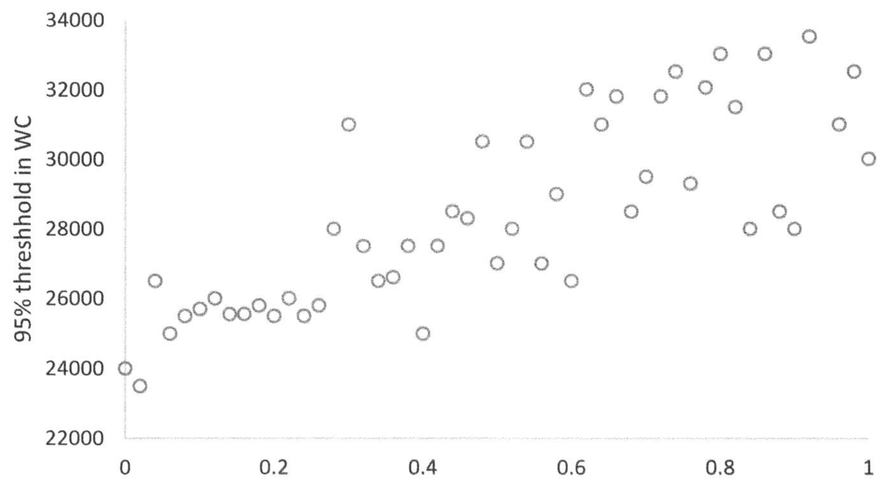

Fig. 4.2 Working capital investments to keep default probability <5% as a function of standard deviation in sales

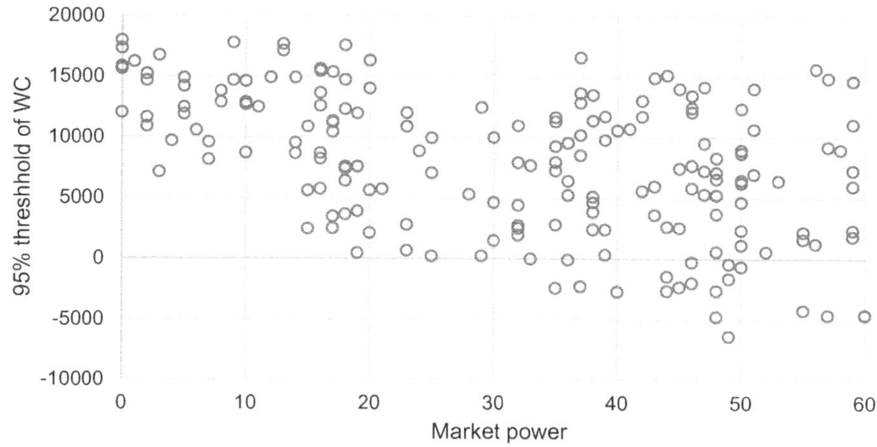

Fig. 4.3 Market power and working capital investment to keep default probability < 5% (*Note* working capital for pushing the default probability below 5% as a function of market power ($\nu_{DSO,Q}$), which varies between 0 and 60. Initial P and Q are still 50)

Based on the simulation shown in Fig. 4.3.

Proposition 2a: The higher a firm's market power, the lower its WCR.

Proposition 2b (corollary): The higher a firm's market power, the lower its CCC.

As for the relationship between market power and an initially negative cash-conversion cycle, given that a negative cash-conversion cycle allows companies to increase cash flow as sales grow, the expected relationship between market power and WCR is clear: their required working capital decreases as companies use their market power.

4.3.4 Empirical Evidence

Lee et al. (2018) investigate the relationship between firms' market power and financial cycles. They hypothesize that a supplier's market share is negatively associated with trade credit provision (of course, conversely, a buyer's market share would be positively associated with trade credit provision), and a supplier's buyer concentration is negatively associated with payment terms. Trade credit provision and the payment terms in a financial cycle are two sides of the same coin. A company that extends payment terms to its customers provides them (trade) credit.

Interestingly, the authors also study the relationship between payment terms and profit margins (specifically, gross margins). Formally, they aim to test if the industry-average trade credit provision is positively associated with the supplier's gross profit and if its abnormal trade credit provision is positively associated with its gross profit.

Their empirical strategy (Fig. 4.4) is based on supplier–buyer pairs in which both companies are publicly-listed as the unit of analysis. They estimate a fixed-effects model in which the variables of interest are the market share of suppliers and buyer concentration. The data set contains 7,274 unique pairs (3,260 suppliers and 1,487 buyers) and 26,647 observations over the period 1976–2010.

The regression results support the study's hypotheses. The coefficients of supplier market share are negative and statistically significant, while they are positive for buyer market share. Finally, the supplier's buyer concentration coefficients are negative and statistically significant. The last result indicates that companies tend to extract cash flow from consumers when their clients cànnot easily substitute their goods from those of other firms.

Some works focus on the credit aspect of trade credit. Of course, in many instances, firms should extend trade credit when other members of their supply chains are credit constrained. However, that is unlikely to be a factor for Lee et al. (2018)' sample, as the authors deal primarily with listed companies. All else being equal, the present dynamic framework of working capital

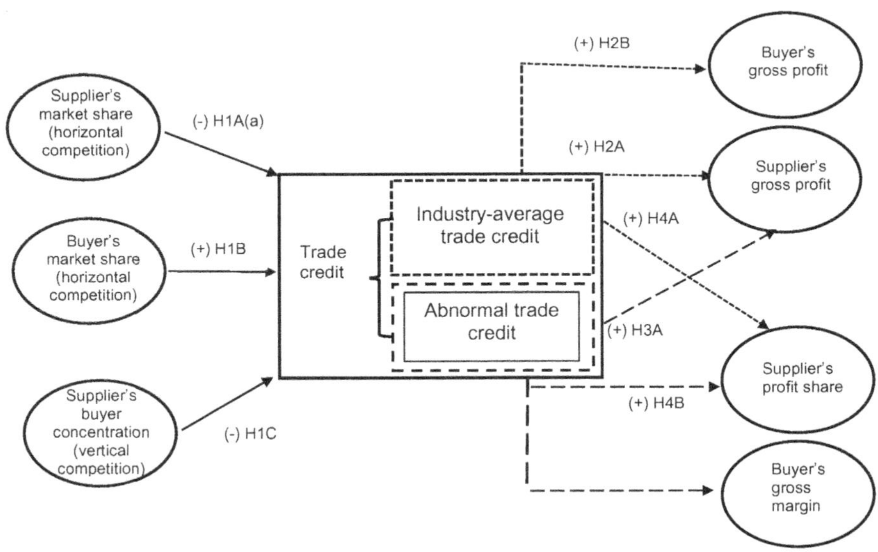

Fig. 4.4 Hypotheses development (*Source* Lee et al. [2018])

management would predict similar results to Lee et al. (2018). We now turn to Chod et al. (2019), who investigate the effects of trade credit extended by suppliers to cash-constrained retailers.

Chod et al. (2019) are interested in the spillover effects of trade credit relationships. In particular, they investigate the possibility that trade credit extended by suppliers to cash-constrained retailers allows the latter to increase cash purchases from their other suppliers, leading to a free-rider problem.

The authors write: "the free-rider problem is especially detrimental to a trade creditor when the free-riding suppliers are its product market competitors, leading to a negative relation between product substitutability among suppliers to a given retailer and trade credit that the former provide to the latter… A supplier that represents a smaller share of the retailer's purchases internalizes a smaller part of the benefit from increased spending by the retailer and, as a result, extends less trade credit relative to its sales. In consequence, retailers with dispersed suppliers obtain less trade credit than those whose suppliers are more concentrated."

Lee et al. (2018) and Chod et al. (2019) study the average behavior of publicly listed companies. Their results are consistent with the present general dynamic working capital management framework. Firms with market power can extract cash flow from their supply chain. Meanwhile, firms that purchase inputs from many suppliers will find it harder to improve payment terms.

However, there is also evidence for the flipside of the use of market power: focal firms as lenders of last resort. Gonçalves et al. (2018) study trade credit and product market power during a financial crisis. They find that firms with high market power provide more liquidity to suppliers during the great financial crisis. Moreover, the authors find that liquidity-insuring suppliers maintain monopoly rents; high market power firms increase sales relative to low market power firms during crises. Finally, these effects are present for liquidity-rich and liquidity-poor firms.

There are subtle confirmations of the expected relationships between market power and working capital management from the scientific literature. On the one hand, firms can exploit market power to reduce their financial cycle when convenient. On the other hand, they can act as lenders of last resort, especially during crises, profiting from either cash buffers or exclusive access to credit.

4.4 The Managerial Lessons

There are five primary lessons from integrating trade credit, working capital management, and market power. Here, it does not matter if

- If the goal is to maximize profits in the short run, companies can yield their market power to reduce their cash conversion cycle.
- If they bring the financial cycle to lower than zero, each additional unit sold will increase their cash flow.
- The main restrictions to the use of market power are the DSO-elasticity of demand and the possible impact of lengthy financial cycles on operating margin.
- Unused market power can function as reserves against illiquidity events or cushion the effects of financial crises.
- The use of market power should change throughout a firms' life cycle.

These five lessons describe the main tradeoffs related to working capital management.

Supply chain finance is costly compared to the alternative of using retained profits as firms' primary sources of funds. It is a common trope to state that small businesses entrepreneurs are too conservative in managing working capital because they lack the financial literacy to make sophisticated trade credit decisions.

Indeed, there are instances in which x-inefficiency is rampant, which is likely more common in small firms. Still, retained profits have one significant advantage over trade credit or other external sources of funds: it increases the likelihood that companies survive over the long run.

This section's model is beneficial for understanding how working capital policies affect the probability that companies will go bankrupt in the long run. Of course, firms may go bankrupt for all sorts of reasons. Still, working capital management may limit the probability of illiquidity events or allow managers to take more risks to leverage sales growth.

Companies that have some market power but don't use trade credit extensively have benefits, including the ability to cushion external shocks to their cash flow. However, it should be noted that this works if shocks are not systemic. For instance, during the great financial crisis of 2008 or the early stages of the pandemic in 2020, credit markets froze. Non-financial companies scrambled for cash to meet their obligations, and the unused market power was not of much use.

The central tradeoff regarding market power is that corporations can choose to extract value from the supply chain with lengthy DPO or short DSO or act almost as financial institutions, lending money to suppliers or customers. There are companies with short financial cycles due to their use of market power. In contrast, others purposedly have long cash conversion cycles, enjoying lower costs or higher prices from supply chain partners for extending credit to them. These dual possibilities are the primary reason why empirical studies of market power and working capital cannot be readily performed in large samples of non-financial companies.

There is one caveat to the use of market power, though. Firms are more likely to extend trade credit if they internalize the benefits to the supply chain. For instance, Petersen and Rajan (1997) argue that a monopolistic supplier is more willing to provide trade credit than if other firms also had market power, all else being equal. A monopolistic supplier is more likely to internalize the long-term benefit of helping customers or suppliers. Here is an intuition behind this argument. Assume that a customer is credit constrained but would purchase much more if they had access to credit. If a supplier were to extend trade credit to the consumer, it might get a slice of the increased purchases from the customer but will not get all of it. If a consumer were to buy more just from that supplier, that supplier would have more incentives to extend credit to the client. We explore the behavior of companies to extend trade credit when they can't internalize most of the benefits from it in Sect. 4.7.

Finally, there are essential lessons regarding trade credit policies throughout a company's life cycle. It is more likely that companies will extend credit to their supply chains when they are mature and profitable. During their high growth phase, organizations should streamline the financial cycle as much as possible. At the end phase, working capital ceases to be necessary strategically, as any credit extended to the supply chain is returned to shareholders eventually.

4.4.1 Mondelez and the (Ab)use of Market Power?

How far can companies push their suppliers? Depending on the company's size and market power, quite a lot. Large companies can squeeze suppliers to improve their cash flow through different strategies, but a straightforward one is extending payments terms significantly. Mondelez, a spun-off subsidiary of Kraft Foods, is an example of a company that maximizes its cash flow at the expense of its supply chain.

In July 2013, the company announced that it was changing its policy and would pay suppliers 120 days after receiving their invoice. Mondelez is by no means the only large company to have such a long payment cycle. A few months before, Procter & Gamble had lengthened its payment process from 45 to 75 days, and Merck was considering a 90-day policy.

That action is not very different from Ambev's during the financial crisis (Sect. 6.5.1): squeeze the production chain (requiring advance payments from customers and extending payment from suppliers) to reduce its working capital investments. Not every company can do that. For example, water and electricity concessionaires cannot reduce DSO below a specific value, as measuring and sending invoices take some time. Moreover, there are regulatory barriers: some rules limiting working capital management are built into public concession contracts.

In other countries, such as Europe, the business model is different, and there is the possibility of prepaid cards for water and electricity consumption. In this case, the OWC of the concessionaires would necessarily be lower than in the countries in which invoices are sent after measurement (in such cases, companies receive payments 30 to 45 days after measuring people's consumption).

In addition to extending payment terms to suppliers, Mondelez maintains a policy requiring that consumers pay invoices in less than 30 days. This period is 15 days for confectionery products, while snack distributors must pay within 25 days. Mondelez, using its privileged position, manages to have a negative OWC. In a note sent to Fortune magazine, Mondelez argued that the 120-day deadline "would align the company with industry practices, increase the transparency and predictability of payments." The company was the most indebted in the industry when it introduced these changes, and decreasing OWC would represent millions of dollars in reduced interest payments.

What were the risks? Lower profits because of higher costs, as suppliers priced in the extended payment terms, and quality control issues, as some firms may stop bidding on contracts to service Mondelez. In the end, Mondelez reduced its cash conversion cycle significantly. In 2017, its CCC was positive, and approximately five days. It became negative in 2018 and remained so until 2021, around ten days (Table 4.1).

Table 4.1 Mondelez cyclical assets and liabilities, in USD million, and financial cycle components, in days

	2017	2018	2019	2020	2021
Sales/Revenue	25,896	25,938	25,868	26,581	28,720
Accounts Receivable	3,526	3,006	2,927	2,954	3,188
Accounts Payable	5,705	5,794	5,853	6,209	6,730
Inventories	2,557	2,592	2,546	2,647	2,708
DSO (days)	49.0	41.7	40.7	40.0	40.0
DIO (days)	35.5	36.0	35.4	35.8	33.9
DPO (days)	79.3	80.4	81.5	84.1	84.4
CCC (days)	5.3	(2.7)	(5.3)	(8.2)	(10.5)

Source Mondelez's financial statements

4.5 The Information Content of Trade Credit

The in-kind model we have seen in Sect. 3.9 describes a static decision on financing a project using trade credit or not. In a sense, even in a world of perfectly liquid financial markets, trade credit facilitates business operations due to the nature of private information. Suppliers have access to information that banks and other financial institutions do not.

Some authors claim that the widespread use of trade credit is a puzzle due to its high implicit costs. But it is clear that trade credit contracts contain information that would be difficult to be collected by financial institutions.

Aktas et al. (2012) analyze the information content of trade credit, focusing primarily on American public companies after deriving a strategic game with imperfect information on trade credit decisions. Like the in-kind model of trade credit, input diversion is a possibility.

Aktas et al. (2012) is a two-period model with four types of agents: managers, investors, suppliers, and banks. The N managers decide between two available technologies, A and B, at time 0. Simultaneously, managers also choose how their chosen technology will be financed, either by trade credit (illiquid inputs from suppliers, TC) or bank loans (BF). Therefore, the set of actions available to managers is {A, BF; A, TC; B, BF; B, TC}. The manager's utility function is:

$$U = (\Delta V)^y (1 + F),$$

where ΔV is the variation of the firm's market value thanks to the investment decision, F indicates the manager's private benefits, and y captures the manager's preference for market value maximization.

Managers have information about their type y and the chosen technology but don't have a way to communicate these credibly to investors. The financing choice is public information.

The investment decision generates a value $(V_1(1+\beta) - V_0)$ when the game ends at period 1. V_0 and $V_1(1+\beta)$ are the firm's market value at time 0 and time 1, respectively. Technology A is more value-creating $(\beta > 0)$ and requires one unit of investment, while technology B is less value-creating $(\beta = 0)$ and requires α units of investment with $0 < \alpha < 1$. The authors also assume $(V_1 - V_0) > 1$, implying no bankruptcy risk.

If the manager chooses technology A, all inputs are invested; there is no input left for private benefits. If the manager chooses technology B, only a fraction α of the input is invested. If the financing source is trade credit, the remainder $(1 - \alpha)$ is an illiquid asset and cannot be diverted. However, if the financing source is bank loans, the remaining $(1 - \alpha)$ is a perfectly liquid asset (cash provided by the banks) and can be diverted for personal benefit. Notably, if managers choose technology B, they select bank financing and capture the $(1 - \alpha)$ private benefits.

One of the crucial features of the model is the manager who is indifferent between technologies A and B (denoted as manager $\hat{y}$). For manager $\hat{y}$, the utility derived from investing in technology A is the same as the sum of the utility derived from an investment in technology B and the input diversion:

$$(V_1(1+\beta) - V_0)^{\hat{y}} = (V_1 - V_0)^{\hat{y}}(1 + (1 - \alpha)$$

Some managers favor technology A $(y > \hat{y})$ and other, B $(y < \hat{y})$. After the investment, the firm's market value is a weighted average of the firm's value under technologies A and B; the weights are the proportions of each manager type in the economy. Investors do not observe y or the manager's investment choice.

The Nash equilibrium of the game is:

1. Managers with $(y < \hat{y})$ choose technology B and use BF.
2. Managers with $(y > \hat{y})$ choose technology A and use TC.
3. Investors value firms that use TC as $V_1(1 + \beta)$ and the companies that take BF as V_1.

There are two significant implications from the model:

1. Trade credit use signals high firm market value.
2. An increase in manager incentives, entrenchment, or firm opacity reinforces the positive relationship between trade credit and the company's market value.

Entrenchment and firm opacity refer to the managers' abilities to capture private benefits (from weaker governance) and the possibility of acquiring information about personal actions, respectively.

Aktas et al. (2012) test their hypotheses on data from American companies from the pre-global financial crisis period, 1992–2007. Most specifically, they test the positive correlation between trade credit use and the quality of the firm's investments, finding support by using several proxies for the firm's investment quality (Z-score, return on assets, and long-run abnormal returns). At the time, suppliers financed almost 10% of the total assets of American listed firms.

In the model, trade credit use informs market agents about the quality of a firms' investments and managers' actions. It should be noted that this is an issue for publicly-listed companies subject to high agency costs. Managers are either ultimate owners for small and medium-sized companies or respond directly to them. Still, it wouldn't be hard to change the model to make trade credit transmit information to financial institutions; one could also tweak model parameters to make the relationship between trade credit use and high firm market value non-linear. Firms that use too little trade credit could be valued highly because they generate enough cash flow to meet their financing needs. Firms that use too much are being monitored by their suppliers, who trust that the company's projects are valuable.

We turn now to other formal models of trade credit and market power.

4.6 Trade Credit, Relationship-Specific Investment, and Product Market Power

This section summarizes Dass et al. (2015). They rely on a model with incomplete contracts and bargaining power to argue that trade credit can be a commitment device for making relationship-specific investments (RSI). They aim to explain how trade credit is affected by firms' bargaining power and the specialized nature of transacted goods. Their empirical results, also using publicly listed firms, show that trade credit increases in upstream firm's RSI and downstream firm's market power.

For our purposes, the primary results pertain to how firms behave to build relationship-specific investments and how competition affects decisions about DPO and DSO.

Their work relies on identifying publicly-listed firms' behavior changes when their credit ratings are downgraded or upgraded. They divide their firm samples into RSI and non-RSI companies. As Dass et al. (2015) observe, RSIs include building a factory close to a downstream customer, purchasing special machinery, developing specific human capital, acquiring specific technology, etc.

The authors plot the mean changes in net TC provided by firms separately for firms whose long-term credit ratings are either downgraded, unchanged, or upgraded (compared with the previous year's ratings). In Fig. 4.5, net TC is receivables/sales net of payables/sales, and the change from one year to the next is calculated as the log difference between net TC and its lagged value. Figure 4.5 also illustrates how ratings upgrades/downgrades change trade credit provision. Other figures not reproduced here do the same, but separately for non-RSI and RSI intensive firms.

In their model, an upstream firm must invest to ensure that the intermediate good meets the expectation of the downstream organization. Trade credit emerges as a commitment device since contracts are incomplete, and downstream firms can only verify RSI over time. The downstream can delay payments or default if the RSI has not been made. Hence the authors predict that the level of trade credit provided by the upstream firm is increasing in the level of RSI.

The second prediction of their model is the same as we have explained at the beginning of the chapter: the more significant the market power of the upstream firm, the less trade credit it will make it available to the downstream firm.

Interestingly, the authors argue that: "it is not clear why stronger firms would seek to extract more TC from trading partners that may be financially

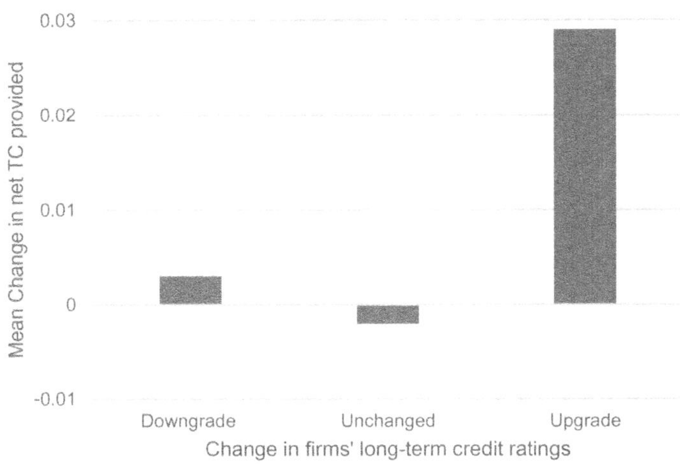

Fig. 4.5 Mean changes in net trade credit provided by firms (*Source* Dass et al. [2015])

weaker. Why do they not simply negotiate for a higher (lower) price from customers (suppliers)?" We have explored this issue deeply in the earlier part of the book. Dass et al. (2015) offer one more explanation for the minimization of the financial cycle. In their model, "RSI generates a surplus and the relative bargaining power of the upstream and downstream firms affects their share of the surplus. We posit that greater the bargaining power of the upstream firm, the larger is the share of the RSI-induced surplus that it captures in trading with the downstream firm. As a result, the bargaining strength of the upstream firm strategically affects its incentive for making the RSI in the following way: since an upstream firm with greater bargaining power is going to capture a greater proportion of the surplus, it stands to lose more by not making the appropriate level of RSI."

Of course, only upstream firms with specific relationship-specific investments have an incentive to lower DSO in their setting. Moreover, we must understand that companies with market power are not indifferent negotiating between lower costs or more extended payment terms. Payment terms affect cash flows, while lower costs reduce profit margins. There are many reasons for preferring one over the other, such as the effects of taxes, credit constraints, growth projection, and life-cycle considerations. Strategies for reducing costs and lowering the financial cycle are not perfect or even close substitutes.

More interesting are other predictions from the authors' model. Trade credit will be less critical when: (i) the supplier and customer have had a longer-term relationship, (ii) the downstream and upstream firms are nearby, (iii) the upstream firm has a better reputation, and (iv) the downstream firm is less dependent on the upstream firm for inputs. We explore some of these ideas in the following sections.

4.7 Trade Credit, Supplier Competition, and Risk-Sharing

Chod et al. (2019) and Lee et al. (2018) explore some of the ideas expressed in the previous subsection by studying trade credit financing under competition. They are the antecedents of trade credit as a risk-sharing mechanism. When companies have bargaining power, risk-sharing can be done forcefully, but potentially this still reduces the impact of crises on the supply chain members.

Chod et al.'s (2019) model features multiple heterogeneous suppliers selling differentiated products to retailers that resell these products to end consumers. All firms in the supply chain face convex costs of bank financing;

each supplier can increase its sales and, potentially, profit by providing the retailer with some trade credit. The main result is that in the presence of multiple suppliers, the benefit of providing trade credit is not fully internalized by the trade creditor, as the retailer can use trade credit to increase input purchases from all suppliers.

Another relevant outcome from Chod et al. (2019) is a positive correlation between a retailer's use of trade credit and its supplier concentration, measured by the Herfindahl–Hirschman index (HHI) of suppliers' shares of the retailer's spending. Again, that is because suppliers with larger shares of the retailer's expenditures are willing to sell more on credit.

However, even though companies without market power have a lower incentive to extend trade credit, other factors may force their hand into extending payment terms to their supply chain. Lee et al. (2018) find that suppliers with smaller market shares are associated with more trade credit; they use it as a competitive tool. They also find that buyers with a more significant market share are associated with more trade credit. In contrast, suppliers selling to a concentrated buyer base are associated with less trade credit.

Companies that use their cash reserves as a competitive tool in emerging economies are familiar. For instance, allowing customers to pay in installments is still common in Latin America, sometimes up to a year. In rich countries, 'buy-now, pay later' is becoming increasingly common. Regarding the supplying side, organizations can win contracts with large companies by accepting to get paid for their services months after they are performed.

Supply chain risks get spread out as firms extend trade credit. Take the example of organizations that allow customers to pay for a product in twelve monthly installments. The customers' default risk is now part of the company's balance sheet.

Firms that extend more trade credit should have better information about the quality of their supply chain. As we have seen, Aktas et al. (2012) derive a theoretical model about the information content of trade credit that predicts a positive correlation between trade credit use and the quality of the firm's investments. Agostino and Trivieri (2014) complement these results and show that trade credit also brings information to financial institutions. That is especially so at the beginning stages of bank-firm relationships when banks do not have good company information. Thus, suppliers' credit availability might be crucial to foster access to institutional funding for new firms. Of course, even after years of financial relationships, most trade credit models assume that suppliers have better customer information than financial institutions.

To sum up, supply chain finance globally cannot converge to predictable patterns, as there are countervailing forces to companies' decisions to extend trade credit to their supply chain. Monopolists have more options, of course, but new companies and those with cash buffers may also act strategically. The more we delve into the subject, the more nuance we should expect from the managers of firms of all sizes.

References

Agostino, M., & Trivieri, F. (2014). Does trade credit play a signalling role? Some evidence from SMEs microdata. *Small Business Economics, 42*(1), 131–151.

Aktas, N., De Bodt, E., Lobez, F., & Statnik, J. C. (2012). The information content of trade credit. *Journal of Banking & Finance, 36*(5), 1402–1413.

Canales, R., & Nanda, R. (2012). A darker side to decentralized banks: Market power and credit rationing in SME lending. *Journal of Financial Economics, 105*(2), 353–366.

Chod, J., Lyandres, E., & Yang, S. A. (2019). Trade credit and supplier competition. *Journal of Financial Economics, 131*(2), 484–505.

Dass, N., Kale, J. R., & Nanda, V. (2015). Trade credit, relationship-specific investment, and product market power. *Review of Finance, 19*(5), 1867–1923.

Fabbri, D., & Menichini, A. M. C. (2010). Trade credit, collateral liquidation, and borrowing constraints. *Journal of Financial Economics, 96*(3), 413–432.

Fabbri, D., & Klapper, L. F. (2016). Bargaining power and trade credit. *Journal of Corporate Finance, 41*, 66–80.

Giannetti, M., Burkart, M., & Ellingsen, T. (2011). What you sell is what you lend? Explaining trade credit contracts. *The Review of Financial Studies, 24*(4), 1261–1298.

Gonçalves, A. B., Schiozer, R. F., & Sheng, H. H. (2018). Trade credit and product market power during a financial crisis. *Journal of Corporate Finance, 49*, 308–323.

Lee, H. H., Zhou, J., & Wang, J. (2018). Trade credit financing under competition and its impact on firm performance in supply chains. *Manufacturing & Service Operations Management, 20*(1), 36–52.

Liu, H., & Hou, C. (2019). Does trade credit alleviate stock price synchronicity? Evidence from China. *International Review of Economics & Finance, 61*, 141–155.

Nadiri, M. I. (1969). The determinants of trade credit in the US total manufacturing sector. *Econometrica, 37*(3), 408–423.

Parekh, R. (2013). *Adland's fears realized: Mondelez piggybacks on P&G's payment terms*. AdAge. Available at: http://adage.com/article/agency-news/mondelez-piggybacks-p-g-s-extended-payment-terms/241546/

Petersen, M. A., & Rajan, R. G. (1997). Trade credit: Theories and evidence. *The Review of Financial Studies, 10*(3), 661–691.

Zeidan, R., & Shapir, O. M. (2017). Cash conversion cycle and value-enhancing operations: Theory and evidence for a free lunch. *Journal of Corporate Finance, 45*, 203–219.

5

The Archetypes: From Mature, Single-Product Companies to Cash-Constrained Organizations

We describe the central dilemmas of working capital management by defining businesses archetypes. That also allows us to investigate what happens when companies transition from one standard to another. The archetypes are mutually exclusive. A growing company with a negative cash-conversion cycle falls into one archetype, while a mature corporation in which most of its sales come from exports is classified into another. It is also likely that the managerial lessons from one classical exemplar are not helpful for companies belonging to a distinct one. Still, there are exceptions to these rules. A company with distinct business units that allow managers to work independently may find that some units will be cash flow generators. In contrast, others make significant working capital investments as they grow. In addition, cash-flow volatility is more painful when unexpected, impacting companies belonging to each archetype.

Capital budgeting rules should be slightly different depending on a company's standard. Working capital investments usually grow with sales, prices, and costs, but not for companies with negative financial cycles. For them, revenue growth brings more cash flows. There is a flip side to it, though. Any dip in sales can be problematic, as it can trigger a negative feedback loop in which fewer sales prompt a cash crunch. That makes it more costly for an organization to get out of a crisis, as it must scramble for credit, which makes it more challenging for managers to spend money to increase sales, and so on.

R. Zeidan, *The General Model of Working Capital Management*, https://doi.org/10.1007/978-981-19-3334-9_5

Table 5.1 The different archetypes

		Financial cycle	
		Negative	Positive
Revenue growth	Negative	Significant cash-flow needs. E.g., tobacco companies; pension funds at disbursement phase	Illusory cash-flow gains. E.g., companies in a recession
	Stable	Risk of cash-flow needs. E.g., service companies; subcontractors	Stable cash flow needs. E.g., Restaurants, most industrial and retail companies
	Positive	Supply chain funded growth. E.g. AB Inbev; Amazon, etc	Predictable cash flow needs. E.g., most growing industrial and retail companies

This chapter has three main objectives: describe how capital budgeting works for companies in each archetype, what should be done if there is an unexpected transition from one model to another, and how to incorporate multi-product working capital budgeting.

The classical exemplars are based on expectations about sales growth and the financial cycle. Firms have a positive cash conversion cycle in the primary archetypes, requiring additional working capital investments to grow sales. That accounts for the largest share of business globally and is the example of capital budgeting in most corporate finance textbooks. However, there are many critical managerial lessons for the business environments where companies have stagnant sales, negative financial cycles, or transitions between different situations (Table 5.1).

5.1 Positive CCC and Sales Growth: The Retailer

The classic example of working capital management practices is a retailer or an industrial company with predictable sales growth and a stable and positive financial cycle. Such a business has predictable cash flow needs and can easily budget the required working capital investments for the year. These additional working capital investments are:

$$\Delta \text{OWC} = \text{CCC} * \Delta \text{Revenue}$$

Of course, throughout the year, sales volatility may require temporary investments. Still, in annualized terms, it is straightforward to estimate how much a company should put aside to fund its growth in operations.

One of the most critical managerial lessons from the paradigmatic case of a company with a constant and positive financial cycle is that a recession may temporarily increase cash-flows, as long as the company can quickly adapt to reduced sales. Figure 5.1 illustrates the changes in operating working capital as sales decrease during a recession.

The intuition is straightforward: if companies sell fewer units, they need to buy fewer inputs and thus require less working capital to maintain operations. Small and medium-sized enterprises that do not keep track of working capital investments, which is the majority, sometimes struggle with the usual swings of business cycles. Managers may not understand why cash balances increase during a recession and fail to prepare for expanded working capital requirements when sales bounce back. The illusory expansion of cash flow is temporary. Companies cannot rely on that for capital investments or returning value to shareholders unless they don't expect sales to return to their pre-recession levels.

Of course, suppose a recession brings higher delinquency rates by customers. In that case, the cash-flow effects are uncertain: cash balances should increase from the revenue effect but decrease from delays in payments from customers.

Figure 5.2 illustrates the uncertain effects of a recession when the cash-conversion cycle rises and revenue declines simultaneously.

The firm must invest working capital if the cash conversion cycle effect is more significant than the revenue effect or gets a respite in terms of cash

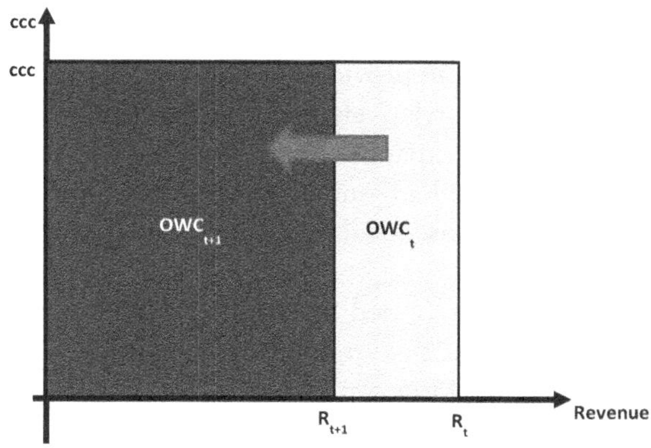

Fig. 5.1 Changes in operating working capital in a recession

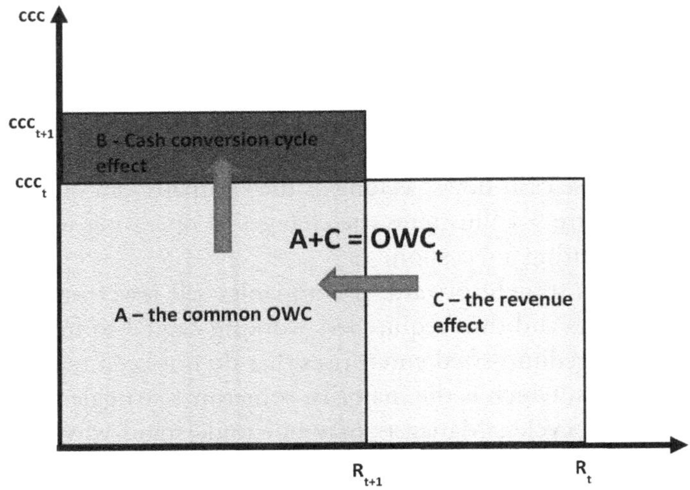

Fig. 5.2 OWC effects of simultaneous recession and increase in cash-conversion cycle

flow otherwise. The figure gives the original operating working capital by the area A + C. As revenues decline, cash is freed (area C). However, because the CCC is higher, operating working capital increases by area B. The OWC in $t + 1$ is now A + B.

For this archetypical company, the managerial lessons are straightforward. Once the company optimizes DSO, DPO, and DIO, it should continue measuring and tracking them alongside sales volatility and keeping its efforts in other business areas.

5.1.1 Ownership of Managerial Targets: Sem Parar

Sem Parar is a company that provides electronic toll and parking collection services. Its business is relatively predictable, and the company grows organically as its client base expands. More importantly, on its creation, the company's ownership group had one clear mandate: the company should avoid issuing debt as much as possible, as the other group's businesses had significant cash-flow needs.

Historically, the company funded its working capital needs with retained profits; the downside was that this strategy limited growth. To unlock growth potential while limiting working capital expenditures, Sem Parar adopted a two-folded approach:

- Introducing a service that would reduce the firm's cash conversion cycle; and
- Hiring a finance executive that would take ownership of the financial cycle's management.

The new service was a pre-paid toll tag. More than bringing loyal customers, the label's goal was to improve the firm's cash flow. The firm would essentially borrow from customers willing to pay for the commodity of passing through booths without paying the toll then or later.

The company's new hire was responsible for, among other things, building and monitoring the financial cycle indicators that the company lacked at the time. At first, the executive's annual bonus was tied to reducing the cash conversion cycle from 42 to 27 days, which was quickly achieved.

Performance pay was tied to keeping the financial cycle around 27 days from then on. More importantly, the monitoring of the financial cycle became standard in the company, and new services were designed with cash flow constraints in mind.

Sem Parar's case illustrates some essential managerial lessons: one can't manage what is not measured; of all possible new services that a firm can introduce, it should pay particular attention to those that can improve customers' experience while reducing a firm's financial cycle; and measures towards the reduction of DSO, DIO and DPO are better done when somebody owns that process.

More importantly, such measures allowed the company to dominate its market without relying on debt to finance its growth. In 2021, Sem Parar held 80% of the electronic toll and parking collection market, with 6 million customers and a solid reputation for delivering efficient and cost-effective service to its customers (Dall'Agnol, 2021).

5.2 Positive CCC and Stable Revenue: The Brick-a-Brack Store

Managerial lessons are usually predicted on a changing landscape. Fads, such as reengineering, outsourcing, consensus management, and delayering come and go. Companies should be lean, adaptable, or customer-centric. Many careers are built on being up to date and repeating ad nauseam corporate jargon such as synergizing, taking it offline, and thinking outside the box, among others.

Still, most business owners do not seek to expand their operations significantly, and their firms exist as a surrogate to life in the corporate trenches. The story of the immigrant family that builds a small firm from scratch to make a living and put their children through school is a storied cliché because it is all-too-common. I should know. My grandparents arrived from Syria with almost nothing, and their brick-a-brack store helped put their five children through college, the proudest accomplishment of their lives. They never wanted to expand; they were content with managing their store to the best of their abilities, as long as they could survive on its profits.

Because many small business owners lack the formal education to develop sophisticated strategies, they choose not to expand their business rapidly, or at all, because of managerial diseconomies of scale.

Managerial diseconomies of scale may be defined as:

$AC = f(k)^*Q$, in which $f(k)$ pertains to positive and increasing values. Thus, the average cost of production goes up with how much companies produce.

This type of diseconomy of scale arises because business owners may find it challenging to manage a more numerous workforce, control the quality of the services or products, establish relationships with more suppliers, etc. "I can sleep soundly only if I know everything going on at the firm" is a familiar feeling for small business owners.

Firms with stable sales, DIO, DSO, and DPO shouldn't expect to invest in working capital. Paradoxically, stability can be the goal of business owners and an obstacle to survival if there is a changing business landscape.

In addition, given that the purpose of many small businesses is to provide a living for the owners' families, predictable dividends are a boon. In addition, small companies tend to be credit constrained, and even when they have access to credit, owners are leary to take on debt.

For businesses with this type of profile, the most critical managerial lesson is:

- Companies should build emergency working capital reserves.
- They should understand their primary source of cash flow risk.

While emergency cash reserves or access to lines to credit are relevant to all companies, they are essential to small family-owned companies. However, it is difficult for small business owners to keep reserves put aside for an emergency, as having money sitting at a bank account goes against the ethos of entrepreneurs who have been cash-strapped for most of their lives.

Should restaurants or small businesses sell on credit? That is the thousands-year-old question. There are examples of bills of exchange on Babylonian tablets dated around 3000 BC. In a poem by the Ancient Roman writer Ovid (sexist by today's norms) in Ars Amatoria (available at: https://courses.lumenlearning.com/suny-geneseo-humanities1-1/chapter/ars-amatoria/):

> "But when she has her purchase in her eye,
> She hugs thee close, and kisses thee to buy;
> "'Tis what I want, and 'tis a pen'orth too;
> In many years I will not trouble you."
> If you complain you have no ready coin,-
> No matter, 'tis but writing of a line;
> A little bill, not to be paid at sight:
> (Now curse the time when thou wert taught to write)."

Throughout history, restaurant and store owners struggled with the decision of extending credit to their customers or not. Nineteen-century posters show this, as do posters stating that one should look for credit tomorrow, but never today, that hang in many stores worldwide (Fig. 5.3).

Yet more than the decision to sell on credit to a returning customer, the primary risk to a company's operations is usually ignored. What is the cash flow shock that can bring down the business for small companies? Are sales concentrated on a few customers? Uninsured inventory in danger of spoiling? Policy changes that can destroy entire supply chains? Suppliers with market power that can raise prices significantly? For most small businesses, survival is paramount, and while operational problems maim, cash flow shocks can kill.

5.3 The Small Volume Service Company

Subcontractors and small volume service companies must make one major decision: should they fund their working capital management or get their customers to do it? It is common for independent contractors to ask for half of their payment upfront. It is straightforward to see why by rearranging the financial cycle in Fig. 5.4.

For small volume service, the minimum efficient scale is a few sales per month or year. Thus, entrepreneurs should be concerned about losing any sales. However, cash flow restrictions also make it difficult for companies to finance their economic cycle without pre-charging clients.

How much should advances be? There is no correct answer for all companies. Companies should consider two main tradeoffs:

Fig. 5.3 Selling on credit

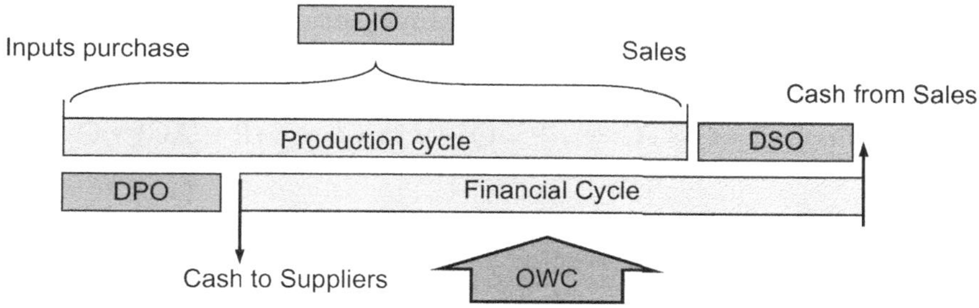

Fig. 5.4 Graphical representation of the linear relationship between the CCC and OWC

1. Potential decrease in revenue from cash advances versus predictable cash-flows.
2. Commitment versus quality issues.

It is reasonable to suppose that companies that do not pre-charge consumers can sell more. But for most small subcontractors, the primary constraint is limited production capacity and not lack of demand. In addition, many live service by service, similarly to workers who live paycheck to paycheck. Thus, small subcontractors rarely have cash reserves to complete a job before getting paid.

Ideally, subcontractors or small service companies should create enough cash reserves to survive a prolonged downturn, but such foresight is challenging. Still, for such companies, even without much reserves, one question must be answered: What minimum resources must a company generate to survive the following year? The answer to that question leads us to the concept of break-even point: What is the sales level that makes a company profitable?

Small companies' accounting, economic, and cash-flow break-even points are similar. Break-even points are estimates of the transition between losses and profits.

Let's assume that total costs (TC) are easily divided into fixed (FC) and variable costs (TVC) and that unit variable costs (VC) are constant (later, we explore the implications of this assumption). Then: Total Costs (TC) = Fixed Costs (FC) + Total Variable Costs (TVC). Average costs (AC) would be:

$$AC = TC/Q => (FC + TVC)/Q => AC = FC/Q + VC$$

For a single-product company, in which profits can be straightforwardly defined as the difference between revenue (TR) and costs (TC):

Profits = TR − TC. As revenue is price times quantity (assuming no excess inventory, for simplicity):

$$\text{Profits} = P * Q - TC => P * Q - AC * Q => (P - AC) * Q$$

The linear functions are simplifications of operations in which a constant profit margin (P − VC) is used to pay for a company's fixed costs. As firms sell more (again, assuming constant prices and unit variable costs), they start covering their fixed costs until they reach the break-even point (Q*) (Fig. 5.5). Graphically, if there are no sales, firms must still settle their rent and other overhead.

A small company with fixed costs of U$40,000 per month must generate gross margins of U$480,000 per year to break even without any considerations for reinvestments, expansion, or interest. Accounting break-even refers to the amount the firm must generate to cover all other direct and indirect costs, so net profits are zero. Cash-flow break-even concerns how much inflows are necessary for a firm to meet its obligations. Finally, the economic break-even incorporates the opportunity costs of shareholders' investments. Detailed cash flow statements are in Chapter 8.

Another example is a company that charges U$50 per hour, has fixed costs of U$12,000 per month, and variable costs of U$20 per hour (including taxes, material, and other direct costs for service provision). The linear minimum efficient scale is given by:

$$Q* = FC/(P - VC).$$

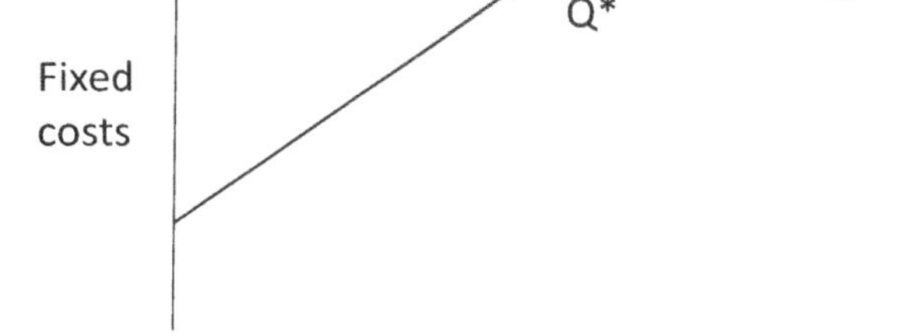

Fig. 5.5 Break-even point

$$\text{Thus: } Q* = 12,000/(50 - 20) = 400.$$

The firm must service customers for a minimum of 400 hours per month to meet its current obligations. Of course, that does not consider the timing of cash flows or the possibility of payment delays. There are two significant risks for such companies: not getting enough orders or accepting too many.

For small service companies, estimating the break-even point and budgeting cash flows for the following months is the only way to determine the percentage of upfront payments they will require from customers. Such budgeting also allows entrepreneurs to understand if they are biting more than they can chew (the case study below explores the possibility of overcommitment).

5.3.1 The Downsizing Decision

Three friends founded the small interactive installation company; its clients were museums in the Americas. Like most niche service companies, there were good and bad years. In 2015, business was good. The company moved offices to a larger space and contemplated expanding further, opening offices in a different country.

The company was doing well, with a growing portfolio of projects. At the same time, it was stretched thin, with the partners flying between the four cities in three countries where their more notable projects were happening.

One of the partners reached out to me: does it make sense to open a new office? Answering the question required simple estimates of cash flow requirements for the following years. My approach was straightforward: "let's forecast the cash flow requirements for expanding the business. If you believe that you will be able to sustain that business level for the foreseeable future, go for it."

Estimating the company's cash flow needs for the year was straightforward. As a small services business, most costs were renting and wages. The managers also used a simple rule of thumb for estimating their gross profit margin: 50% of the contracts' total values should be set aside for taxes, transportation, purchase of service-specific types of equipment, subcontractors (paid by the hour), and other variable costs. Thus, the firms' break-even point was the total contracts that equaled twice the projected fixed costs. Opening a new office would require hiring full-time employees and renting new premises. These new costs would double the firm's fixed costs, even ignoring new computers and other equipment outlays.

The partners had to answer one and only question then: would they believe it would be sustainable to win contracts that would bring twice the revenue they had gotten on that year? And the answer was no. Once they stopped to think about their market and future opportunities, they realized they were at the height of their industry's business cycle, and it was likely that future orders would dry up.

Worried about their current structure and cash flow commitments, the partners decided to reorganize the business by moving operations to smaller offices and transitioning some full-time employees into contractors. They worked to maximize cash flow and started bidding on long-term maintenance contracts, something they avoided in the past in favor of setting up new museum exhibitions. That strategy worked. The market was indeed at its peak, and they downsized at the right moment. To be clear, the company did not downsize in the traditional sense of cutting capacity. It shifted fixed costs and cash flow commitments into variable costs. Such a move was risky. If demand increased, they could lose market share and see their costs increase. But as new projects dwindled, the reduced cash flow commitments meant that the company could survive the downturn.

5.3.2 Bootstrapping

Sometimes, firms find it difficult to obtain external financing from traditional outside parties due to information asymmetries and transaction costs.

The academic literature has developed the concept of bootstrapping to explain start-up financing decisions. Bootstrapping can be defined as when entrepreneurs start a business with only financial capital possessed by the business owners or family members (Rutherford et al., 2017). For start-ups, most entrepreneurs finance new ventures themselves. According to Rutherford and Phillips (2021), few entrepreneurs (20%) take on external debt at startup, and far fewer (5%) launch with external equity.

The follow-up strategies to keep companies out of credit markets are more important than the initial decision. Still, bootstrapping leads to interesting managerial insights that emerge from the decision to self-finance. The concept complements the type of in-kind model (Sect. 3.9), in which the entrepreneur must decide on self-financing a project versus relying on bank credit.

Under bootstrapping, firms should find creative ways to avoid the need for external financing through reducing the overall cost of operation, improving cash flow, or using financial sources internal to the company.

Some of the reasons for bootstrapping are similar to those related to trade credit in later stages of companies' life cycles, including the pecking order theory, as discussed in Sect. 6.3). Entrepreneurs prefer control and generally avoid debt and external equity from the demand side. On the supply side, financial institutions cannot accurately gauge the underlying quality of the entrepreneur/venture due to asymmetric information (Rutherford & Phillips, 2021).

In addition, according to Rutherford and Phillips (2021), there seems to be no significant difference in performance between bootstrappers and non-bootstrappers. Of course, non-bootstrappers usually take more risks and thus are more likely to fail. However, for our work, bootstrapping is an example of a cautious financial strategy, which is common in many companies. Of course, not all companies are going to extremes of early payments of invoices to avoid any credit, but entrepreneurs will often choose to self-finance their projects.

Bootstrapping is connected to the pecking order theory described in Sect. 6.3. Here, what matters is how bootstrapping restricts working capital management. It puts a ceiling on growth, as companies must fund new investments, fixed or working capital, with retained profits. It also makes any adverse financial cycle shock much more painful than companies with access to credit. Finally, bootstrapping is intrinsically linked to the "crying CEO" case study in Sect. 3.2.1. Gladly, that CEO abandoned its convictions and knocked on banks' doors to borrow money; if he didn't, it is likely his company would have folded.

5.4 Supermarkets and the Implications of Negative Cash-Conversion Cycles

Negative cash-conversion cycles allow companies to grow without using much capital, or sometimes any capital at all. Because cash from the production and sales process enter a firms' coffers before suppliers must be paid, sales growth results in cash inflows that may distort decision making.

When companies have a positive cash-conversion cycle, the effects from recessions are smoothed by a reduced need for working capital investments. That is not the case for firms with negative financial cycles: recessions may trigger cash implosions. The adverse effect of lost sales is compounded by sudden cash outflows as bills eventually come due.

The condition for negative cash-conversion cycles is:

$$\text{CCC} < 0;\ \text{DIO} + \text{DSO} - \text{DPO} < 0;\ \text{DPO} > \ \text{DIO} + \text{DSO}.$$

Industrial companies rarely have negative cash-conversion cycles. Negative cash conversion cycles result from companies powerful enough to extract significant concessions from the supply chain for regular industrial companies. For that to happen, days payable outstanding must be long enough to cover both the production cycle and credit to consumers. Thus, negative financial cycles are more common in service industries with very short DIO. Conversion cycles lower than zero may also arise in specific business models, usually tied to particular industry characteristics.

It is unclear for industrial companies with market power if they should minimize their cash-conversion cycle. Such companies may have the ability to pay suppliers in sixty, or ninety, or even 180 days. Still, they risk facing higher input prices, losing previously loyal suppliers, or even finding that they are getting lower quality products than competitors that pay promptly. Moreover, firms with market power tend to be larger and more credit-worth, finding it profitable to extend credit to the supply chain if, in return, they get more favorable prices than other companies (for more, see Chapter 4).

Firms that manage to transition from positive to negative financial cycles discover that sales growth stops requiring additional working capital investments and now swells cash reserves. For instance, assume the following:

- A company with an initial positive cash-conversion cycle of 60 days.
- Current sales are U$1 million per month.

The firm's operation working capital is U$2 million. If for some reason, the cash-conversion cycle were to go down to −30 days, cash reserves would go up by U$3 million, as the firm would recoup all its working capital investments and would start being financed by its supply chain. Now, if sales were to double, the company's cash flow would increase, to the tune of U$1 million.

Figure 5.6 illustrates the transition from positive to negative cash conversion cycle and operating working capital as sales grow. As the initial ccc (ccc_t) becomes negative (ccc_{t+1}), the operating working capital also turns negative (from OWC_t to OWC_{t+1}). If sales grow, from R_t to R_{t+1}, the OWC generates cash flow (note that the resulting working capital is the whole area: $OWC_{t+1} + OWC_{t+2}$.

Companies with negative financial cycles can get addicted to growth. After all, higher revenue increases cash flows. Some business models are based on that premise. We discuss this in detail in the following subsection.

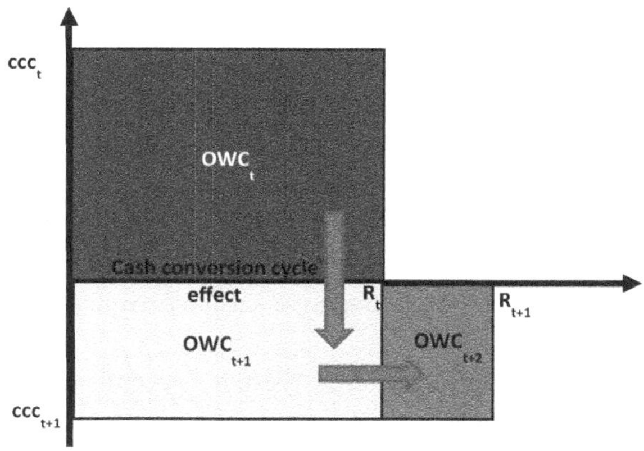

Fig. 5.6 From positive to negative cash-conversion cycle

5.4.1 Exponential Growth: Sustainable Business Models or Ponzi Schemes?

Some business models are based on the premise that new facilities can fund previous ones. Thus, companies would be viable only if they opened new stores, clubs, restaurants, or other units contributing to their cash flow.

These business models are usually capital-light in terms of fixed asset investments. The necessary condition for exponential growth is that the operating working capital of a new business unit is higher than its setup costs. In other words, exponential growth can be achieved if:

$$|OWC| > \text{Set up costs}$$

For instance, assume that an existing gym chain is deciding on opening a new unit. A new gym requires a total initial investment of U$200,000, and, for simplicity, it will sell only annual memberships for U$500 per year. As long as the entrepreneur believes that 400 people will sign up immediately (or, preferably, before the initial investment must be made), there is no cash outflow for expanding the chain.

Is this unrealistic? Not at all. It wouldn't be hard for a gym chain to market a new unit to potential customers, sign them up, and only then make the necessary arrangements to open it. Now, having no net cash outlays to set up a new unit does not mean it is a good decision. Additional gyms will generate profit if revenue exceeds costs, but it is impossible to know beforehand if a gym should be opened. However, from a cash flow perspective, entrepreneurs have a solid incentive to open new units if there is an inkling that they can be profitable.

For the typical firms, more units sold generate more profits, but they must first invest in supporting this growth. Companies with negative cash conversion cycles see their cash flow decline in a recession, all else being equal—conversely, more revenue turbo-charges cash flows. Sales become self-funded, with the supply chain supporting revenue growth. Thus, it is tempting for companies with negative cash conversion cycles to pursue growth at all costs.

Later, we discuss how governments regulate several industries with long negative operating capital cycles. Of course, not all companies with negative cash conversion cycles swell uncontrollably, but we must discuss the dangers and benefits of relying on the supply chain to fund growth. Companies that can expand without cash outlay may become Ponzi schemes or leverage unwisely.

If a company is not viable, growth will only increase the size of the hole left behind when it folds. Sometimes, negative cash conversion cycles also lead to unusual survival strategies.

In one example of a small auto repair chain, the company found itself without credit and cash reserves due to conflict between the two brothers who owned the business equally. The company charged customers before performing the services. Thus, it began a cycle of discounting its services to increase revenue to finance its cash flow needs. At one point, the company was selling its services below cost. It would spend U$100 in material and labor to perform a service and charge U$90. Of course, it had all the business it could muster, but such a scheme was only viable for so long. The problem was only solved through mediation. An external shareholder bought out one of the brothers and injected enough cash to meet payroll without resorting to selling below cost.

The main issue for a company with a negative cash conversion cycle is: how does it come about? Suppose it is part and parcel of the company's business model, and there is no sacrifice in terms of costs, prices, and operational efficiency. In that case, it may be an excellent opportunity for sustainable growth. However, suppose the company uses it as a crutch to run from low-profit margins and ensure it can meet its short-term obligations, such as paying dividends to shareholders. In that case, it may lead to bankruptcy later. Worse, it can also be used as fraud. Sell below cost to attract consumers who must prepay for their purchases, use the cash flow to grow the business, pay out huge dividends, and do it as long as the firm can expand unimpeded.

Of course, this strategy is only viable for asset-light companies. Still, regardless of how firms manage their negative financial cycles, it is much easier to invest and grow when the supply chain finances your sales than if companies must invest in working capital on top of other assets.

5.4.2 Tesco: Why a Negative Financial Cycle Matters

Supermarkets are notoriously tricky businesses due to low margins, economies of scale, diseconomies of scope, and customers who can quickly check for lower prices among competitors. The average profit margin of grocery store chains is around 2%. Tesco, a British supermarket founded in 1919 as a market stall, has had a better than average profit margin, about 3.1%, during the 2010s, but faced stiff competition to generate total shareholder return.

For supermarkets, short or negative financial cycles are almost a requirement. Since firms compete on prices and thus pass along cost savings to consumers, optimizing inventory and payment terms to suppliers is the only way to mobilize as little capital as possible. In addition, grocery stores carry many different items, making it particularly difficult to optimize inventory. Too many units of a particular item of a specific brand and the store are tying capital unnecessarily and run the risk of spoilage; too few items and customers get disgruntled when they find empty shelves.

Operationally, supermarkets target quick inventory turnover. Well-managed grocery stores maintain a lean inventory but stocked-up shelves.

Usually, supermarkets aim to reduce the working capital requirements by extending days payable outstanding and reducing days sales outstanding without affecting gross margins. That includes taking products on consignment and negotiating long payment terms for brands that would like to position their products in more favorable aisles. Some measures may potentially run afoul of competition authorities. For instance, in 2021, the National Grocers Association (NGA) highlighted anti-competitive behavior impacting independent grocery retailers in a Federal Trade Commission's public meeting. The association claimed that, among over violations, powerful supermarket chains did not only enjoy more favorable supply terms but negotiated for the first call on high-demand items (Redman, 2021), which allowed them to limit competition for these items while not tying their capital. In Turkey, practices such as listing fees, shelf fees, advertising and announcing fees, discount pressure, and unconditional product restoration are typical (Koç et al., 2010). In an executive education class where I was the instructor, a supplier from a supermarket in Brazil described how an advertisement fee worked. His firm must contribute a percentage of its sales to an advertisement pool to be repaid in 365 days or more. The advertisement fee works as a zero-interest one-year forced lending of around 5% of its sales to the supermarket chain. This particular practice is likely illegal, but small firms find it hard to bring complaints to antitrust authorities.

Regardless of the legality of some practices in the industry, supermarket chains aim for low or negative cash-conversion cycles without sacrificing operating margins. Negative operating working capital allows these companies to expand without mobilizing huge pools of financial resources. Tesco is an excellent example of that. Table 5.2 presents data on the balance sheet and the income statement for the company during the 2019–2021 period.

Data are consolidated for the whole group, but we will assume that it refers mainly to its retail stores for the analysis that follows. We want to estimate Tesco's cash conversion cycle and operating working capital

There are some caveats. Some operational data are found in Tesco's financial statements' noncurrent assets and liabilities. It may be that these data do not relate to the companies' operations, but these numbers do not change the final values much. Another caveat is related to current tax liabilities and

Table 5.2 Tesco financials, 2019–2021, £m

	2019	2020	2021
Trade and other receivables (current)	1,550	1,396	1,263
Trade and other receivables (noncurrent)	243	166	170
Current tax assets	6	21	41
Inventories	2,617	2,433	2,069
Trade and other payables (current)	(9,131)	(8,922)	(8,399)
Current tax liabilities	(325)	(324)	(79)
Trade and other payables (noncurrent)	(365)	(170)	(109)
OWC	(5,405)	(5,400)	(5,044)
DSO (days)	11.3	9.8	9.2
DIO (days)	16.4	15.1	12.9
DPO (days)	61.5	58.4	53.4
CCC (days)	(33.8)	(33.5)	(31.4)
Revenue	57,493	58,091	57,887
Cost of sales	(54,092)	(53,810)	(53,538)
Impairment loss on financial assets	(49)	(183)	(384)
Gross profit/(loss)	3,352	4,098	3,965
Gross profit margin	5.8%	7.1%	6.8%
Administrative expenses	(1,633)	(1,892)	(2,229)
Operating profit/(loss)	1,719	2,206	1,736
Operating margin	3.0%	3.8%	3.0%

Source Tesco PLC Annual Report and Financial Statements, available from Tescoplc.com

assets. The normal operations of grocery stores generate both tax assets and liabilities. However, it may be that some of these taxes are related to non-operational issues such as asset sales. One significant account not classified as derived from operations is "Loans and advances to customers," which goes from £7 billion in 2019 to £3 billion in 2021. This line is most likely related to the financial services part of the business. If that is the case, we should ignore it, as our interest is in the performance of the retail stores.

Data limitations are expected when estimating the financial cycle from published financial statements, which is not a significant issue as long as we understand those limitations.

Tesco's cash flow benefitted from sales growth in 2020 compared to 2019. Sales increased from £57.5 billion to £58 billion, while the OWC changed from negative £5.04 billion to £5.40 billion. All the components of the financial cycle went down significantly throughout the period. DSO and DIO changed from 11 and 16 days in 2019 to 9 and 13 days in 2021. That would usually reduce the cash conversion cycle, but that is not what happened, as DPO also went down from 61 to 53 days in the same span. Given that the reduction in DPO was higher than that of DSO and DIO combined, the cash conversion cycle increased.

Still, Tesco's financial cycle remained firmly negative, changing from −34 days in 2019 to −31 days in 2021. Meanwhile, Tesco's gross and operating margins changed some but averaged numbers ahead of its competitors - approximately 6.5% and 3.2%, respectively - throughout this time.

As usual for supermarket chains, Tesco's negative financial cycle is due to extended payment terms to suppliers. Trade and other accounts payable was never lower than U$8 billion in the 2019–2021 period, while receivables and inventories didn't average half that amount.

The benefits of this type of financial cycle are clear, but what about the costs? It is impossible to build a counterfactual scenario where Tesco pays its suppliers quicker for lower prices using financial statements alone. Tesco may not optimize its cash-flow and profit margins simultaneously, but it is almost unfeasible to find real-life situations in which companies are astoundingly efficient. Even Tesco's managers cannot ensure that they are not leaving money on the table. They don't have complete access to the financial situation of their suppliers and can't be sure if there are cost savings to be made by renegotiating payment terms.

Notably, sales decline puts pressure on cash flows when companies have negative financial cycles. Thus, when downsizing, these firms should do it as fast as possible, understanding that they will need extra cash to settle their outstanding payable accounts. In the 1970s, Tesco restructured its operations,

Table 5.3 Tesco financials, selected years, £m. Financial cycle indicators in days

	2014	2015	2019	2020	2021
DSO	14.0	13.8	11.3	9.8	9.2
DIO	22.7	19.0	16.4	15.1	12.9
DPO	70.4	64.5	61.5	58.4	53.4
CCC	(33.7)	(31.7)	(33.8)	(33.5)	(31.4)
OWC	(5,311)	(4,923)	(5,405)	(5,400)	(5,044)
Revenue	56,695	55,900	57,493	58,091	57,887

considering these cash flow effects in revamping its business. The company closed 500 stores in 1977 and updated the aisles' designs and lighting of the remaining stores. Sales reached £1 billion in 1979 (*The Guardian*, 2015) and grew steadily until the early 2010s. The company had several crises during the 2010s. The company abandoned its operations in the US and was fined due to overstating profits by £250 million in 2014. Tesco went into another restructuring in 2015, closing stores, cutting the range of products by 30%, and even getting rid of its fleet of corporate jets (*The Guardian*, 2015).

From 2015 to 2021, Tesco grew little, and the financial cycle, other than a few minor observations, as seen above, has not changed much. Table 5.3 details the components of Tesco's financial cycle in the crisis years of 2014 and 2015, contrasting them with those of the 2019–2021 period.

If we take a long-term perspective, Tesco's overall financial cycle becomes remarkably consistent, even if the company went through lean years in 2014 and 2015 and faced the effects from the covid pandemic in 2020 and 2021. Its cash conversion cycle in 2014 was almost the same as in 2019; similarly, between 2015 and 2021. Nevertheless, there are clear trends regarding the individual components of the CCC. All go down steadily. The most likely reason is that the company is shortening the entire economic cycle. If a company can reduce its DIO, it will start buying inputs earlier. Even if payment terms are the same, DPO will naturally fall.

A negative cash conversion cycle allows companies to grow while financing part of that growth through the supply chain. Shocks to companies' sales may trigger cash-flow crises, as working capital requirements rise in tandem with reduced revenue. Any restructuring will require more resources than a company with a positive financial cycle; likely, a restructuring is better done swiftly. It is crucial to understand which indicator is driving the behavior of the cash conversion cycle over time. Finally, it is essential to connect the financial and economic cycles (is the reduction in the financial cycle accompanied by lower margins? Is the company losing sales?).

5.4.3 The Adjusted Inventory Turnover

One of the main lessons of the current approach to working capital management is that performance indicators should not be analyzed individually. Reductions in inventory turnover that impact firms' costs, their ability to serve consumers, or the quality of their products and services may generate immediate cash inflows but cost the firm dearly.

Gaur et al. (2005) provide a framework to adjust inventory turnover to the possible negative consequences of optimizing it. Their framework considers three relationships between inventory management and the rest of the business processes. Specifically, they refer to firms with different capital intensity, unexpected sales growth, and the impact of inventory management on gross margin. Considering these factors, the authors build a trade-off curve that computes the expected inventory turnover of a firm for given values of sales surprise (SS), gross margin (GM), and capital intensity (CI). A firm's distance from its trade-off curve is defined as the adjusted inventory turnover (AIT).

$$\mathrm{AIT} = \mathrm{IT} * \mathrm{GM}^{\beta 1} * \mathrm{CI}^{\beta s} * \mathrm{SS}^{\beta 3}$$

The different β coefficients represent the adjustment to each factor that modifies the initial turnover. In their empirical specification, these coefficients arise from the difference in logs across firms and years in their sample. Thus, AIT is not a managerial performance indicator but an empirical measure to compare inventory productivity across firms and years by controlling for differences in gross margin, capital intensity, and sales surprise. The authors claim that benchmarking is relevant and that firms with low AIT should investigate whether they are less efficient than their peers. However, building AIT from published financial data requires strong assumptions, such as similar business compositions across companies, product homogeneity, etc.

The authors use the Ruddick Corporation as a case study. Ruddick Corporation is a holding company that owns Harris Teeter, a regional supermarket chain in the southeastern United States with 137 stores and sales of $2.7 billion in 2000. Figure 5.7 shows time-series plots and linear trends of IT and AIT for Harris Teeter from 1987 to 2000. The inventory turnover of Harris Teeter does not show any significant trend. During the same period, the gross margin of Harris Teeter has increased steadily from 23.4% to 30.9%, and its capital intensity has increased marginally. After applying their adjustment, the adjusted inventory turnover of Harris Teeter has expanded significantly at an average rate of 0.055 per year. Thus, the adjusted inventory turnover shows that the lack of time trend in the regular version of stock turnover does not necessarily imply that firms are not better at managing

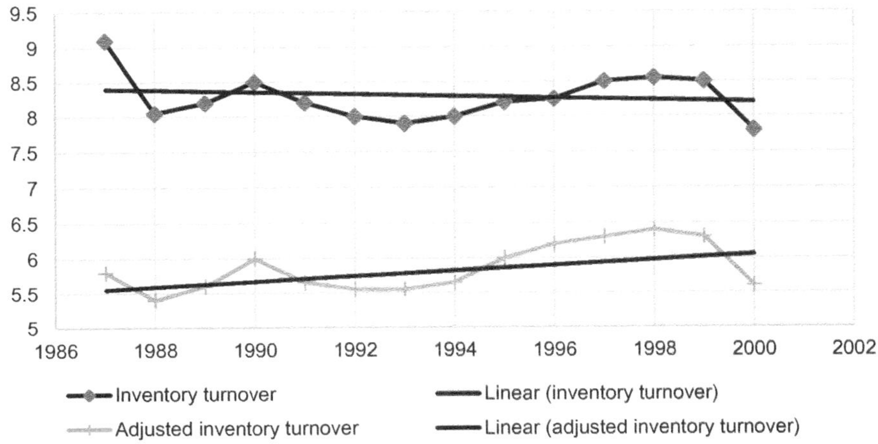

Fig. 5.7 Plot of inventory turnover and adjusted inventory turnover for Harris Teeter (*Source* Gaur et al., 2005)

inventory. Indeed, Harris Teeter switched to private-label brands during this period. Because private-label brands have higher gross margins, Harris Teeter increased the service level for private-label merchandise in its stores without reducing inventory management efficiency.

As we have seen, optimizing inventory turnover from a cash flow perspective requires minimizing inventory turnover, as long as there are no significant changes in operating margin and the ability of the company to fulfill orders. It is important to note that we can't rule out that accounting manipulations drive these changes over time. Still, benchmarking may allow companies to improve their inventory productivity.

The main managerial lessons from the AIT are not that there should be benchmarking or that firms should be careful about using inventor turnover as the barometer of operational efficiency by itself. Managers have better information than analysts or researchers who build indicators from public financial statements.

An internally applicable adjusted inventory turnover should be tied to the current operations of the company and its strategic plans. For cash-flush companies battling for each percentage point of market share, the ability to fulfill orders can be prioritized over inventory turnover. For others, supply-chain fulfillment risks may lead to a build-up of inventories that are considered inefficient in standard times.

5.4.4 Corporate Hoarding and the Bullwhip Effect

Companies usually aim to low inventory turnover numbers to avoid trapping more cash flow than necessary into the production process. However, the supply-chain disruptions caused by recurrent waves of covid in 2021 generated a rare phenom: hoarding of inputs by cash-constrained small companies, which is the opposite of these companies' typical behavior. Disruptions that reverberate through supply chains generate what has been defined as the bullwhip effect, the amplification of demand variability along a supply chain. A company bullwhips if it purchases from suppliers more variably than it sells to customers. Order variability increases under the bullwhip effect as the orders move upstream in the supply chain (Wang & Disney, 2016). The amplification of demand variability can lead to mismatches between demand and production and lower supply chain efficiency (Bray & Mendelson, 2012).

Maheshwari and Marcos (2021) describe the case of the owner of two shops, one among some independent stores that ordered in bulk well in advance of the holiday season and were then hoping they could sell their wares. The two running stores in Connecticut would typically have about 3,000 pairs of shoes in stock ahead of the holiday season. But as she watched supply chain concerns in Vietnam mount during the year, she secured a new storage facility to expand inventory capacity to 4,100 pairs. That has been costly for the company, as the owner tied U$165,000 more than she would typically do in November because of worries about potential shortages.

The owner was gambling on hoarding inputs to guarantee that the company could fulfill unimpeded orders.

As Maheshwari and Marcos (2021) write, "the unpredictability of 2021 has forced many small businesses to make buying decisions months or weeks earlier than they normally would and to tie up more of their cash in inventory, which can be risky. "The big thing is you really have to order in advance," said Dan Quinn, an owner of What We Make, a furniture business in Algonquin, Ill., which sells tables and other wares through Etsy. "I've got 14 weeks of projects. I need to get most of that material in house as fast as possible and keep buying it until you have a stockpile basically." The range of shortages can manifest themselves in unusual ways. Isabel Amigon, the owner of the online store Sololi, was still waiting on an order of Christmas tree ornaments she placed in April. The manufacturer alerted that the order would be delayed because of a shortage of strings to tie the decorated orbs. Ms. Amigon was worried that if she didn't get it in time for the holiday season, she would have to wait until next year to use the inventory. The string shortage has also led her to remove specific home goods items from her websites, such as table runners and washcloths. “Even if I get them by the end of November, I won't be able to sell all of them because most people have already bought their ornaments,” Ms. Amigon said. “I placed the orders early, and I still have to face this situation.”

The bullwhip effect is relatively standard. Bray and Mendelson (2012) investigated the bullwhip effect in a sample of 4,689 public U.S. companies over 1974–2008 and found that about two-thirds of firms bullwhip. The mean and median of bullwhip effects relate to 15.8% and 6.7% of total demand variability, respectively. Hence, upstream orders' mean quarterly standard deviation exceeds demand by $20 million. The authors decompose the bullwhip effects, finding that demand signals firms observe with more than three-quarters' notice drive 30% of the bullwhip, and those with less than one-quarter's notice drive 51%. However, bullwhip has decreased over time. From 1974–1994 to 1995–2008, their sample's mean bullwhip effect dropped by one-third. The Fig. 5.8 illustrates the bullwhip effect in four industries, defined as the increase of variation between demand and production orders (or shipments) (Wang & Disney, 2016).

Two possible managerial responses to the bullwhip effect are hoarding (seeking extensive safety stocks) and phantom ordering (purchasing more than they need to meet demand). Sterman and Dogan (2015) investigate the behavioral causes of phantom ordering in supply chains, as epitomized by the quote in the title of their article: “I'm not hoarding, I'm just stocking up before the hoarders get here.”

Their work is valuable because they help explain why managers deviate from rational decision-making. In the case of the CEO, who liked to proclaim that he was always debt-free, the irrational decision to pay bills the moment they arrived in the finance department was quickly changed. However, repeated stressors such as large orders, backlogs, or late deliveries may trigger hoarding and phantom ordering even when these behaviors are irrational. Sterman and Dogan (2015) designed an experiment where participants place orders. In their investigation, hoarding and phantom ordering are never rational because there is no horizontal competition, randomness, or capacity constraint; customer demand is constant, and participants have common knowledge of that fact. Nevertheless, 22% of participants place orders more than 25 times greater than the known, steady demand.

Of course, in their experiment, the incentives for getting the order size correct are not the same magnitude as managers who must do that in real life. Still, their results provide an underpinning for decision-making that falls short of rational behavior. We shouldn't expect companies to behave according to some programmed rules found in a textbook. For instance,

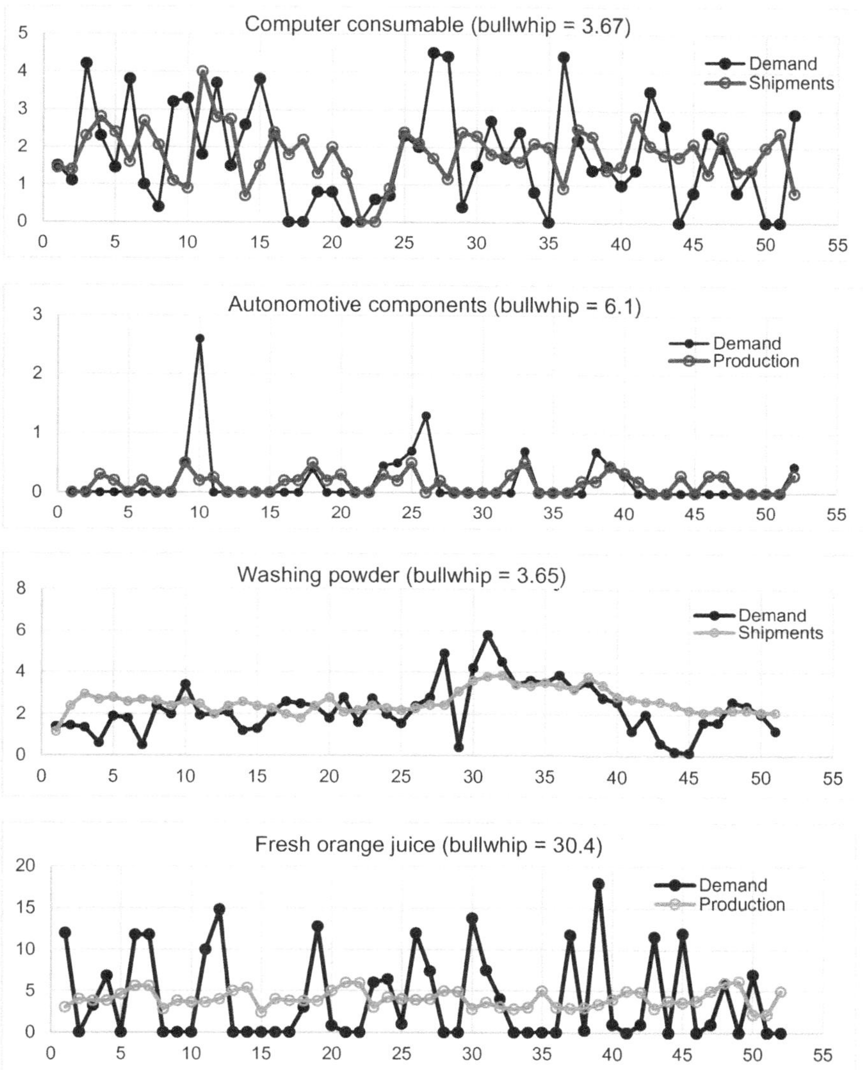

Fig. 5.8 The Bullwhip Effect (thousands of units and weeks) (*Source* Wang & Disney, 2016)

should we expect industrial managers who have grown up in countries that experience hyperinflation to maintain higher inventory levels than their counterparts who have never experienced it? Most likely, yes. The administration of inventory in particular and working capital, in general, are learned behaviors affected by the environment.

Wang and Disney (2016) summarize some critical observations about the bullwhip effect and how it changes with the evolution of supply chains.

- Bullwhip can be observed at various supply chains' industry, firm, and product levels.
- Bullwhip can be induced by both rational and irrational decision-making behavior.
- Under certain circumstances, bullwhip can be reduced or even eliminated.
- More accurate forecasts, smaller batch sizes, and shorter lead-time help reduce bullwhip.
- Supply chain integration, collaboration, information transparency, and centralized decisions are also beneficial.

Coordination and even technological changes such as adopting blockchains to record and publicize orders for supply chain participants can reduce the bullwhip effect. Still, it is unlikely that order variability will disappear. Markets are too dynamic, with companies entering and exiting markets and supply chains changing constantly, and coordination is too costly for demand variability not to be amplified as orders move upstream.

Thus, it is okay if companies want to purchase more inputs than necessary, as long as managers understand the reasons behind that decision. Buying more commodities because prices may seem particularly low may be acceptable, but doing so because the sales director feels comfortable having a full range of quasi-finished products at the disposal of the sales team may not be tenable.

5.5 Dancing with the Wolves: The Multinational Corporation

Multinational corporations don't fall under a single archetype. Some business units may have positive financial cycles, while others can extract funding from the supply chain. In addition, large companies must choose between centralization and decentralization of working capital management. The former limits cash flow volatility, while the latter allows business unit executives to maximize profit (or cash flow). Finally, these companies may choose to act as lenders for the rest of the supply chain or look to borrow funds from the other supply chain members, forcefully or not.

Usually, multinational companies have more choices regarding their financial cycle than the level of sales. Many can pick between positive and negative financial cycles and shift between them, allowing the cash conversion cycle to increase as sales decrease and vice versa. Companies that expect to enter high growth phases would benefit from reduced or negative cash conversion cycles, as they would need to mobilize fewer resources for operational expansion. Multinational corporations can even customize trade credit policies. They can create special payment terms for new products payment suppliers six months before the launch and reduce times to the same as the rest of their products (say, two months) after the product has reached consumers. Doing so would limit working capital investments during the most cash-intensive part of a product's life-cycle, the weeks and months while the product's design is wrapped up and production starts, but there are no sales to offset the development and distribution costs.

It is hard to describe all the possible options for multinational companies regarding trade credit policies. Mostly, multinational corporations face a few tradeoffs: rules vs. discretion, lending vs. extracting, profit vs. cash flow, predictability vs. flexibility, and accommodation vs. aggression.

Let's start with the last tradeoff. Multinational corporations usually face entrants in several of their markets. We can use game theoretical models to analyze the possible responses of incumbents to potential entrants. A typical model has the incumbent deciding on some investment or price-setting anticipating the possibility of entry that depends on the strategic effect of this investment and the type of product market competition. If a firm wants to prevent entry, it will over-invest or cut prices to dissuade potential competitors. If it does not carry out such practices, it will accommodate the entrant, sharing the market with new competitors.

Typical entry deterrence games consider that incumbents might aggressively pursue trade credit policies to challenge potential entrants. Assume that a firm wants to make it more costly for another company to enter its market. Instead of decreasing prices, it may simply extend credit to customers, creating another barrier to entry. Or prepay expenses to suppliers, purchasing present and future inventory promptly.

When an incumbent makes their financial cycle longer, it is more difficult for competitors to enter their markets, as potential entrants need more funds to operate in the same conditions. There is also an added benefit. While predatory pricing might invite regulatory scrutiny, longer payment terms are usually ignored by competition commissions.

We deal with rules vs. discretion in Sect. 7.6.1. We have also explored lending vs. extracting and profit vs. cash flow at length in previous sections. The final significant advantage of multinational corporations with some measure of market power is predictability vs. flexibility. Predictable payment terms have been the same for decades or even centuries in some markets. In others, terms change according to market conditions. Take inflation, for instance. In countries that experience bouts of surging prices, payments terms usually shrink unless cash-rich companies act as lenders to the supply chain. Firms that face more competition tend to extend more favorable terms to suppliers and customers. Some multinational corporations may want to retain the flexibility of payment terms by announcing that DPO and DSO will be revised periodically. Others may find it more accessible for all parties to have stable payment terms. As with most issues in working capital management, there is no universal preferable policy. We should note that the rules vs. discretion dilemma is about internal incentives to a firm's executives, while the predictability vs. flexibility tradeoff involves external actors.

For instance, if companies renegotiate contracts often, they should prefer flexibility regarding payment terms. Moreover, if transaction costs, such as coordination between supply chain members, are significant, organizations should prefer transparent and stable compensation intervals.

5.5.1 Bank Credit and Corporate Working Capital Management

One of the reasons multinational corporations can choose between different working capital strategies is their cash reserves and access to external finance. One relevant study investigating how bank credit affects working capital policies by corporations is by Chen and Kieschnick (2018). They study how changes in the availability of bank credit influence aspects of a firm's working capital policies, finding that effects often differ across firms that are more or less dependent on bank financing.

Unsurprisingly, bank-dependent firms are more restricted regarding their available working capital policies. More interesting is the evidence that younger and smaller firms appear to adjust their use and extension of negative cash conversion cycles to fluctuations in the availability of bank credit and that R&D intensive firms are more likely to extract funds from the supply chain.

Formally, the authors test hypotheses such as expansions of bank credit lead public firms to reduce their extension of credit to their suppliers, whereas contractions of bank credit lead public firms to increase their extension of credit to their suppliers; and expansions (contractions) of credit lead bank-dependent firms to reduce (increase) their extension of credit to their suppliers by less; expansions (contractions) of bank credit lead firms to reduce (increase) their dependence on advanced payments by customers, and expansions (contractions) of credit lead only lead bank-dependent firms to decrease (increase) their dependence on prepayments.

As with most empirical studies on trade credit, the authors use data from listed companies in the US. Still, we shouldn't expect that their results are specific only to US firms, as the relationship between bank credit availability and the alternatives of working capital strategies should be universal. Large corporations have a multitude of alternative schemes than credit-constrained firms. One emblematic example is that of Ambev. The company moved from a positive financial cycle to a negative one, with significant implications for its growth strategy. Most companies would not be able to reduce DSO and extend DPO to the extent that Ambev did without significant adverse consequences.

Yet not all multinational corporations have the same degree of freedom in designing trade credit policies. Companies in commodities markets are more likely to be "payment terms-takers." Take mining companies whose products are exported to China, for instance. If Chinese consumers make a significant share of a firm's exports and prices are established in international exchanges, there may be no space to negotiate specific payment terms.

One of the reasons working capital management is not a more significant part of the financial literature is because it focuses on studies of American liquid and relatively efficient markets. There, companies' survival is not as overtly tied to access to finance as in the rest of the world, and thus working capital efficiency does not matter as much.

5.6 The Effects of Transitions Between Archetypes on Cash-Flow and Firm Survival

Companies' regular operating working capital management strategies follow their business model. Shocks to sales or the financial cycle might lead to illiquidity events. Still, as long as companies are aware of these possible shocks, they can set up contingency plans, such as capital buffers or special credit lines. More problematic are unexpected transitions between working capital management archetypes that are long-lasting. A company with a negative financial cycle that finds itself vying for market share with a suddenly positive cash conversion cycle will encounter an extra competitive barrier.

Figure 5.9 illustrates the situation in which the financial cycle of a company ceases to be negative. For the same revenue, a change in the financial cycle, from negative to positive, requires significant operating working

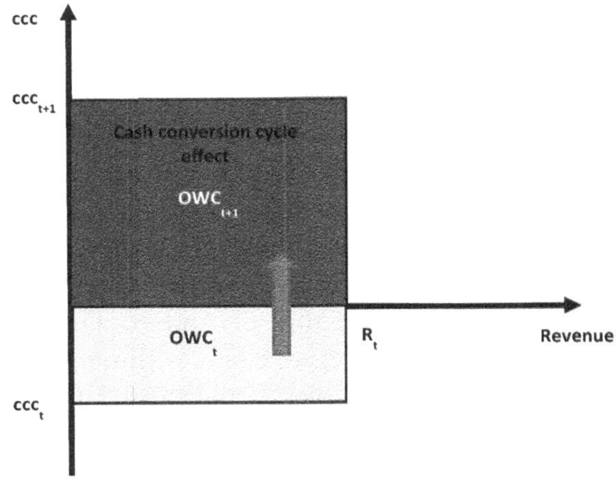

Fig. 5.9 A sudden change in the financial cycle, negative to positive

capital investments. The company must return to the supply chain the capital borrowed in the form of long DPO or short DSO (OWC_t) and invest a corresponding amount that depends on the new financial cycle (OWC_{t+1}). Thus, the total working capital investment necessary for the company to continue operating when the financial cycle suddenly turns positive is $OWC_t + OWC_{t+1}$. For instance, assume that before this abrupt change in the C2C, sales are U$20 million per quarter, and the C2C is −30 days. Thus,

$$OWC_t = \frac{24,000,000 * -30}{90} = -8,000,000$$

If sales remain the same, the financial cycle is now 15 days.

$$OWC_{t+1} = \frac{24,000,000 * 15}{90} = 4,000,000$$

Thus, the change in OWC is

$$\Delta OWC = OWC_{t+1} - OWC_t = 4,000,000 - (-8,000,000)$$
$$= 12,000,000$$

More importantly, the managers must change their current behaviors to adapt to a negative cash-conversion cycle transition. In this example, the company is selling the same amount but now must invest U$12,000,000 to maintain current operations. Before the shift, more sales enhanced cash flows, but after the C2C turns positive, the company must fund growth by investing in working capital.

Such a change may cause significant ripple effects if a negative cash-conversion cycle is ingrained in the current business processes. Before, much of sales growth was self-funded, so everything from budgeting to sales incentives could have been geared towards promoting growth, with minor cash flow restrictions. For instance, it would be natural to have a budgeting process focused on capital expenditure in that scenario. In addition, a company would be wise to invest such as bottlenecks to sales growth would be rare. After all, a company with a negative financial cycle has much lower opportunity costs from excess capacity than firms that must invest in working capital alongside fixed assets to sell more units of their products and services.

There is a scant need to worry about the impact of sales growth on operational cash flows when the C2C is negative. Sales reductions would be almost unacceptable, bringing a decrease in cash flow, alongside profits. Sales teams would be incentivized to fill as many orders as possible, with the only constraint being the firm's ability to fulfill them. Production teams would not be much concerned about placing large orders to their suppliers. Again, fulfilling new orders would take precedence over almost everything else. However, as the financial cycle turns positive, excess input purchases become costly or unappealing, periods of stagnation or decrease in sales are not cash-draining anymore, and the budgeting process is likely to need to be revamped.

Transitions from positive to negative financial cycles may seem beneficial and bring some challenges. Using the same assumptions of quarterly sales of U$24,000,000 and a change of CCC from −30 days to 15 days, but now in the opposite direction, the difference in operating working capital would be:

$$\begin{aligned}\Delta \text{OWC} = \text{OWC}_{t+1} - \text{OWC}_t &= -8,000,000 - (4,000,000)\\ &= -12,000,000\end{aligned}$$

Therefore, the company would find itself flush with cash, with U$12,000,000 hitting its coffers. That event would be a good thing only if managers understood its reason. Otherwise, two things could happen: capital misallocation and failure to plan for another financial cycle reversal.

The former is common in companies that do not track cash flows' underlying mechanisms. Firms that focus on profits instead of cash flows may find themselves scrambling for credit even when business is booming (or because of it). When the funds hit the firm's bank accounts, managers may go on a spending spree or issue a special dividend to shareholders without realizing this is not a one-off. But any increase in the CCC may require that part of that amount is reinvested. For instance, if the financial cycle moves from −30 days to −15 days, then:

$$\begin{aligned}\Delta \text{OWC} &= \text{OWC}_{t+1} - \text{OWC}_t \\ &= \frac{24,000,000 * -15}{90} - \frac{24,000,000 * -30}{90} \\ &= -4,000,000 - (-8,000,000) \\ &= 4,000,000\end{aligned}$$

Therefore, even if the CCC remains negative, the firm must invest U$ 4 million as working capital. If the company issues a special dividend with the formerly trapped working capital investments plus the amount the supply chain is now lending the company, what should be a positive liquidity event may turn into a cash crunch.

That is a not far fetched scenario. Around the world, small companies increase capacity by funding capital expenditure with internal funds. Many business owners have more project ideas than funds for them, so investments are made when a business is generating enough cash for the project to get off the floor. A sudden cash inflow should be expected to be distributed as special dividends if managers do not grasp the origins of that money.

The most common regime transition in corporate finance textbooks is a recession. Weak economic activity affects companies through lower demand. Fewer sales mean fewer profits. However, a recession usually enhances cash entries while reducing outflows to suppliers from a cash-flow perspective, as long as the companies can adapt quickly to decreasing orders. Moreover, a recession is temporary. Here, we are concerned about permanent transition working capital regimes. We have described the cash flow impacts. But what drives these changes?

Given the two dimensions that determine the operating working capital, sales growth, and changes in the financial cycle, regime transitions usually follow substantial changes in the economic landscape and the firms' business model.

Table 5.4 describes some external issues that may trigger working capital regime changes alongside other managerial effects. Take consumer behavior, for instance. Of course, changes in demand can impact sales positively or negatively. However, when consumer behavior changes significantly, companies may struggle to adapt. In the first months of the global covid pandemic, the demand for online services exploded. That benefitted many companies, such as Zoom Video Communications and Examity. But for the latter, the increase in demand did not lead to smooth sailings. Examity had to drop

Table 5.4 External trigger to financial cycle changes

Source	Revenue	Financial Cycle
Consumer behavior	Strong sales effect	May change DSO
Supplier's bankruptcy	–	Changes on DIO and DPO
Use of market power by other companies	–	Changes on DPO
New technologies	May change sales	Changes on DIO and maybe DPO
New competitors	Sales effects	May change DSO and DPO

many of its clients as it struggled to expand fast enough to meet their needs. There were two reasons for that: operational bottlenecks and credit constraints.

Regarding the former, Examity struggled to find and train examiners and expand bandwidth capacity to cope with the flood of requests for online exams. As for the latter, the sudden influx of orders from regular customers and new ones created a conundrum: would the transition from a stable to a favorable sales regime be transitory or permanent? Suppose the surge in demand was transitory and the firm invested significant amounts in expanding capacity. It could lead to substantial business risks if the business experienced a sales growth reversal.

Examity would need to find funds to increase operations by orders of magnitude. Even if the company chose that route, it would be impossible to time expansion precisely. It could be that as new employees are trained and ready to work, demand would be back to its pre-covid levels, leading to excess capacity.

Companies in supply chains with powerful focal corporations share such cash flow risks. When Mondelez increases payment terms to 180 days, announcing to their suppliers that it would take them half a year to receive payment for their wares, the financial cycles of hundreds of small companies rise in tandem.

Operating working capital regime transitions, from negative to positive, stable to negative, or everything in between, are major cash flow events. Is your company prepared to deal with the possibilities of working capital regime transitions? The answer to that question may be the difference between survival and bankruptcy for credit-constrained firms.

5.6.1 Who is Stealing from Me?

This short case is about the intersection of agency theory, working capital management, and executive compensation, which arises from a transition between positive and negative financial cycles.

The CFO of a small beverage distributor implemented a plan to reduce the company's financial cycle. That involved operational efficiency measures to reduce inventory turnover, new payment terms to customers, and renegotiating terms with suppliers. The reduction in the financial cycle freed up a considerable amount that was trapped in previously inefficient operations.

At the end of the quarter, the financial statements revealed that the company's cash balance was U$1 million higher than in the previous quarter. As the CFO later recalled: "I went to the owner's office to tell him the good news. I explained that the extra funds could be paid out as dividends or be used for expanding the business, as the goal was to keep the renegotiated payment terms moving forward." His response? "Who was stealing from me?"

For the owner, the idea that the supply chain could finance the company and that growth could increase cash flow was absurd. Thus, instead of celebrating the newfound efficiency, he was set on finding out who was diverting funds from the company. After a few meetings with the CFO, the owner finally relented on this pursuit. He asked that the company maintain most of the extra funds as reserves; the rest was used to pay off some debt.

The case study illustrates a common issue in financial management: unless executives understand the drivers of cash flow changes, it will be harder to optimize production and sales. There is no such thing as a free lunch until there is.

5.7 Fraud, Moral Hazard, and Seedy Working Capital Strategies

There is a reason why pension funds and health insurance plans are heavily regulated: fraudsters could fill such markets without government action. Long negative cash conversion cycles open the possibility of fraud. Companies that charge customers early for products and services to be delivered years later may simply take people's money and run. Most people have had experiences with pre-paying a contractor's fee and never having the service performed, getting it late or of lower quality than expected. Once a company is paid for its services, it has few incentives for the timely execution of its duties other than maintaining its reputation.

The business models based on negative cash conversion cycles but require relatively high capital investments are unlikely to fall prey to bad actors. After all, one can collect money and fail to deliver its products or services, but the expenditures on fixed assets must still be accounted for. For instance, setting up a gym requires purchasing numerous types of equipment, paying for rent deposits, and more. Even if members first pay before using the services, it is unlikely that gym owners will collect membership fees and vanish. Of course, some fraudsters may purchase equipment in installments and find a way to set it up before spending significantly on rent and fees, but we should not expect that shenanigans are standard in that type of business.

Other than business models that allow companies to charge customers today for services years down the road, a few situations encourage deleterious working capital policies. We highlight the cash crisis loop and the shareholder exit dilemma.

There are many reasons for a cash crisis, from overexpansion to a large customer's default, from increased competition to shareholders requiring special dividends.

The cash crisis loop for companies with negative cash conversion cycles happens when managers trade margin for sales to plug a hole in a company's finances. Assume that a firm is credit-constrained and must meet payroll but does not have enough cash. Since it first collects from customers before delivering the final products or services, managers announce a mega-sale to pay its employees. Of course, that will widen the gap managers must plug in the future. Growth turns detrimental, and the company cannot afford a period of stagnant or declining sales. In this instance, operating working capital becomes even more negative, and it becomes harder for executives to pay their bills without resorting to even higher revenue. Solutions to this cash crisis loop include selling assets and finding new long-term funding sources (for instance, bringing new partners to the fold).

Regarding shareholders' exits, they can be traumatic if the result of conflict between partners. The strategy of growth at all costs is often used to cash out disgruntled shareholders, leading to similar problems as the cash crisis loop. Cashing out unsatisfied owners can drain a company's cash reserves.

Companies with negative financial cycles may be careful regarding their growth strategies. Not every company is Amazon, sustaining double-digit revenue growth for decades. Any recession can be problematic for a company that generates cash as sales grow; it reduces profits and cash flow simultaneously, even if the company can adjust its inventory downwards quickly.

References

Bray, R. L., & Mendelson, H. (2012). Information transmission and the bullwhip effect: An empirical investigation. *Management Science, 58*(5), 860–875.

Chen, C., & Kieschnick, R. (2018). Bank credit and corporate working capital management. *Journal of Corporate Finance, 48*, 579–596.

Dall'Agnol, L. (2021). *Com 80% do mercado, Sem Parar chega a 6 milhões de clientes no Brasil, Veja*. https://veja.abril.com.br/coluna/radar/com-80-do-mercado-no-brasil-sem-parar-chega-a-6-milhoes-declientes/

Koç, A. A., Boluk, G., & Kovaci, S. (2010). Concentration of food retailing and anti-competitive practices in Turkey. *Food Economics-Acta Agricult Scand C, 7*(2–4), 151–162.

Gaur, V., Fisher, M. L., & Raman, A. (2005). An econometric analysis of inventory turnover performance in retail services. *Management Science, 51*(2), 181–194.

The Guardian. (2015). Tesco timeline—The retail giant's rise and fall. *The Guardian*. https://www.theguardian.com/business/2014/dec/09/tesco-timeline-the-retail-giants-rise-and-fall

Maheshwari and Marcos. (2021). Supply chain problems have small retailers gambling on hoarding. *The New York Times*. https://www.nytimes.com/2021/11/30/business/small-retailers-hoarding-supply-chain.html

Redman, R. (2021). *NGA speaks up on anticompetitive practices in FTC meeting*. Supermarket News. https://www.supermarketnews.com/issues-trends/nga-speaks-anticompetitive-practices-ftc-meeting

Rutherford, M., & Phillips, D. (2021). Bootstrapping: Complementary lines of inquiry in entrepreneurship. In *Oxford research encyclopedia of business and management*.

Rutherford, M. W., Pollack, J. M., Mazzei, M. J., & Sanchez-Ruiz, P. (2017). Bootstrapping: Reviewing the literature, clarifying the construct, and charting a new path forward. *Group & Organization Management, 42*(5), 657–706.

Sterman, J. D., & Dogan, G. (2015). "I'm not hoarding, I'm just stocking up before the hoarders get here": Behavioral causes of phantom ordering in supply chains. *Journal of Operations Management, 39*, 6–22.

Wang, X., & Disney, S. M. (2016). The bullwhip effect: Progress, trends and directions. *European Journal of Operational Research, 250*(3), 691–701.

6

The Managerial Decisions

6.1 Minimizing Bankruptcy Costs

If a company's goal is to squeeze every little bit of profit from its operations, managers will refrain from keeping idle capital. However, companies that minimize working capital investments will be more subject to shocks or limited growth opportunities unless they have unrestricted access to credit.

Let's consider the example of H&M, a clothes retailer in which seasonality is clear when we trace operating working capital over time. Figure 6.1 presents a simple estimate of the working capital investments of H&M in the years before the great financial crisis. Working capital investments are calculated as:

$$\text{OWC} = \text{Inventories} + \text{Receivables} - \text{Current liabilities}.$$

A more precise estimate would require operational data on inventories, receivables, and the parts of current liabilities related to everyday purchases, production, and sales processes. However, we don't have a breakdown of the current liabilities for this period, so we consider all short-term liabilities part of operating working capital. Despite the data limitations, the figure clearly shows the seasonal pattern of working capital investments. Working capital usually hits its apex in the third quarter and its nadir on the fourth. The reason for that? Christmas sales. For the company to stock its stores for the season's busiest days, purchases increase significantly in the preceding months, while receivables follow later.

R. Zeidan, *The General Model of Working Capital Management*,
https://doi.org/10.1007/978-981-19-3334-9_6

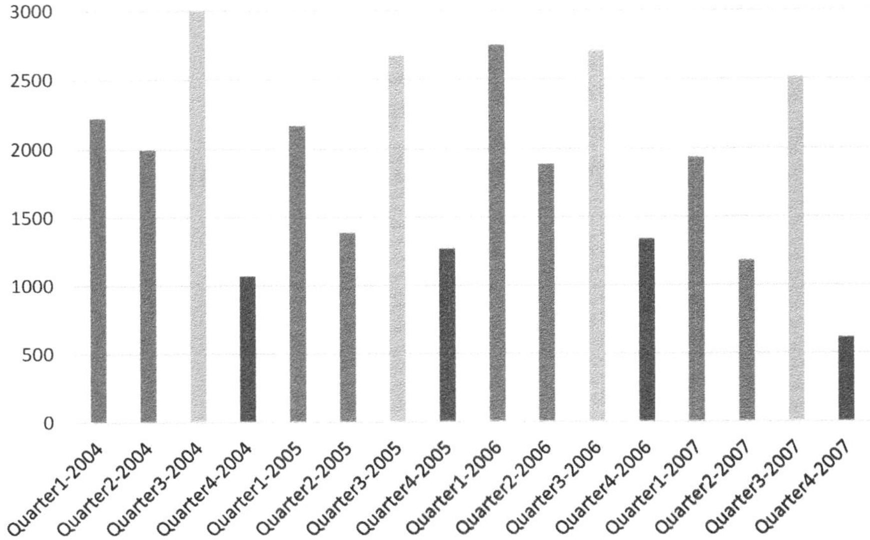

Fig. 6.1 Operating working capital, H&M, thousand SEKs (*Source* H&M financials)

Hence, working capital is the lowest in the fourth quarter since input purchases have already been paid, and sales increase manifold. If we zoom in on a single part of the financial cycle, we can see the seasonal pattern playing out in the financial reports from the company.

Figure 6.2 displays H&M's variation of inventories for the 2003–2021 period. Positive values indicate that inventories are increasing, and negative values mean a reduction in the value of goods yet to be sold. It bears reminding that the company is expanding globally during this period, so we shouldn't expect a regular pattern revolving around stable inventories, year

Fig. 6.2 Simplified inventory changes, H&M, 2004–2021 (*Source* H&M, financial statements)

on year. Still, the figure illustrates that H&M's operations are remarkably predictable, with stocks growing the fastest during the two last quarters of each year. Such a pattern is not affected by the usual vagaries of the retail business. For instance, in their 2000 annual report, H&M management noted that "despite that, the warm weather in December 2000 had a negative effect on sales, the Group results were in line with December 1999." Warm or cold weather does not change that the company is likely to purchase more products in the second half of each year. The only exception is 2008. On September 14, 2008, Lehman Brothers filed for bankruptcy, with the Federal Reserve choosing not to rescue depositors. The ensuing panic froze capital markets around the world. On the real side of the economy, consumers reduce discretionary purchases. H&M managers, observing the combination of a financial crisis and economic recession, reduced orders from suppliers, resulting in the company's total inventories going down.

Otherwise, there was almost a clockwork pattern of rising inventories in the third and fourth quarter of every year. In 2005, there were 1,200 stores in 22 countries, while that number was close to 5,000 in 2021. Such a predictable pattern indicates that the company can expect cash-flow needs to peak in those quarters. Given the foreseeable changes in operating working capital, what should H&M and other companies in a similar predicament do? There are two reasonable strategies: early investments to match working capital needs during the year or the use of credit lines to deal with cash-flow volatility. The main tradeoff regarding working capital volatility arises from the opportunity cost of holding excess cash and access to credit lines.

If a company has easy access to credit lines, cash-flow volatility can be smoothed out by management tapping banks whenever needed. However, suppose an organization relies on credit to deal with cash-flow volatility. In that case, there are two sources of market risks, from financial systems and the determinants of the cash-conversion cycle. Internally, sales growth may also require extra working capital investments, but firms can never insure against sudden financial crises or market movements.

Unexpected changes in the financial cycle may come from customer payment delays, production bottlenecks, suppliers being late in shipping inputs, and other factors. Regarding credit markets, credit lines may be sensitive to financial market developments that catch companies and banks unprepared. A company may agree on a specific credit line with its banks, but the onset of panic in financial markets can freeze credit and cut firms out of much-needed capital. Thus, credit-constrained firms should choose cash balances that limit the possibility of running out of cash based on:

expected sales growth, negative scenarios regarding the financial cycle, credit availability, and estimated default costs.

6.1.1 Sales Volatility

Dealing with expected sales volatility means choosing a cash balance that falls in the interval between the required investment to meet expected average sales growth and the investment necessary to allow the company to finance the maximum expected sales during the year.

Assume, for instance, that for H&M, sales have averaged SEK 1.44 billion in the current year, and the financial cycle is constant at 15 days. For the following year, the sales are projected to be SEK 300 million in the first quarter, and 400, 500, and 600 million in each subsequent quarter. How much should be the company's working capital investment for the next year?

H&M's current operating working capital is:

$$\begin{aligned} \text{CCC} &= \frac{\text{OWC}}{\text{Daily Revenue} * 360} \\ &= \frac{\text{OWC}}{\text{Annual Revenue}} \Rightarrow \text{OWC} = \left(\frac{15}{360}\right) * 1.44\,\text{billion} = 60\,\text{million} \end{aligned}$$

Given that expected sales for the following year are 1.8 billion, changes in operating working capital, assuming that the CCC remains constant at 15 days, are:

$$\Delta\text{OWC} = \text{CCC} * \Delta\text{Revenue} = (1.8 - 1.44) * \frac{15}{360} = 15\,\text{million}$$

Thus, the company would need to invest an additional SEK 15 million to meet the working capital needs of higher expected sales for the year. However, this is the amount related to the average sales during the entire year. For each quarter, the operating working capital related to the sales for the period are:

$$\text{Quarter 1}: \text{OWC} = \left(\frac{15}{90}\right) * 300\,\text{million} = 50\,\text{million}$$

$$\text{Quarter 2}: \text{OWC} = \left(\frac{15}{90}\right) * 400\,\text{million} = 66.66\,\text{million}$$

$$\text{Quarter 3}: \text{OWC} = \left(\frac{15}{90}\right) * 500\,\text{million} = 83.33\,\text{million}$$

$$\text{Quarter 4 : OWC} = \left(\frac{15}{90}\right) * 600\,\text{million} = 100\,\text{million}$$

In this scenario, the expected OWC for the first quarter is below the previous year's investment in working capital. However, the cash inflow is temporary, as working capital investments rise each quarter. Thus, if managers are not keeping track of working capital investments, the company's bank account will suddenly be flushed with cash in the first quarter, but it will be drained in subsequent months. The two most straightforward strategies for H&M, given the expected volatility of cash flows, are the conservative and the aggressive strategies.

6.1.2 The Conservative Strategy

In the conservative strategy, the company maintains as cash reserves the amount necessary to meet all the year's working capital needs, including, and especially, the peak of its business activities.

In the example above, H&M's sales would increase during the year, and the respective working capital investments would reach U$100 million by year-end. The firm ended the previous year having invested U$60 million to fund its operations. Thus, the conservative strategy would require that the company put aside U$40 million at the start of the year to finance its production and sales cycle during the following 12 months.

Formally, the working capital requirements for the following year would be:

$$\text{WCR} = \text{Max}\{\Delta\text{OWC} = f(\Delta Q, p\text{DPO}, i\text{DIO}, s\text{DSO})\}$$

If there is no uncertainty, the maximum WCR needed for a certain period is given by the working capital investment associated with the highest combination of CCC and sales.

Of course, shocks in the components of the financial cycle may require extra investments. For instance, a firm must access funds to meet a surge in demand. Still, the conservative strategy limits the possibility of illiquidity events.

In this example, H&M should budget US$100 million as the required working capital investments for the year. If there are already U$60 million invested, the company must put aside an extra U$40 million to meet the U$100 million target for the year.

This extra financial cushion should not be funded with short-term debt, as is usually believed. Working capital investments, after all, do not depreciate and are a perennial requirement for companies to operate seamlessly.

The main drawback of the conservative strategy is the opportunity cost of the extra U$40 million, which is necessary just for a quarter. These funds could be used for capital expenditures, special dividends, or reduction of interest-bearing debt.

It bears repeating that so far, the conservative strategy is based on the known expected sales volatility and nothing else. It is assumed that the financial cycle is invariant during the year. There are no changes in the variables that determine the conversion cycle, such as the percentage of late customers with their payments.

Implementing this strategy in real life requires modeling the financial cycle and sales components and creating a working capital buffer.

6.1.3 The Aggressive Strategy

The aggressive strategy maintains the required amount for operations and growth, taking advantage of credit lines to deal with sales volatility. For instance, for a company for which sales peak at a particular month, credit lines are used to fund the spike in inventory and credit to customers.

There is no unique way to implement that strategy. Still, a straightforward one is to fund the expected WCR related to sales growth and use credit lines to finance any changes in the operating working capital from sales volatility or an unexpected variation in the components of the financial cycle.

For instance, for the H&M's fictitious example in which the OWC is projected to be:

$$\text{Quarter 1}: \text{OWC} = \left(\frac{15}{90}\right) * 300 \text{ million} = 50 \text{ million}$$

$$\text{Quarter 2}: \text{OWC} = \left(\frac{15}{90}\right) * 400 \text{ million} = 66.66 \text{ million}$$

$$\text{Quarter 3}: \text{OWC} = \left(\frac{15}{90}\right) * 500 \text{ million} = 83.33 \text{ million}$$

$$\text{Quarter 4}: \text{OWC} = \left(\frac{15}{90}\right) * 600 \text{ million} = 100 \text{ million}$$

The company should use long-term funds totaling U$50 million to support sales in the first quarter and prepare to make additional investments of U$16.66 million in each of the following quarters. Any shocks to the financial cycle would need to be absorbed by reducing cash reserves or accessing external funding.

The aggressive strategy aims to limit any unnecessary working capital investments. Firms should put aside the minimum amount of capital to support sales growth. Thus, for any two periods t and $t + 1$, a firm must invest an additional: $\Delta OWC = OWC_{t+1} - OWC_t$; no more and no less.

6.1.4 Personality Traits and the Role of National Culture on Trade Credit Decisions

How do managers make working capital management decisions in real life? That is an unexplored question in the scientific literature. Many ultimate owners pay little attention to working capital. There is nothing wrong with that per se. In fact, bloated operating working capital may serve a purpose: it works as insurance in a financial crisis.

Paradoxically, some entrepreneurs, risk-takers overall, may behave conservatively regarding working capital management. In middle-income countries where business cycles tend to be more volatile, and institutions weaker, it is easy to find instances of ultimate owners behaving conservatively from past traumas. For instance, Alforria was created in 1986 by Edna Thibau amidst rising inflation in Brazil; it soon turned into hyperinflation. Managing a company during hyperinflation likely scarred Alforria's managers. For years, the CEO aimed to pay all its bills when they were received, even weeks before their due date. Thus, even though it is easy to criticize the behavior of the current Alforria CEO, his desire for a company without debt is understandable.

Behavioral economics has a long tradition of investigating how people deviate from instrumental decision-making. Maybe working capital management in listed companies can be studied as rational decision-making, as larger companies can devote more resources to mitigate the effects of individual cognitive biases. However, when firm-related and family-related risks are intertwined, as is often the case in SMEs, one can't expect managers to behave instrumentally. It shouldn't be a surprise that the cognitive biases in executives limit their abilities to manage working capital following economic theories.

However, many executives that ignore working capital management leave money at the table. Inertia has a price. So, how do managers behave regarding trade credit decisions? The answer is that not even the CEOs of publicly listed companies behave similarly.

Xu et al. (2021) study the relationship between personality traits and working capital decisions. Like most scientific literature, their study is based on publicly-listed companies, but they devise a neat strategy to investigate that relevant relationship. They use a pilot license as a proxy for the sensation-seeking personality trait, building a sample of pilots and non-pilot CEOs from U.S. listed firms from 1993 to 2016. They find strong evidence that firms led by pilot CEOs are more likely to use trade credit. More importantly, the positive relationship between pilot CEOs and trade credit is more pronounced for firms with high investment growth opportunities.

They argue that companies would invest more than similar firms to satisfy the CEOs' desire for sensation. Their results seem consistent with the conjecture that firms with pilot CEOs tend to have a higher level of trade credit.

Of course, CEOs and entrepreneurs don't necessarily share the same psychological traits. According to Kerr et al. (2019), entrepreneurs display more tolerance of risk, even in small gambles, stronger self-efficacy, internal locus of control, and need for achievement than non-founder CEOs/leaders, inventors, and non-inventor employees, the other groups studied. They also find that non-founder CEOs/leaders typically sit between entrepreneurs and employees for personality traits. Finally, entrepreneurs, non-founder CEOs/leaders, and inventor employees all show more innovative personalities than the non-inventor employees in the same companies.

If part of the differences in manager behavior of SMEs is due to personal traits, it would be expected that the same holds for bankers and loan officers. Cole et al. (2015) find evidence for that. They designed a randomized experiment with professional loan officers with many years of experience in credit assessment. The controlled laboratory environment closely matches the approval process of low documentation loans in an emerging credit market. They show that career concerns are a critical nonmonetary determinant of loan officer behavior and strongly affect baseline screening effort. In addition, personality traits interact, albeit weakly, with monetary incentives in lending decisions, which indicates that personality traits can help identify conscientious screeners.

If we look at more aggregated behavior, El Ghoul and Zheng (2016) study the relationship between trade credit provision and national culture. They find that trade credit provision is positively related to collectivism, power distance, uncertainty avoidance, and masculinity, the famous (albeit flawed but still practical) Hofstede's four cultural dimensions. More interesting is how trade credit provision evolves. The authors find that international trade openness mitigates the relationship between trade credit provision and national culture. As firms are more exposed to international markets, their behavior somewhat converges to the average global firm.

What are the implications in the present context? We need to understand that working capital management will not be a set of rules that all companies must follow blindly. Some companies will prefer to limit illiquidity events, while others will look at every opportunity to reduce the cash conversion cycle, keeping as little reserves as possible. And owners' preferences matter.

6.2 Working Capital Buffering

Working capital budgeting is a cornerstone of budgeting processes in general. The usual practice is to focus on the revenue effect. If sales go up, so should working capital investments. However, changes in the financial cycle can significantly alter the required amount to support a firm's operation. Some of it may be expected, such as sales shifting to products with longer DIOs compared to the rest of the firm's portfolio,

More damaging are unexpected changes related to customers' defaulting or paying late, especially if it is not a one-off.

How much cash should a company hold if it does not want to count on credit lines? That is one of the most critical questions for owners of small companies who want to avoid borrowing if possible.

Working capital investments necessary to finance revenue growth are a staple of capital budgeting. Suppose the goal of a company is to reduce the probability of running out of cash. In that case, it must put aside enough resources to finance changes in operating working capital due to the revenue effect. Less specific are the possible changes from the cash-conversion cycle effect. Are delinquency rates stable? Can the organization count on suppliers to deliver inputs without delays? What is the probability of production delays? These and other questions are company-specific, but a general framework for estimating a safety margin for working capital investments has the following functional form:

$$\Delta\text{OWC} = f(\Delta Q,\ p\text{DPO},\ i\text{DIO},\ s\text{DSO}),$$

in which p = change in payment terms to suppliers, i = change in production time, s = change in payment terms from consumers.

The standard approach to economic risk is to consider demand uncertainty. Business cycles are represented through production and sales going up and down. However, in the present case, unexpected changes in payment terms may limit a company's ability to meet its obligations.

Take financial issues with a significant customer, for instance. The client may not change the size of its orders, but payment delays percolate throughout the supply chain.

In Chapter 4, we simulate changes in operating working capital due to changes in market power over time. Here, we discuss the implications of changes in delinquency rates and other variables related to payment terms.

There are several rules of thumb for setting up working capital buffers. Boehlje and Langemeier (2020) write that: "a frequently suggested goal is a 20–35% buffer or working capital that is 20–35% of gross revenue or total expense. A firm facing more volatility in the business climate needs a larger buffer." They write regarding the context of farmers. However, it is not a good rule of thumb for managers of all companies if there are no significant expectations of a credit crunch soon.

A more comprehensive working capital buffering procedure is given below. It requires assumptions about the statistical distributions regarding revenue and payment terms. For payment terms, a practical statistical distribution is a triangular distribution (for revenue, there is also a case for a lognormal distribution).

A triangular distribution is a straightforward continuous probability distribution with well-defined lower, mode, and upper limits. The main advantage of triangular distributions is that the minimum and maximum values of parameters such as DPO and DSO are limited to a pre-determined interval (for normal distributions, these values have no boundary). Another benefit is that managers can skew the distribution to make larger or smaller values than the mode more likely.

For instance, assume that a is the minimum, b is the expected, and c is the maximum expected revenue for the following year (Fig. 6.3).

Once these values are estimated for a company's revenue, they can be extended for DSO, DIO, and DPO. For instance, assume that a firm requires its customers to pay in 30 days, but 10% settle in 50 days, and 5% on average in 90 days. Managers expect that pattern to hold for the following year. However, they devise a pessimistic scenario in which 30% of their sales are settled in 120 days. They also estimate an optimistic scenario in which only 10% of clients delay their payments for only ten days.

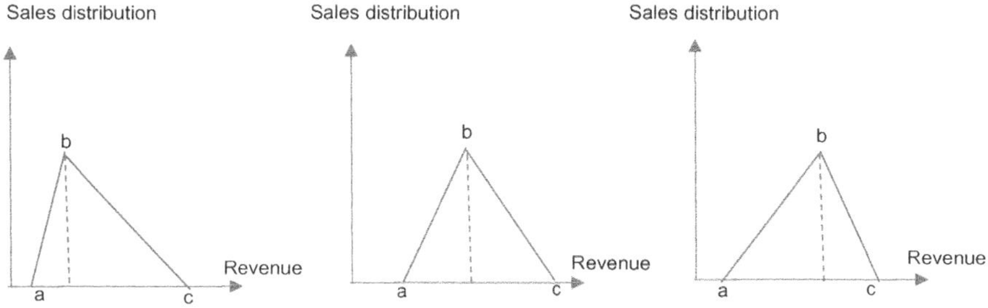

Fig. 6.3 Three examples of triangular distributions

Thus, the mode is 35 days (given by 0.85*30 + 0.1*50 + 0.05*90), the maximum is 57 days (0.7*30 + 0.3*120), and the minimum is 31 days (0.9*30 + 0.1*40). Figure 6.4 illustrates these estimates.

Of course, there are limitations to this approach, such as the truncated possibilities. However, it is a straightforward manner of estimating payment terms that is easy to communicate to other employees.

Formally (feel free to ignore the definitions below, as they will not be of interest to anybody but the most statistically inclined), the parameters of a triangular distribution are:

- Mean: $(a + b + c)/3$
- Mode: b
- Variance: $(a^2 + b^2 + c^2 - ab - ac - bc)/18$

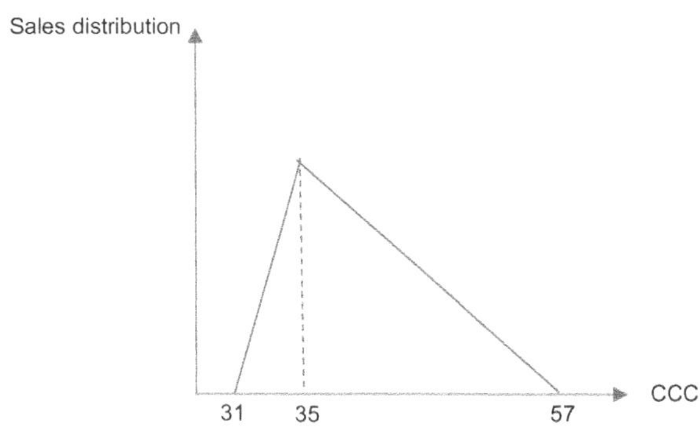

Fig. 6.4 An example of triangular distribution with $a = 31$, $b = 35$, and $c = 57$

- Probability Density Function: $p_X(\mathrm{x}) = \begin{cases} 0 & \text{for} \quad x < a \\ \frac{2(x-a)}{(b-a)(c-a)} & \text{for} \quad a \le x < b \\ \frac{2}{c-a} & \text{for} \quad x = c \\ \frac{2(c-x)}{(c-a)(c-b)} & \text{for} \quad b < x \le c \\ 0 & \text{for} \quad c < x \end{cases}$
- Cumulative Density Function: $F(x) = \begin{cases} 0 & \text{for} \quad x \le a \\ \frac{(x-a)^2}{(b-a)(c-a)} & \text{for} \quad a \le x \le b \\ 1 - \frac{(c-x)^2}{(c-a)(c-b)} & \text{for} \quad b < x < c \\ 1 & \text{for} \quad c \le x \end{cases}$

When more than one parameter in the cash conversion is drawn randomly from different statistical distributions, it is challenging (and likely impossible in most cases) to come up with joint probability and cumulative density functions.

A straightforward way to estimate the feasible range of operating working capital is to set up minimum, mode, and maximum CCCs and revenue, ascribing random probabilities for intermediary values. An example follows below.

Assume that a company has sales of U$2,000,000 and believes that its revenue cannot fall below U$1,200,000 and should not surpass U$2,500,000. Regarding its DIO, the company's current term takes 38 days, and managers believe they cannot reduce it below 35 and don't find any good reason for it to take longer than 50 days, even with supply-chain delays. For DSO and DPO, managers make simple estimates in which minimum, mode, and maximum are, respectively: 15, 22, and 35, and 24, 29, and 32.

Thus, a, b and c for CCC are:

- Minimum: 35 + 15 − 32 = 18.
- Mode: 38 + 22 − 29 = 31.
- Maximum: 50 + 35 − 24 = 61.

Given the expected range of revenue, the parameters for a triangular distribution of OWC would be:

- Minimum: 18*1,200,000/360 = 60,000.
- Mode: 31*2,000,000/360 = 172,222.
- Maximum: 61*2,500,000/360 = 423,611.

Graphically, in Fig. 6.5.

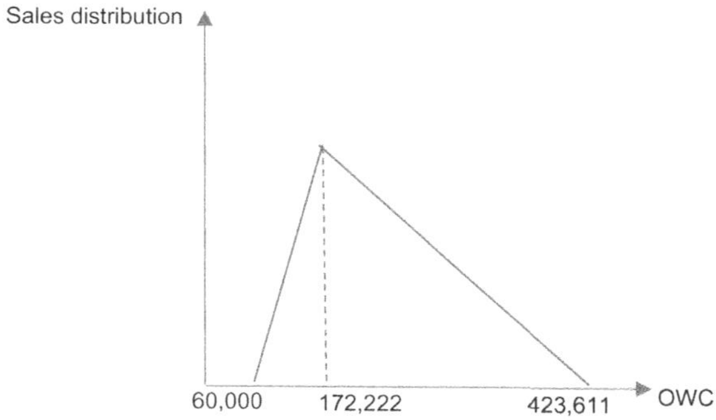

Fig. 6.5 Example of OWC from triangular distribution

As we can see, the interval of possible OWC is substantial, maybe to the point of being useless. Nevertheless, if necessary, one could quickly reduce the probability of more extreme events.

Thus, according to the cumulative density function above, to find the probability that the firm's OWC is higher than U$300,000:

$$\begin{aligned} P(X > 300,000) &= \frac{(c-x)^2}{(c-a)(c-b)} \\ &= \frac{(423611 - 300000)^2}{(423611 - 60000)(423611 - 172222)} = 16.7\% \end{aligned}$$

That type of information shouldn't be used as point estimates, in that managers should necessarily put aside resources to meet the pessimist estimates of operating working capital. After all, these pessimistic scenarios refer to extended payment terms but strong revenue growth. If companies can appropriate profits from the sales growth to meet changes in payment terms, the growth in operating working capital can be funded by an increase in economic activity.

Still, as in the case of the crying CEO (Sect. 3.2.1), the timing of cash outflows matters. The interval of OWC above is best used as an initial guide and benchmark by managers. Improving on it, managers could set up Monte Carlo simulations with values taken randomly from the intervals for each parameter to estimate cash flow needs and illiquidity events. For instance, for simplicity, let's assume that the firm is reasonably sure that its revenue will be around U$2,000,000 next year, but it is uncertain about the length of payment terms.

It could use some mode, minimum and maximum parameters for DSO and DPO (also leaving DIO constant or allowing it to vary) and simulate the resulting working capital requirements by plotting 10,000 random draws of the selected parameters.

Moreover, simulations can be more precise by allowing some sales and payment terms combinations to be more likely. For instance, sales drop and DSO go up simultaneously in a recession. Thus, the probability of a worst-case scenario regarding working capital investments in which sales explode but DSO increase in tandem can be made lower.

In this section, the goal is not to exhaust the options available to forecast working capital requirements. Triangular distributions are amenable to direct simulations but suffer from disallowing extreme values; minimum and maximum values are pre-determined. It also does not consider how financing costs rise with working capital requirements. Many companies have enough reserves to fund all their working capital needs, even in stressed scenarios. For a treatment of financing costs that increase non-linearly when payment terms are extended, see Van der Vliet et al. (2015).

Finally, we consider working capital buffer a financial variable, but companies should relate it to inventory buffering. For instance, all else being equal, companies should not invest in working capital unless necessary. However, safety stocks are part and parcel of the production process. Moreover, supply chain uncertainty may temporarily lead managers to overstock raw materials.

For instance, a study by Darby et al. (2020) reveals that firms accumulate more inventory as a buffer against policy risk under conditions of high policy uncertainty and high industry dynamism.

As with every aspect of financial management, proper working capital buffering management should be customized to a firm's realities. This section describes the foundations of sound working capital forecasting and leaves the application to the readers.

6.3 When Should a Company Borrow, and the Options to Fund Working Capital?

There is a widespread belief that working capital management is about short-term funding. It is not the case. Working capital is akin to capital expenditure; it is best funded with long-term sources. Of course, firms can finance the acquisition of machinery with short-term debt, rolling it over constantly, but that is not ideal. Similarly, firms shouldn't finance working capital with momentary borrowing.

Here, we will not formalize an optimal debt theory but will describe executives' main tradeoffs in real life. While CFOs of multinational companies might have the correct incentives to pursue an optimal debt ratio, owners of small and medium-sized companies usually prefer lower debt levels rather than maximize their firms' values.

We summarize decades of sophisticated finance theories in a simple Fig. 6.6. As we can see, the relationship between the debt level and the firm's value is non-linear.

There are three stages in the relationship between debt level and firm value:

1. A firm with no debt has a specific value (FV_0), also known as Enterprise Value (the sum of total debt and equity). As it starts to issue debt, its value rises, as the marginal benefits from debt are higher than the marginal costs. That goes on until;
2. The firm reaches its optimal debt level (DL*), where marginal cost and benefit are the same. The firm's value starts to decrease until;
3. At a particular debt level (DL_{max}), the firm's value is the same as it would be if the company had no debt. Any additional debt destroys value until the firm's capital structure is composed solely of debt. After that, there is excessive indebtedness.

The optimal debt level equates to the marginal interest tax shield and the expected marginal cost of default (Abel, 2018). In essence, sophisticated optimal debt theories balance debt costs and benefits, summarized in Table 6.1.

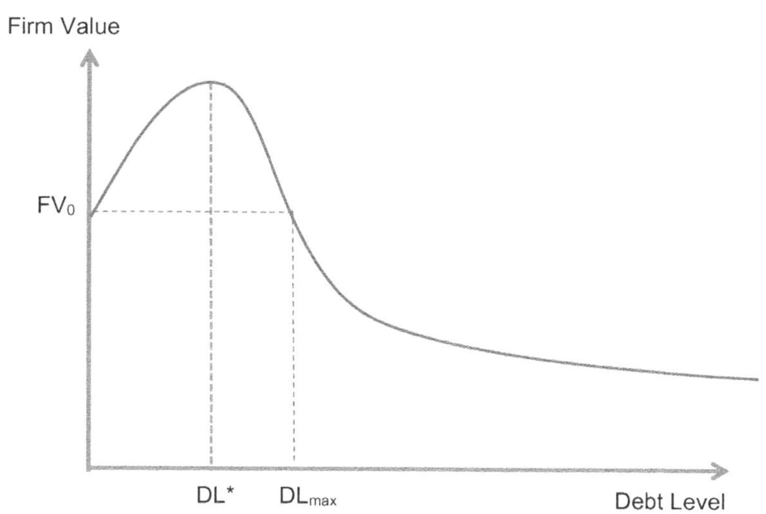

Fig. 6.6 The optimal debt level

Table 6.1 Advantages and disadvantages of debt to non-financial companies

Advantages of indebtedness	Disadvantages of indebtedness
Tax Shield—the company can lower its tax burden by deducting the amount paid as interest to service its debt from the operating profit	Bankruptcy costs—greater indebtedness increases the probability of bankruptcy. There are significant costs associated with restructuring a business
Growth—firms can usually grow quicker if they have access to debt markets	Transaction costs—Costs associated with debt issuance include preparing specific financial statements and others
Discipline—managers must make better decisions, as interest and amortization must be paid off regularly	Monitoring—there are direct and indirect costs for borrowing. That includes even the executives' time for administering relationships with debtholders. There also may be restrictive covenants to debt contracts

The non-linear relationship between firm value and debt levels arises because the benefits outweigh the costs for the lower valuer of debt. Companies benefit from the discipline that debt brings, the growth opportunities, and the tax shield. Of course, debt also brings direct (transaction) and indirect (monitoring) costs and the possibility of default. As the likelihood of default increases as debt increases, so do the costs of issuing more debt.

Debt tends to be cheaper than equity, but that may not matter much to ultimate owners who value survival over marginal benefits. A finance theory called the pecking order posits that owners have strong preferences for using retained profits to finance expansion and borrow only as a last resort. Zeidan et al. (2018) found, in a direct survey with 159 ultimate owners of small and medium-sized firms, that they even prefer retained profits over subsidized loans. The preference for retained profits is also invariant to debt constraints, and robustness checks show that the pecking order holds even for firms with no debt.

So, how should a company fund its working capital needs? Managers, regardless of a company's size or ownership structure, should follow three simple rules:

1. Working capital should be financed by long-term sources, be it equity or debt.
2. Retained profits are a natural tool to fund working capital investments.
3. The optimal debt structure should be disassociated from specific funding of working capital requirements.

The search for the optimal level of debt is the search for the best capital structure of the company. As with the search for an optimal working capital strategy, there is no magic formula for all sectors, and DL* depends on the company's business model and other factors. However, the lesson that organizations are better off mustering long-term funds to finance working capital is universal. Accounts receivables are not short-term assets, and accounts payable are not short-term debt unless we focus solely on accounting rules. As long as firms continue to operate, they will exist.

As we have seen before, working capital grows due to the revenue, the financial cycle, and the mixed effects. Let's assume that the company's revenue and cash-conversion cycle grows over three years and then stabilizes, as demonstrated in Fig. 6.7.

The total working capital invested grows steadily, stabilizing at OWC_{t+3}. Companies have a few options to mobilize resources to support this expansion: retained profits, issuing equity, short-term borrowing, and long-term borrowing. The critical assertion is that managers should not look at short-term lending for working capital investments.

We leave the discussion about the trade-off theory and other models of optimal debt ratios to other textbooks but note that capital structure policies should be pursued holistically. Specific debt target ratios should not discriminate between fixed assets and working capital investments. Suppose a firm projects its investments to be U$10 million in the next few years, and the

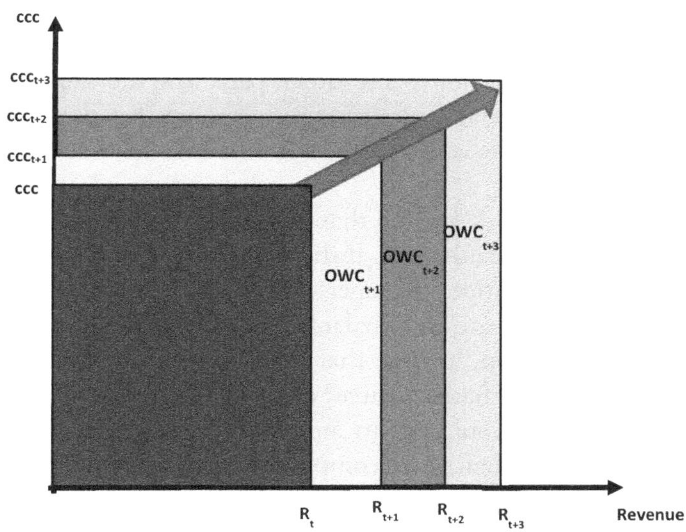

Fig. 6.7 Simultaneous increase in financial cycle and revenue

goal is to achieve a capital structure of 40% debt and 60% equity. It doesn't matter if the outlays are directed towards fixed assets or working capital.

No matter how a company administers its capital structure, working capital investments are long-term investments, and it behooves executives to treat it as such. Savings from a reduction in operating working capital can be used towards expansion and are remunerated at the company's WACC. The same holds for projects that reduce the financial cycle sustainably. Unfortunately, many small business owners do not understand this and rely on factoring and other types of short-term borrowing if they face liquidity problems without preventing such events from happening in the first place.

6.4 Trade Credit Finance, Factoring, Discounted Trade Bills, and Anticipation of Receivables

Associated with the optimal debt policy, a central question regarding working capital management is: should companies ever use trade credit finance? Like most relevant issues in finance, the answer is: it depends.

Here, we concentrate on trade credit finance in which companies borrow using their receivables as security. These factoring transactions can be done in spot markets, or they can be options embedded in specific contracts, such as public procurement. In addition, in reverse factoring, the retailer's payment guarantee and the credit rating differential between a small supplier and a prominent retailer enables the supplier to receive financing at a more favorable rate (Kouvelis & Xu, 2021).

The selling firm must notify the other party on the sales contracts it intends to enter for several factoring arrangements (Smith & Schnucker, 1994). Factoring contracts can lead to moral hazard, adverse selection, and fraud.

Regarding moral hazard, assume that a firm has private information that its customer will likely default soon. If they sell their rights to collect on their sales to a financial institution, managers would be taking advantage of their private information to create an unbalanced trade.

As for adverse selection, assume that for some reason, factoring is a bit more expensive than alternative sources of financing. Then, only companies without many options would try to anticipate their due revenue. If these companies were riskier than their competitors, financial institutions would hike rates to compensate for the additional risk, and only more desperate firms would demand such services.

Finally, assume that the owner of company A is indirectly the owner of company B, but that is private information. Firm B can be bankrupted on purpose, but not before "buying" vast quantities of products from firm A. These sales, delivered or not, priced at a fair price or not, can now be used by firm A to borrow against them.

However, borrowing from the factor can compare favorably to other interest cost and flexibility alternatives. That is because the factor is already involved in managing the seller's trade credit (Smith & Schnucker, 1994).

The main difference between factoring and other types of trade credit, such as staggered discounts for payments at specific dates, is that interest rates become explicit. When a firm extends payment terms, they usually use an implicit interest rate to determine prices. However, loans from financial institutions in which guarantees are receivables have perspicuous prices.

For a company borrowing against receivables, the instrumental decision should be straightforward: if borrowing terms are similar to those of other types of debt, managers should use it; otherwise, they should pass on it. However, in real life, factoring is usually used by credit-constrained companies that have difficulties accessing other types of debt. Especially in countries where credit is scarce and expensive, trade credit financing plays a significant role in allowing firms to deal with sales volatility or a sudden influx in orders.

There are four main reasons companies use factoring, three that may create value and one that is just a survival strategy: sales volatility, growth bottlenecks, asset-specific procurement (public and private), and severe credit constraints.

In Sect. 10.3, we describe the factoring model by Kouvelis and Xu (2021). In their model, recourse, non-recourse and reverse factoring depend on the supplier and retailer's credit rating and the supplier's liquidity risk. Figure 6.8 illustrates the boundary conditions that make these choices feasible for the supplier.

However, factoring feasible for all parties involved does not mean companies should use it indiscriminately. The first value-enhancing use of factoring is dealing with sales volatility. Assume that a company expects a spike in sales for a short period (for instance, a restaurant during a major national holiday). For that purpose, it must place large orders of supplies. The restaurant manager may find getting an advance for their table reservations easier than mobilizing funds. In that case, even if factoring has a higher interest rate than other sources, the short-term nature of the loan can make it cost-effective in terms of opportunity costs.

Growth bottlenecks are similar to sales volatility, giving companies a solid reason to use factoring as cash advances. Suppose companies are entering a

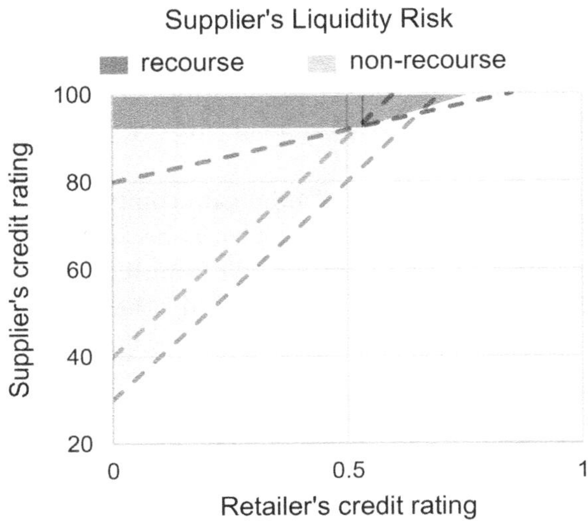

Fig. 6.8 Supplier's financing choice for a given payment extension (*Source* Kouvelis and Xu [2021])

period of high growth planned to last a few months but must ensure enough liquidity to fund working capital investments. In that case, factoring can be a relief to strained coffers.

The last primary value-creating reason for factoring is procurement. Companies and governments often design procurement auctions with bank financing attached to the process to attract more competition. The contract is used as collateral for banks to lend funds so the winning firms can provide the goods and services. Companies that bid on large contracts may not have the necessary capital to provide the goods and services adequately.

Finally, we have firms in distress. It is relatively common for small companies to enter a cash crunch spiral. They start getting cash advances from future sales, limiting future money inflows. Later, the company resorts to factoring again, and the cycle continues. A short-term debt becomes permanent. Some firms use factoring for years without finding other ways to survive. After companies enter the factoring cycle, it is usually the case that the hole in their cash flow is approximately one month of sales. The primary way to break the value-destroying factoring cycle is to muster long-term funds to pay off the entire debt. The exception is for companies that do not have access to other types of credit. If the only debt that firms can issue is collateralized receivables, it may be optimal to do it indefinitely. Usually, debt is cheaper than equity, and it includes a tax benefit (although this is less clear for some types of credit in emerging markets).

One significant result in the different aspects of working capital financing is that of Wu et al. (2019). The authors study a supplier decision on two issues regarding the payment mechanism: (a) the payment term, whether to collect payment early or late and (b) the payment approach, to collect personally or through a third party. They compare the influence of three supply chain finance schemes: early payment, delayed payment, and reverse factoring. They found delayed payment offers additional benefits to the supplier and retailer when the supplier has a lower cost of capital. Early payment and reverse factoring offer additional benefits to the supplier and retailer when the retailer has the financing advantage. Also of note is that with the bank's involvement and intermediation role, the increase in profits for the supplier and retailer of reverse factoring is higher than under early payment. The more significant the difference in capital cost between the supplier and retailer, the greater the efficiency of the three financial schemes.

To sum up, factoring is usually seen as an expensive source of credit for most companies, especially SMEs. However, it can play an important role in firms' abilities to manage their cash flow volatility, as long as companies don't rely on it perennially.

6.5 Operating Margin or Extended Payment Terms

The central concern of working capital management is the balance between cash generation and profit margin. Should a company negotiate extended payment terms with suppliers or extract as much value as possible from the supply chain?

Here, we can't provide a definitive answer, but we develop a heuristic for managers to decide their primary targets. These involve five steps: estimating elasticities, determining the firm's stage in the business cycle, dividing suppliers into specific categories, considering short versus long-term negotiations, and designing optimizing strategies.

First, companies must estimate the DSO and DPO elasticities. In other words, what is the discount for early payment to suppliers, and the changes in prices one can expect if customers are allowed to pay later? There are three main ways to estimate such elasticities: historical data, simulations based on benchmarking, and experimentation.

As the term implies, historical data requires delving into the company's past information to analyze the effects of earlier price changes. Were the company able to extend payment terms to suppliers without pressuring its costs? Is the number of suppliers decreasing, making the organization less able to negotiate terms?

Profit maximization is usually a simple story: companies should make as much money as possible, once and often. Of course, even for the leading indicator of a firm's performance, strategic considerations can make companies sacrifice earnings today for profits in the future. However, all else being equal, more profits are better than fewer earnings.

Things are also clear-cut regarding financial cycles, with all else being equal; shorter cycles are better than long ones. However, companies without any influence have their cash conversion cycle determined by the market conditions they encounter. In that case, their goal is to be as efficient as possible, reducing the only variable under their control, days of inventory outstanding, while keeping costs low.

What is the ideal cash conversion cycle for companies to negotiate terms with suppliers and consumers? The easy answer is the number of days compatible with a firm's business model and growth strategy. Of course, business models and growth strategies can be vaguely defined, turning into useless terms.

Chapter 4 presents the main variables for analyzing the tradeoffs between operating margins and cash flow generation. Chapter 7 includes the steps for building a comprehensive working capital management strategy. Here, we are interested in the managerial implications and the possibility of operational strategies reducing the cash conversion cycle without loss in profit margins. Below we describe some situations that highlight these issues.

6.5.1 The Reputational and Long-Term Risks of Negative Cash-Conversion Cycles

How can an industrial company achieve a negative cash conversion cycle? Here, we discuss the case of Ambev, the precursor of AB InBev, the largest brewing company in the world. Ambev itself is the result of a merger between Antarctica and Brahma, owners of the biggest two beer brands in Brazil at the time, in 1999. The company has always had an aggressive commercial reputation and has a similar work culture to investment banks. "You either stay two months, two years, or more than twenty years," mentioned one of the executives to the author in the past. The first milestone comes from new employees learning quickly if the corporate culture is for them. The second milestone comes after the second round of bonuses and promotions. Some employees feel dejected from toiling hard and not getting rewarded or are told matter-of-factly that their performance was subpar. Finally, those who survive these brutal two years tend to build a career in the company and become workers for life (as long as they never lose their edge, of course).

Ambev's share of the Brazilian beer market has hovered around 60% since the original merger, giving the company clout in negotiating with suppliers and large customers, such as supermarkets. Ambev is known for being aggressive in its relationships with the supply chain. The company may even overstep its boundaries. More than once, Ambev has been accused of anti-competitive behavior, such as forced bundled sales. In 2019, the industry association of beer distributors (Confederação Nacional das Revendas Ambev, Confenar) entered a formal complaint against the company with antitrust agencies in Brazil.

Regardless of formal proceedings, the company has a history of squeezing its suppliers. Informal interviews with CEOs of large distributors and supermarkets reveal a similar pattern: "They don't want to leave anything on the table," "If I could afford to, I would never do business with them again," "I try to steer my customers away from their products, just to see if they lose sales in the future." The CEO of a trucking company related that he refused to let his firm's managers bid on Ambev's contracts. He claimed that "no company should ever service another that proposes to pay only after 180-days after the service is performed. We will never work with them again, but not every company can afford to lose such a large client."

These executives also point out a turning point in Ambev's history: 2008. In July 2005, InBev Holding Brazil and AmBev merged, with the resulting company acquired Quinsa in August 2006. In 2008, Ambev made successive offers to the shareholders of Anheuser-Busch. On June 11, 2008, Ambev's offer was accepted. The final price tag was 39.9 billion euros, and the company announced the completion of its acquisition of Anheuser-Busch on 18 November 2008 (rebranding itself as Anheuser-Busch InBev).

On September 7, 2008, the American Treasury nationalized Fannie and Freddie, and later in the month, Lehman Brothers filed for bankruptcy, triggering global panic. Financial and non-financial companies scrambled to survive the credit crunch in the ensuing months. For Ambev, cash flow was more important than ever, given the massive bill for the acquisition of Anheuser-Busch. However, the great financial crisis sped up in the middle of the acquisition process, and capital markets froze worldwide, even for large multinational corporations. Operationally, how did the company react? By reducing payment terms to consumers and lengthening it to suppliers.

Throughout the first half of the 2000s, the recently formed Ambev proactively reduced its cash-conversion cycle. In 2000, its CCC hovered around 164 days. By 2003, the company had managed to reduce it to 53 days.

From 2004 to 2008, the company strategy was to limit any investment in working capital. The company's cash conversion cycle hovered around zero. During the financial crisis, things changed. There was a strong push towards extracting as much cash flow as possible from the supply chain (Figs. 6.9 and 6.10).

One customer recalled that Ambev's delivery trucks were retrofitted with safes. The reason? A change in payment terms, from 14 days to cash or checks for small customers. Ambev reduced DSO from 28 to 14 days for supermarkets and more prominent customers. Combining shorter payment terms from customers with an increase of payment terms to suppliers to more

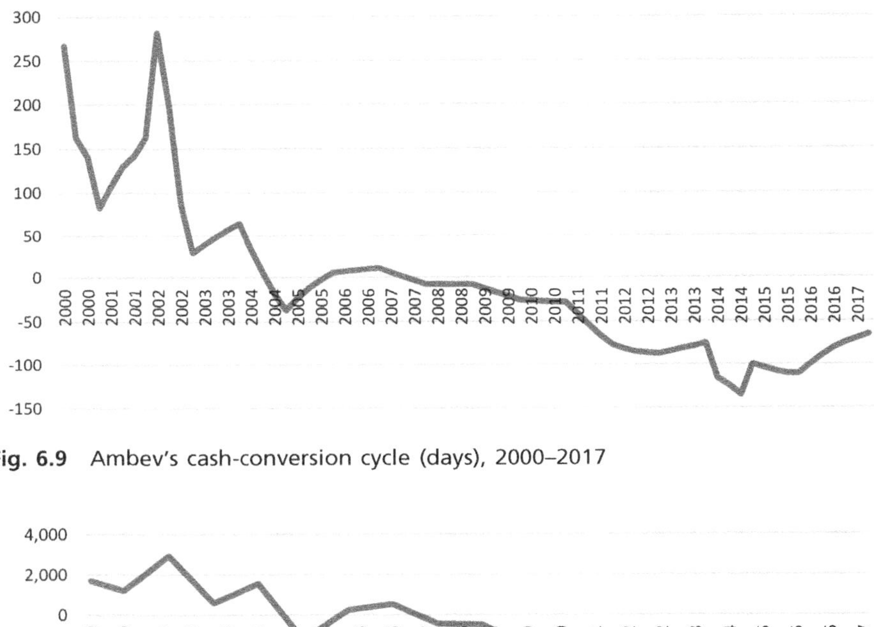

Fig. 6.9 Ambev's cash-conversion cycle (days), 2000–2017

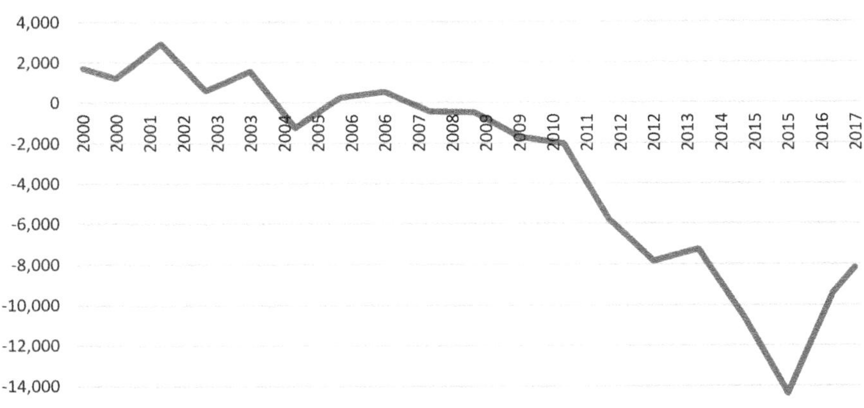

Fig. 6.10 Ambev's operating working capital (U$ billion), 2000–2017

than 180 days is clear why the company turned a positive CCC into negative operating working capital.

Some of Ambev's strategies to reduce its cash-conversion cycle were deemed illegal, and antitrust authorities fined the company in 2009. On July 22, 2009, the leading antitrust agency in Brazil, CADE, handed the company the largest fine in Brazilian antitrust history at the time, approximately U$350 million. Partly, the penalty was due to an exclusivity agreement in which, for every U$100 worth of beer, customers were required to purchase U$90 of Ambev's products.

In addition to bundled sales, the company also had some creative policies regarding marketing budgets that were de facto loans from their customers. Part of the discount that customers were due from the exclusivity agreement with Ambev was retained as a marketing expenditure. It worked somewhat like this: if the cost for a beer was U$3, customers ended up paying U$3.20, with the U$0.20 classified as a marketing expense. Customers were entitled to get that amount back one year later. Ambev was borrowing U$0.20 for a year from each bottle of beer sold. The bundling of a loan in each sale helps explain the turnaround of operating working capital; in 2011, the CCC of the company was −50 days, and it had not since then risen above that threshold.

What is the main risk of that strategy? Over time, the loss of market share, with customers and suppliers seeking business elsewhere. In the 1980s, a company in Brazil held 90% of the retail sugar market in Brazil. It also extracted as much cash flow from customers and suppliers. Supermarkets started to deemphasize the brand when arranging products in their aisles to fight back. Store managers couldn't refrain from offering the most popular brand of sugar, but they could and did put the product in the least visible area of the stores while giving the premium space to the smaller competitors. It is common for companies to pay large retailers for premium space, but, in this instance, store managers were willing to advertise other brands indirectly. Over time, the market became more fragmented, and the market leader was forced to abandon its most egregious business practices, as it did not have the market power required to enforce strict control over the behavior of its consumers and suppliers.

It is unlikely that Ambev will share the same fate, as the company advertises heavily and works hard at creating loyal customers. Still, the case highlights the main tradeoffs in working capital management for companies with market power.

6.5.2 Nudge

This case is about a family-owned supermarket chain that has been through its ups and downs. Their first crisis was related to their eighth unit. It took the company twenty-five years to grow to six stores, but then came a period of rapid expansion, with the chain going from six to eleven stores in approximately two years. This expansion was a feat for a middle-sized company that avoids borrowing unless strictly necessary, like most family-owned companies in emerging markets. The company had never contracted; its business model was based on growth by converting other-use commercial properties into supermarkets in upscale areas in Sao Paulo.

However, things changed with the eighth store. There were never enough customers, goods were turned over slowly, and marketing efforts failed repeatedly. The store never broke even and routinely required cash infusions from headquarters.

Sunk costs are straightforward: once certain investments are made, decisions should consider only future cash-flows and not past expenditures if the money spent cannot be recovered. The executives invested even more time and money to turn things around instead of containing the damage from that store by limiting cash infusions from the more profitable units. They had never dealt with a cash-draining operation before and allowed sunk costs to dictate their behavior.

The sunk cost fallacy leads to many common mistakes, from hanging on to losing investments, such as stocks, for too long or, as in the present case, spending good money after bad.

Because managerial effort was focused on one unit, the others suffered. Eventually, the decision was made to close the unit and move on, but delaying that decision had almost bankrupted the whole chain. In the year that the underperforming was closed, the EBITDA margin was negative 4.4%, and cash outflows were higher than inflows for every month but October.

Once the unit was closed, the executives solved issues with the remaining stores. They deemed the cash flow problem more critical than the lack of profitability because shareholders were willing to defer dividends. Smoothing firms' cash flow through limiting dividend payments is another common type of behavior from shareholders of medium-sized companies. "Rich companies, poor shareholders" is a situation that does exist, even though no business owner should aim for that.

The company tried many measures to reduce its cash-conversion cycle and improve its cash flow. An unusual but surprisingly effective one was to nudge consumers away from using their credit cards. In October, the company rolled out changes about how cashiers greet customers. Table 6.2 shows how sales were broken down by payment method for the year's first ten months.

In Brazil, when handed a card, cashiers would usually ask either: "Should I charge it to your credit card?" or "Credit or debit?". Most upper-middle-income and wealthy people in Brazil have credit cards, while few have mortgages (Bertran & Echeverry, 2021).

The everyday use of credit cards to pay for groceries is most likely a leftover of hyperinflation in the country (for more about how the hyperinflation that ended in 1994 has molded financial decisions, see Zeidan, 2018). Consumers should be mostly indifferent about buying groceries with their credit or debit cards in a low-inflation scenario. Still, before the intervention that would nudge consumers towards debit cards, credit cards users answered for 34% of total sales.

The central intervention could not be more simple. It consisted of managers training cashiers to greet customers by asking: "Debit?" as in "are you going to pay with a debit card?". Some additional training aimed at improving customer service in general. Cashiers did not have formal targets regarding clients' payment methods; the goal was to nudge customers gently, not cause any disruption in the checkout process or risk losing consumers altogether.

The training is likely to have worked. The use of credit cards as a payment method fell, on average, 20%, with some stores seeing reductions of almost 30% a year after the intervention. In only one of the 17 stores, the use of credit has not budged. We can't establish direct causality between the intervention and the shift towards debit cards, as external factors, such as the business cycle and broad changes in consumer behavior, could have explained the reduction in credit card use. However, soon after, Brazil entered its worst recession in decades. While consumers looked to postpone paying for groceries in other supermarkets, credit card use remains lower than before in the company's stores (Table 6.3).

What was the effect on cash flow and working capital investments? Financial institutions took 35 days to pay vendors for credit card sales and three days for debit card purchases at the time. For an average of U$300 million in annual sales, a permanent shift from credit to debit card of 6%, from 33 to 27%, the operating working capital investment reduction was a tad over U$1.5 million.

$$\begin{aligned}\Delta \text{OWC} &= \Delta \text{DSO} * \text{Daily Sales} * \text{\% Sales affected}\\ &= 27\ \text{days} * \text{U\$822,000} * 6\% = \text{U\$1,578,082}\end{aligned}$$

Table 6.2 Sales by payment method

Item	January	February	March	April	May	June	July	August	September	October	Total	%
Sales	25,573	22,678	25,331	27,619	23,967	25,315	21,270	26,696	27,092	27,244	252,785	
Checks	484	328	320	359	404	430	291	404	308	328	3,655	1
Cash	5,974	5,551	6,307	5,907	6,011	5,766	5,959	6,319	6,384	6,500	60,678	24
Credit card	8,622	7,737	8,018	11,509	8,416	8,203	4,913	9,812	8,849	9,630	85,710	34
Debit card	10,477	9,050	10,462	9,206	8,589	9,822	9,380	9,935	10,283	10,178	97,383	39
Food ticket	16	11	214	629	541	1,088	722	222	1,262	604	5,310	2

Table 6.3 Credit card use before and after nudging intervention

Store	Before intervention (%)	After intervention (%)
1	33	27
2	35	31
3	27	26
4	34	31
5	34	28
6	37	30
7	28	25
8	31	24
9	35	30
10	37	24
11	38	30
12	33	33
13	36	27
14	40	29
15	25	24
16	29	27
17	24	21
Average	33	27

For 6% of the sales, DSO is reduced by 32 days. As daily sales were U$822,000 (U$300 million divided by 365 days), approximately U$1.5 million trapped as operating working capital was converted to cash.

As long as credit card use does not rise back to its original levels, the company can use the freed-up cash as it pleases. Executives decided to reduce the company's debt, as headquarters relied on expensive short-term bank credit to finance the growth of its store's retail sales per square meter.

The main lesson from the nudge strategy is not that it worked but that there are many opportunities to improve the efficiency of a company's operations if the goal is to optimize cash flow. If a company needs credit, it should first streamline processes; maybe the money was available all along.

6.5.3 Limiting Working Capital Investments: Just-In-Time

Just-in-time or lean production methods were famously created by Toyota in the 1950s and 1960s and spread out far and wide over the decades. The essence of just-in-time is straightforward: inputs arrive at the precise time needed in each step of the production process. Toyota developed the original just-in-time (JIT) system for its automotive manufacturing plants, but nowadays, nothing is standing in the way of retail businesses implementing similar strategies.

The usual advantages of JIT production are eliminating waste and continuous improvement (Benton Jr., 2010). Other potential benefits include lead times, quality, labor productivity, employee relations, inventory, and manufacturing costs. Costs to companies that switch their *modus operandi* include capital equipment, employee training, and administration (White et al., 1999). Moreover, it is well known that there are significant organizational culture challenges in lean manufacturing implementation, as such systems put more pressure on workers and managers (Alkhoraif et al., 2019). Figure 6.11 presents a conceptual framework for just-in-time and lean production systems, illustrating the critical conditions and challenges for the transition to these types of modes of production.

Just-in-time production methods work better when there is trust between suppliers and customers and somewhat predictable demand. However, previous researchers have overlooked one dimension: the relationship between JIT and the cash conversion cycle. Benton Jr. (2010) states that JIT is focused on waste from overproduction, waste of motion, waste of time, waste of

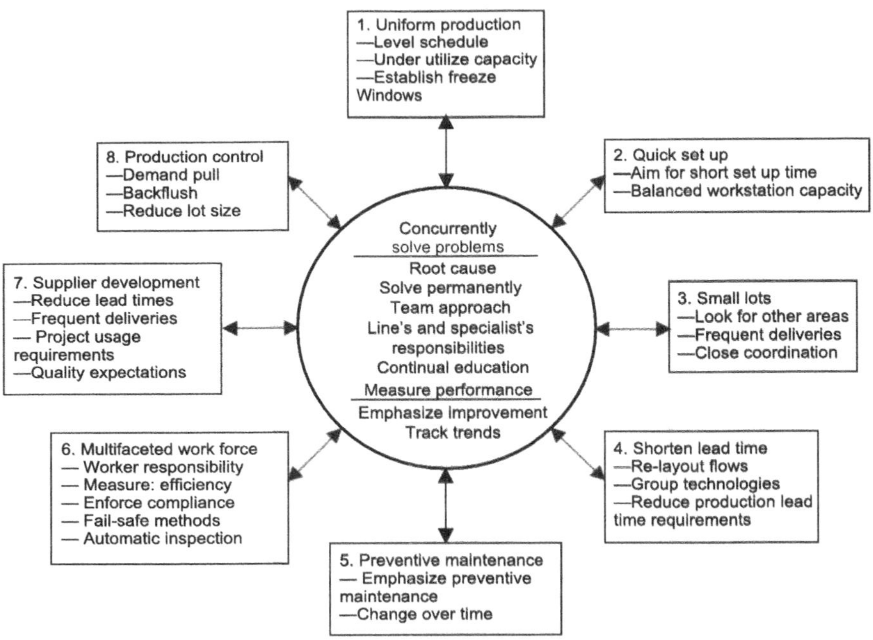

Fig. 6.11 Just-in-time/lean production systems (*Source* Benton Jr. [2010])

movement, waste due to excessive inventory, and the waste resulting from poor quality. However, the author is missing one type of waste: cash trapped in operations. Reducing accounts payable is not necessarily less important than the waste of excessive inventory in lean production systems. It is understandable that because JIT is such a paradigmatic shift in manufacturing operations, the folklore of "zero waste" has been built on descriptions of the manufacturing process. It should also be noted that pure JIT production systems are rare birds due to all the technical requirements for its implementation, and not even Toyota has relied solely on that type of system (Benton Jr., 2010). However, the financial dimension of JIT cannot be ignored. Lean production systems are, maybe above all, cash-saving systems. The more credit constraints a company has and the greater its growth prospects, the higher are the benefits of shifting current practices to just-in-time.

For large companies, the transition to lean production brings two critical benefits that are disconnected from labor productivity, employee relations, quality issues, and other aforementioned potential rewards. Lean production, when it succeeds, allows for a reduction in working capital investments and the transference of demand risk to other parts of the supply chain. It saves companies money from a reduced financial cycle, from postponing working capital investments, and from outsourcing some cash-flow effects of sales volatility.

It is no coincidence that a rapidly expanding manufacturing company in a credit-constrained environment developed JIT. It is not serendipitous that other companies started copying the system introduced by Toyota after the oil crisis of 1973.

Interestingly, the mythology of the just-in-time production process refers to reduced costs from streamlined operations. However, it is unlikely that adopting lean production processes reduces costs significantly. While the focus on efficiency and reducing waste should decrease input prices, the piecemeal nature of ordering inputs from suppliers may lead to increased expenditures. Companies that adopt JIT usually mitigate the risk of disruptions by establishing long-term guaranteed contracts with clauses related to the quality of components, guaranteed delivery times, and contingency plans to issues such as weather calamities, trucker strikes, and others.

Lean production processes are notoriously difficult to implement. N. Radziwill (2008) and Polito and Watson (2006) identify five "major constraints" on the JIT process:

- Customer-Driven and Economic Conditions: effective JIT also depends on capital availability and relative stability of customer demand.

- Logistics: economic turmoil, rising energy costs, labor disruptions, and catastrophic weather events like hurricanes and floods.
- Organizational Culture and Conditions: workers must have the autonomy to improve the manufacturing processes.
- Intractable Accounting and Finance Practices: disparate financial systems between supply chain partners.
- Minor Supplier Difficulties: one of the criticisms of JIT is that it silently offloads costs from larger companies onto the smaller partners, and many small suppliers have implemented "JIT premiums" to offset this effect. Relaxing JIT requirements could positively impact these members of your supply chain.

Lean manufacturing processes can be highly complicated. Implementing such systems include opportunity costs considerations such as comparing the costs of stockouts with the benefits of not having stockouts, re-examining the risks from upstream and downstream partners, and assessing the resilience of smaller suppliers.

One of the real benefits of just-in-time processes is the reduced operating capital necessary for regular operations, the outsourcing of working capital needs due to sales volatility, and the freeing of money to expand operations. Such systems may deliver ancillary benefits such as better ways to manage product quality. Lean manufacturing is in many ways a financial management strategy and not a manufacturing optimization one. Chief Operation Officers find it much easier to manage processes that do not require utmost efficiency at all times. However, the financial benefits of such systems may make it worthwhile the hassle of incorporating just-in-time practices, negotiating supplier contracts that require small batch real-time deliveries, and more.

When Toyota started implementing just-in-time processes, its sales were increasing rapidly, consuming precious capital. Throughout the 1950s, auto production grew at 29% per year, going from 10,126 vehicles in 1951 to 127,444 in 1960. The expansion was still robust during the 1960s, at 20% per year and culminating in 1,110,448 vehicles in 1970 (Fig. 6.12). Throughout this period, the revenue effect from Toyota's financial cycle was only second to capital expenditures, requiring vast sums of money from the company. Japan was also a middle-income country at the time, and capital was not plentiful.

Just-in-time, when done right, becomes the standard mode of production that allows companies to manage production with minimum working capital

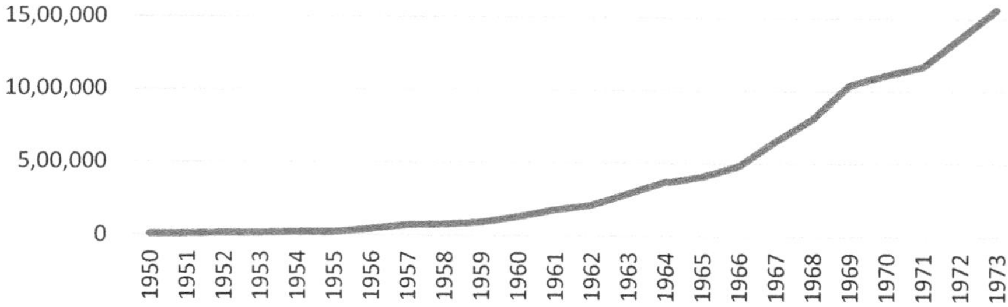

Fig. 6.12 Total passenger cars, trucks, and buses produced by Toyota, 1950–1973 (*Source* Toyota's history from Toyota's main website)

investments. Like the best types of cash conversion cycle strategies, the main challenge is for managers to keep the system running smoothly once set up.

Graphically, Toyota's goal of introducing just-in-time is represented in Fig. 6.13.

The initial operating working capital is defined as the areas A + B. The revenue effect (C) requires additional working capital investments as sales grow. To free up capital for helping expansion go smoothly, the company optimizes its cash conversion cycle, reducing OWC by area B. Of course, we are not claiming that the introduction of just-in-time production processes is solely due to the minimization of working capital requirements. However, given that at the time, the capital was relatively scarce in Japan as the country was industrializing, it seems sensible to posit that limiting the need for additional capital to fund the expansion of operation played a role in Toyota's development of lean manufacturing. More importantly, its competitors started copying this manufacturing process right after the first

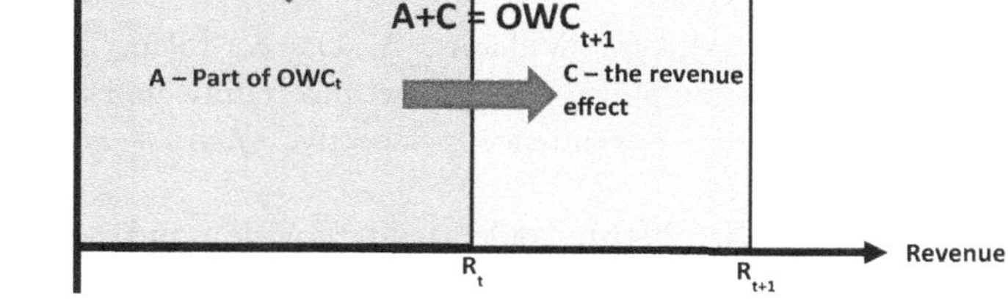

Fig. 6.13 OWC changes from the implementation of just-in-time

oil crisis of the 1970s and the collapse of the Bretton Woods system of fixed exchange rates. Suddenly, imports became more expensive, and tying capital to inventories with fluctuating currencies prices became more costly. Implementing just-in-time processes helped alleviate working capital requirements to Japanese companies during the 1970s, and the practice became standard in many industries in the country.

Finally, winding down just-in-time measures requires additional working capital investments in inventories and the internalization of the sales volatility. Just-in-time optimizes the financial cycle when it works, and firms can divert funds to other business areas. When it doesn't, costs go up, and production fails to meet demand. Regardless, one thing is clear: just-in-time is not only about searching for maximum efficiency in manufacturing and enhancing product quality; it is also about saving cash. Firms in credit-constrained countries should take note of that.

References

Abel, A. B. (2018). Optimal debt and profitability in the trade-off theory. *The Journal of Finance, 73*(1), 95–143.

Alkhoraif, A., Rashid, H., & McLaughlin, P. (2019). Lean implementation in small and medium enterprises: Literature review. *Operations Research Perspectives, 6*, 100089.

Benton, W. C., Jr. (2010). *Just-in-time/lean production systems*. Wiley Encyclopedia of Operations Research and Management Science.

Bertran, M. P., & Echeverry, D. (2021). What is the size of credit card debt in Brazil? Reporting thresholds, interest rates and income distribution. *Journal of Behavioral and Experimental Finance, 30*, 100460.

Boehlje, M., & Langemeier, M. (2020). *Working capital: What is it and do you have enough*. Center for Commercial Agriculture, Purdue University. https://ag.purdue.edu/commercialag/home/wp-content/uploads/2015/09/202009_BoehljeLangemeier_WorkingCapital.pdf

Cole, S., Kanz, M., & Klapper, L. (2015). Incentivizing calculated risk-taking: Evidence from an experiment with commercial bank loan officers. *The Journal of Finance, 70*(2), 537–575.

Darby, J. L., Ketchen, D. J., Jr., Williams, B. D., & Tokar, T. (2020). The implications of firm-specific policy risk, policy uncertainty, and industry factors for inventory: A resource dependence perspective. *Journal of Supply Chain Management, 56*(4), 3–24.

El Ghoul, S., & Zheng, X. (2016). Trade credit provision and national culture. *Journal of Corporate Finance, 41*, 475–501.

Kerr, S. P., Kerr, W. R., & Dalton, M. (2019). Risk attitudes and personality traits of entrepreneurs and venture team members. *Proceedings of the National Academy of Sciences, 116*(36), 17712–17716.

Kouvelis, P., & Xu, F. (2021). A supply chain theory of factoring and reverse factoring. *Management Science, 67*(10), 6071–6088.

Polito, T., & Watson, K. (2006, March). Just-in-time under fire: The five major constraints upon JIT practices. *Journal of the American Academy of Business, Cambridge, 9*(1), 8–13.

Radziwill, N. (2008). *Shocks to the system: Financial meltdown and a fragile supply chain.* Quality and Innovation. https://qualityandinnovation.com/2008/10/12/shocks-to-the-system-financial-meltdown-and-a-fragile-supply-chain/

Smith, J. K., & Schnucker, C. (1994). An empirical examination of organizational structure: The economics of the factoring decision. *Journal of Corporate Finance, 1*(1), 119–138.

Van der Vliet, K., Reindorp, M. J., & Fransoo, J. C. (2015). The price of reverse factoring: Financing rates vs. payment delays. *European Journal of Operational Research, 242*(3), 842–853.

White, R. E., Pearson, J. N., & Wilson, J. R. (1999). JIT manufacturing: A survey of implementations in small and large US manufacturers. *Management Science, 45*(1), 1–15.

Wu, Y., Wang, Y., Xu, X., & Chen, X. (2019). Collect payment early, late, or through a third party's reverse factoring in a supply chain. *International Journal of Production Economics, 218*, 245–259.

Xu, H., Nguyen, D., & Dao, M. (2021). Pilot CEOs and trade credit. *The European Journal of Finance, 27*(6), 486–509.

Zeidan, R. (2018, September 23). Still Haunted by grocery shopping in the 1980s. *The New York Times*. https://www.nytimes.com/2018/09/22/opinion/sunday/brazil-venezuela-hyperinflation-economics.html

Zeidan, R., Galil, K., & Shapir, O. M. (2018). Do ultimate owners follow the pecking order theory? *The Quarterly Review of Economics and Finance, 67*, 45–50.

7

Building a Comprehensive Working Capital Strategy

This book's main departure from previous approaches is that it integrates finance and operations. There is often a perception within companies that financial management is disassociated from operations.

> Over the past five years, the typical S&P500 non-financial company has experienced considerable pressure on the amount of inventory and receivables carried. Had this pressure been left unchecked, it would have added $130Bn of additional net working capital to corporate balance sheets." "Over this same period, U.S. companies were able to extend payment terms (reflected in DPO) – which mitigated the underlying pressure on working capital assets." (Ahearn & Bruce, 2019)

Any strategy to reduce the financial cycle must be done in a manner compatible with the company's business model. Service companies can improve the average collection period by obtaining constant advances; industrial companies can exercise their market power to extend payment terms, and retail companies can improve their inventory management. These will result in more efficient resource allocation, freeing up cash and making companies more profitable; profit margins go up with fewer assets (Table 7.1).

Here, this relationship is straightforward. The management of the financial cycle, through the management of inventories and payment and receipt deadlines, is the responsibility of the company's operational managers. Although

R. Zeidan, *The General Model of Working Capital Management*,
https://doi.org/10.1007/978-981-19-3334-9_7

Table 7.1 Change in WC metrics by region, 2017–18

	C2C change 18/17	
	US (%)	Europe (%)
DSO	−2	-4
DIO	−3	-1
DPO	−3	-3
C2C	−2	-2

Note DSO (days sales outstanding), DIO (days inventory outstanding), DPO (days payable outstanding), and C2C (cash-to-cash), with metrics calculated on a sales-weighted basis
Source Ernst and Young (2019)

there are economic effects of changes in the average storage period, operations management determines variables such as minimum inventory level, just-in-time policies, batch negotiations, purchase minimums, etc.

The first approach we've found helpful is to help managers deeply understand the financial impacts of working capital management. Organizational inertia, or business-as-usual, is a strong force. All managers must actively look for parts of the financial cycle that are poorly managed. Working capital optimization will fail without ownership of the process by all parties involved.

It is also essential to understand the boundaries of any working capital management optimization project. For instance, at MRV, there was no attempt to improve the construction process. The reasoning by Rafael Albuquerque was straightforward: MRV was founded and run by engineers. It is the heart and soul of the company. It would be almost impossible to start his project by changing procedures in the most vital part of the company. Hence, Rafael's focus on the other processes to reduce MRV's cash-conversion cycle.

For some companies, the first stage should be to create managerial data and monitor changes in the financial cycle before designing any project for improvement. The key is to produce measures for the determinants of OWC that are meaningful to business managers of different business areas. For example:

- A construction project company can produce payout charts to allow project managers to monitor actual costs and payments received against contracts.
- A service company that takes orders from thousands of customers can benefit from reporting cash or check payments from each order.
- A manufacturing company can use specialized software to identify supplier problems if quality control or deadline issues exist.
- Retail businesses can monitor patterns of how customers return products.

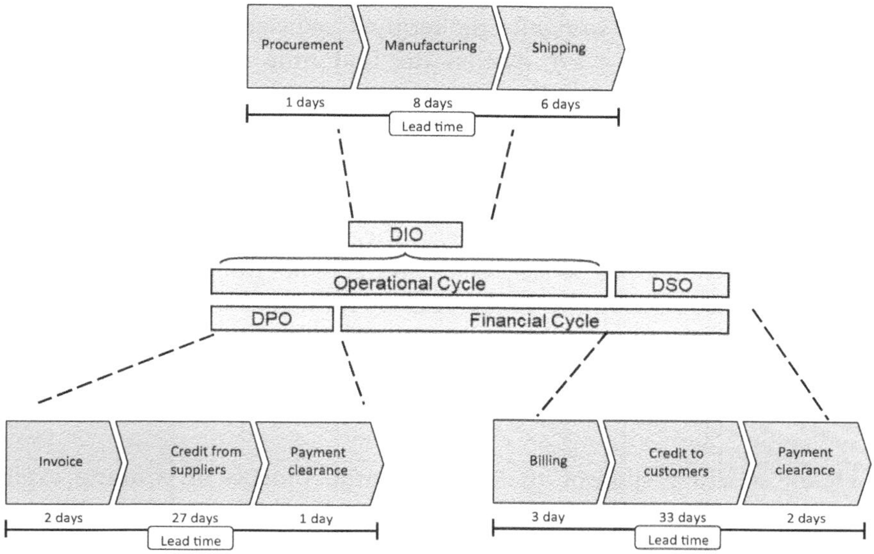

Fig. 7.1 DIO, DPO, and DSO processes

Any working capital optimization project must be aligned with the rest of the organization. Optimization can be hampered by several "diversion" tasks that do not add value to the business. Such tasks deviate managers and staff from those that matter and add value to the company.

The second stage is to pick at the low-hanging fruit. One obvious step is to tighten up the management of receivables and accounts payable. Simple measures such as standardizing payment terms and forwarding invoices quicker can often reduce the sales cycle by two to four days.

Companies can avoid dealing with working capital management by taking other short-term actions. For example, many companies routinely use factoring, securitization, or invoice discounting. These actions are costly and unlikely to generate the same economic value as improvements in operations and payment terms that could permanently reduce working capital investment. Securitization doesn't decrease OWC but is used to finance part of a company's short-term debt.

The managerial focus should be on tightening the financial cycle's control and undertaking substantial operational changes. But which parts of the cash conversion cycle can be optimized? We have seen earlier that not everything can be optimized.

In Fig. 7.1, DIO is 15 days, DPO is 30 days, and DSO is 38, which means that the firm's financial cycle is 23 days. Where should the company focus its efforts? It has several options.

Would it be possible to reduce the term of credit granted? Maybe streamline the billing process? Or shorten the lead time for production? It all depends on the company's business model and its constraints.

If managing the financial cycle and the need for working capital is so important, why don't companies generally do it as part of their daily routines? There are many reasons for this, from lack of training to fixation on traditional liquidity measures. However, the main culprit is the notion that only sales growth matters; as long as revenue goes up, things will be fine. That is not true, of course. Business cycles can be ruthless, and companies cannot grow their sales forever.

For the management team to commit to managing working capital effectively, executives should:

- Define a senior sponsor to lead the entire process of working capital optimization;
- Create a cross-functional team of people with a similar mandate and authority to effect changes.
- Disseminate the working capital customized concepts throughout the organization, making key people aware of the importance of their roles in the broad strategy.
- Create metrics that explain the causes of changes in the OWC.
- Establish targets for each component of the financial cycle.
- Monitor compliance with policies and practices to ensure no impact on quality, costs, or margins.

Tightening control of the financial cycle should be like painting the Eiffel Tower: an ongoing process. You start at the bottom and go up, starting over after the last coat of paint at the top of the tower. Companies should continually strive for better payment terms. They should also regularly improve purchasing operations and accounts payable processes by extending lead times with critical suppliers.

A firm might consider, for example, collaborating with customers and suppliers in the "extended enterprise" (the concept that the firm does not operate in isolation because its success depends on its network of relationships with partners).

Take the idea behind streamlining supply chains. Usually, such a decision would be considered non-financial; it would be done for strategic or operational reasons. However, reducing the supplier base to gain more influence in negotiations, improving transportation, and reducing logistics costs can dramatically reduce working capital investments. There is no reason for such important decisions to be made in silos inside the companies.

The same applies if the company decides to index the variable compensation of sales representatives not to orders placed but to actual payments or margins. Finally, decisions such as reorganizing production chains to reduce inventories or outsourcing and offshoring manufacturing operations assume that the company is committed to further structural changes. All these decisions impact the financial cycle and, therefore, can release or necessitate cash from the company.

7.1 The Basics of DSO and DPO Management

The primary payment terms for companies' goods and services are a mix of competitive pressure, internal decision-making, and customers' behavior. A firm may decide that customers have up to 14 days to pay an invoice, but companies cannot know the delinquency level or the number of late payments beforehand.

For companies in perfectly competitive markets, payment periods should be similar if not identical to that of competitors. Also, business culture plays a role. In some countries, suppliers require almost immediate payment, while in others, small companies may have months before sending a check over for a past invoice.

Payment terms, for example, are longer in Asia, Europe, and Latin America than in the US. Payment terms also vary between sectors: in many public procurement contracts, firms can securitize receivables if they need capital to meet their contractual obligations.

Take water and sanitation, for instance. In some countries, customers prepay for those services. Household consumption is measured twice a year, and any discrepancy is paid for in the next billing cycle. In other countries, measurements are done quarterly, the bill comes, and people have two weeks to settle. Finally, some households are visited monthly, and people are supposed to pay for water and sanitation every 30 days. The working capital implications of these different social norms are significant. Companies in countries with prepaid services invest on average much less on working capital than firms in regions where they must provide services for months before being paid for them.

Companies may also offer special payment terms and conditions for some customers but not others. They should not do this without compensation, for example, in exchange for the customer to pay a higher price or buy a higher volume. The opposite can also happen: a company can give discounts to pay faster. In the US, it's standard to offer customers the option to pay in 30 days or pay in 10 days and get a 2% discount.

Not every company is Alforria, where the CEO paid all invoices immediately upon receipt to boast his company was debt-free. Changing the process to pay suppliers on the invoices' due dates was instantaneous once the decision was made. Still, many companies have numerous opportunities for improving internal processes.

Companies' payment sectors are still far from the ideal vision of automated and efficient departments. A survey on 550 accounts payable departments internationally has found that over a third (35%) of A/P departments have left suppliers unpaid. Almost a quarter (24%) know that their own invoices have not been settled for the same reason – a substantial weakness on both sides. In addition, 26% of A/P departments had paid the wrong supplier when processing an invoice (Lees, 2010). And the surveyed departments have the necessary resources to invest in efficiency, as they processed an average of 93,000 invoices per year, with an average processing time of 18 days. Out of these 93,000 invoices, an average of 6,000, or 7%, contained errors (Lees, 2010).

This survey must be relatively old, but it is unlikely that things have improved dramatically since then. A 2020 survey on 100 Nordic companies that analyzed over 26 million invoices found 0,53% errors of one type, erroneously posted invoices (Qvalia, 2021). To make matters worse, 25% of these errors went undetected, they cost 1/3 of the total invoice posting cost, and it took an average of 31 full-time working days per organization to correct erroneous posting. They also generated losses due to under-deducted VAT, overpayments, and double-payments (Qvalia, 2021).

Below are some of the best practices that could reduce a firm's financial cycle perennially:

- Invoice as soon as possible after completing the job, preferably within a week. The shorter the delay in issuing the invoice, the faster the company is paid.
- Send polite reminders no later than 15 days after the invoice is due, followed by a second reminder 15 days after that and a final reminder 15 days after the second reminder before taking any legal action or turning over the debt to a collection agency. The faster you have a record of reminders, the quicker you can take more drastic actions if necessary.
- Contact key customers (more significant amounts) by phone 15–30 days before invoices are due to remind them of the due date. Due Reminders

also allow you to check that all invoices sent to a particular customer have arrived on time.

- Identify customers who systematically delay payments or regularly develop tactics to delay payment.
- Understand each customer's payment process and know who to call and when a particular 'block' may be causing delays.
- Identify customers who have a long and complicated internal system for paying invoices.
- Create a dispute resolution procedure.
- Establish checks to ensure that the invoice has the correct address and that the invoice is identical to the requested quantity. According to Robert McDonald, President and CEO of Procter & Gamble in 2011, "The GS1 industry association did a study a few years ago and found that 70% of orders between retailers and suppliers had some error." It is unlikely that business practices have eradicated this type of error since then.
- Set a maximum credit limit for each major customer. Credit limits allow the company to limit the amount it can lose for each customer. Firms can also place two credit limits, with the lower one alerting when the limit is breached, leading to an investigation into the client's creditworthiness. If the second limit is breached, then orders from this customer will no longer be accepted unless he agrees to pay on receipt.
- Require indebted customers to provide a bank guarantee to honor their payments.

"We will do it on Monday" is a typical sentence uttered in finance departments worldwide if an invoice is supposed to be posted on a Friday. However, working capital is trapped inefficiently when this becomes a regular occurrence. Sometimes, the failure to have an invoice arrive on time can extend receivables by almost 30 days if invoices approved for payment are paid once a month. Companies may benefit from adapting their processes to customers with multiple delivery locations for centralized charges paid in batches.

7.2 MRV: DIO and DPO Management to Unlock U$1 Billion

In Chapter 2, we described the results of MRV's project to reduce its working capital investments. The company unlocked over U$1 billion in shareholder value by reducing its financial cycle sustainably. How did the company do it?

The project was designed and managed by Rafael Albuquerque, one of the company's top finance executives at the time, and had four phases:

- Benchmarking.
- Prioritization.
- Design.
- Implementation.

Below we summarize part of Zeidan and Shapir (2017). Previously, we have been introduced to the benchmarks, seen again in Table 7.2.

The central information from the benchmarking is that MRV had the "best" DPO among the companies that competed in the Minha Casa Minha Vida market. Only another company, Cyrela, had days payable outstanding of more than 200 days. Of course, some differences between MRV's DPO (212 days) and competitors such as Ez Tec (88 days) can be attributed to distinct business models. Ez Tec does not have the land banks of legacy real estate companies and builds smaller, easier-to-put-together buildings. Internally, MRV had a long-standing policy of associating payment of its invoices with the delivery of the completed services. The external benchmarking and analysis of the company's DPO practices led Rafael and his team to conclude they shouldn't design DPO-specific policies.

Abandoning part of working capital management is not a decision taken lightly. Since MRV's DPO was the longest among its peers, it was felt that any possible gain would be marginal, at best, bringing the risk of higher costs. Since the goal was to revamp the company's processes so that changes were permanent, the focus should be on actions that could yield better outcomes. Hence, leaving DPO management aside was the correct determination at the time.

Here is a simple description of the company's economic cycle. The property must be regularized, and the project design must be ready before MRV applies for bank financing (only one primary lender, Caixa, a public bank, is responsible for managing the program). Onde financing is approved, the company is allowed to market and sell units. Sales do not lead to cash flow yet. Consumers apply for a loan, yet the company does not receive it. Then, the financial Institution measures a percentage of the construction, and the property rights are transferred to the final consumers. Only then is the firm paid for the share of the project built.

Thus, for the prioritization stage of the DSO and DIO reduction project, the economic cycle was broken into its components: Purchasing and land

Table 7.2 CCC and other financial measures, Brazilian companies, 2012 (US$ '000)

	MRV	Cyrela	Gafisa	Brookfield	PDG	Rodobens	Even	Ez Tec
DSO	440	386	354	485	644	386	339	506
DIO	280	251	240	359	382	157	177	329
DPO	212	198	142	202	190	181	66	88
CCC	508	439	452	642	836	362	450	747
OWC	2,647,035	3,383,908	1,736,856	2,406,621	5,000,311	476,505	293,110	647,127
Revenue	1,901,905	2,813,500	1,402,550	1,368,250	2,183,150	480,454	237,745	316,200
EBIT/Revenue	15%	16%	4%	-5%	-42%	16%	15%	39%
Profits/Revenue	13%	13%	-2%	-12%	-50%	11%	13%	42%

Table 2.1 reports data for the CCC of MRV and its direct competitors, along with OWC, annual revenue, EBIT/Revenue, and Net Profits/Revenue. All variables are calculated using firms' balance sheets and income statements for 2012. Values are converted from BRL to US$ at 2 to 1

Source Zeidan and Shapir (2017)

registration; Project design; Financing; Commercialization; Registration of individual contracts; Construction.

A thorough analysis of MRV operations identified five possible areas to improve its CCC: a reduction in average purchasing and land registration times, project design, financing, commercialization, and the registration of individual contracts. Interestingly, the first four stages were part of DIO and not DSO. Usually, DSO starts being counted after a sale is made. But that was not the case in the MCMV business model, as MRV was paid a percentage relative to how much of the buildings were completed. Remember that in the economic cycle of MCMV, construction came after approximately 50% of the units were sold (Fig. 7.2). None of these processes involved building housing units. The next step was to develop possible interventions to reduce the average execution time for each area.

In the case of purchasing and land registration, some actions included creating a checklist with all possible variables that could affect the lifecycle aspects of the project, from purchasing to construction; consulting with water and sewerage companies to check for potential emerging issues before committing to land purchases; offering incentives to land buyers to attach their bonus to the lifecycle of the investment project.

Project design actions incorporated determining two "shepherds" of each project, one from the engineering and architecture departments. Shepherds would oversee projects to ensure all deadlines were met and minimize rework. Additionally, the company designed a new process in which project design is developed alongside the material and equipment purchasing for the buildings to reduce repeated works on projects. Financing solutions entailed registering a "pre-project" with the financial institution and interventions to minimize the internal processing of consumer applications.

Regarding commercialization, the company restructured the operations of sales teams by giving scaling-up incentives on the speed of sales rather than

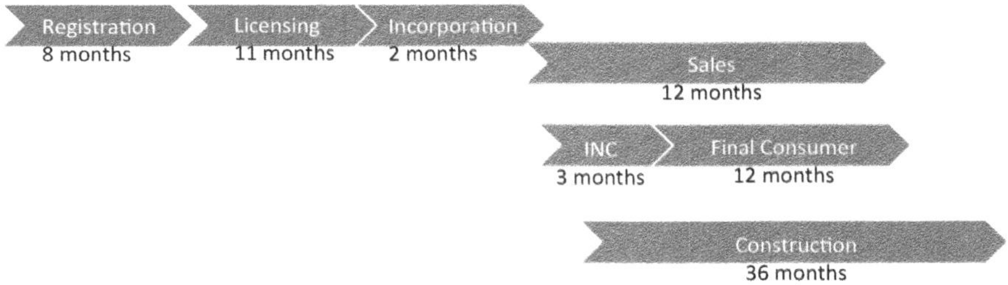

Fig. 7.2 MRV's economic cycle (*Source* Albuquerque [2014])

only on general revenue. Finally, in the case of individual contract registration, the company hired new contractors to speed up registration with local notaries, hired new employees to support the sales teams in the checklist of documents for mortgage applications, and established a pre-validation of standard mortgage contracts with local notaries before the beginning of sales.

Take purchasing and land registration, for instance. Bulan et al. (2009) show that the irreversibility of investments affects how developers make decisions related to price uncertainty and exposure to market risks. Gehner (2008) analyzes developers' many risks when competing for land banks. MRV and many other companies in the Brazilian market face bureaucratic issues related to construction permits and other measures, resulting in sales and building delays. Reducing delays by restructuring internal processes decreased DIO without losing sales or inventories.

Mortgage applications are another example in which it was possible to reduce CCC without impacting the operating margin. The usual process at MRV was for salespeople to check the documents included in the mortgage application. Yet, incentives were skewed towards sales rather than checklists. Many applications arrived at the bank with incomplete or illegible records. Thus, the applications were returned to the salespeople, who had to contact the buyers to return with more documents, which significantly delayed the registration of mortgage applications with banks and thus tied up the company's funds.

There are three central points: low or insignificant costs, minimal risks, and no action represented a significant restructuring of the company's processes. Essentially, steps that wouldn't work would keep the financial cycle unchanged. Costs may have even decreased, as the project design team was likely to have become more efficient in avoiding duplication of work.

All changes started to be implemented in January 2013. Table 7.3 presents the impact of the restructuring of MRV's operations on its financial results in the subsequent years. For the results of 2015, we create a simple counterfactual in which the CCC would be at the same level as 2012 to compare actual OWC with that with a constant CCC.

Revenues increased by 25% from 2012 to 2015. One should expect working capital to rise in tandem, but this dropped by 13.5%, or US$ 358 million. We can see that even if DPO decreased, both DSO and DIO also dropped sharply. DSO was 29% lower when one compares the value from 2015 to 2012, and DIO was 27% lower between these two years. Let's compare the 2015 CCC results with our counterfactual. We arrive at a lower working capital requirement of US$ 1.02 billion, a strong case for improvements in working capital management and its effects on free cash flow.

Table 7.3 CCC and OWC at MRV, 2010–2015 (US$ '000)

	2010	2011	2012	2013	2014	2015	2015*
DSO	389	419	440	371	339	313	440
DIO	227	244	280	233	212	203	280
DPO	134	174	212	176	172	165	212
CCC	482	489	508	428	379	351	508
OWC	1,994,655	2,689,540	2,647,035	2,269,468	2,175,112	2,289,024	3,314,553
Daily Revenue	4,139	5,500	5,211	5,302	5,735	6,525	6,525
Annual Revenue	1,510,475	2,007,530	1,901,905	1,935,305	2,093,093	2,381,519	2,381,519

Note Values are converted from BRL to US$ at 2 to 1. 2015* represents the OWC that the company would have if it maintained the same CCC as in 2012

Source Zeidan and Shapir (2017)

7.3 Classifying Suppliers and Customers to Change DPO and DSO

For medium-sized companies with multiple suppliers, optimizing DPO requires getting them to extend payment terms as much as possible without impacting costs. Conversely, for DSO, the goal is to have consumers pay quickly without sacrificing sales or profit margins.

For internal changes to the company, refer to the previous section. Here, we describe a basic framework for companies' actions with their supply chain. This book is not a consulting-focused tome, but we develop a simple framework for classifying suppliers to lift payment terms strategies and customers regarding prompt payments. Table 7.4 divides input sellers and customers into four categories: untouchables, good soldiers, friction rapport, and irrelevant.

The main division criteria are the dependence and importance of suppliers and customers. Dependence refers to the companies' position in their customers' and suppliers' businesses. Do customers rely on the company to a large extent, or do they have alternatives? Importance is the opposite: does losing a customer hurt the company's bottom line? Is it straightforward to replace a supplier?

If customers can easily switch to other companies, but their business is fundamental to their survival, the firm is a "payment terms taker." In microeconomics textbooks, a price taker is a firm that must meet the market conditions and cannot influence market outcomes. Here, a "terms taker" has no space to negotiate better payment terms and must accept the industry's standards.

Such customers or suppliers form what we call the "untouchables" part of a company's supply chain. Take a small commodities exporter to China, for instance. For that company, customers pay the invoice 28 days after the products arrive at the port in Ningbo. The firm cannot do anything about it other than use factoring to collect money from its sales earlier.

The untouchables may trigger cash crises in their supply chains if they change payment terms unilaterally. More importantly, it is unlikely that a firm can get much better payment terms from an untouchable supplier or customer; thus, it should avoid opening negotiations for better payment terms.

On the other side of the spectrum are the firms' "dance partners," parts of the supply chain that depend on the companies' business. Firms have market power against "dance partners" and have multiple strategies available. They can try to squeeze as much cash as possible from the supply chain, but that

Table 7.4 Classifying suppliers and customers

Consumers				
	Untouchables	Dance partners	Friction Rapport	Irrelevant
Customers' dependence and importance	Low/High	High/Low or Medium	Medium/Medium	Low/Low
Approach	Nothing	Proactive negotiation	Proactive negotiation	Non-priority communication
Initial contact	Nobody	Senior executives	Senior/Junior executives	Junior executives
Suppliers				
Dependence and importance on supplier	High/High	Medium/High	Medium/Medium	Low/Low
Approach	Nothing	Proactive negotiation	Proactive negotiation	Non-priority communication
Initial contact	Nobody	Senior executives	Senior/Junior executives	Junior executives

risks losing clients or suppliers in the long run. These options have been discussed in previous sections. Here, the crucial message is that companies must be proactive in determining the payment terms in relationships with these parts of the supply chain. We use that metaphor because dance partners must accommodate each other somewhat but can look for new partners if their relationships are not mutually beneficial. Given the strategic objectives of setting up payment terms with dance partners, firms are better served by negotiating with the senior executives of their clients or input sellers.

Another part of the supply chain in which being proactive should be the norm is the one populated with suppliers and customers with whom the company has a frictional rapport. These are the most challenging trade-credit negotiations. Firms and their partners have incentives for extracting better terms from each other. Negotiations should be proactive but not necessarily done with the most senior executives.

Finally, the "irrelevant" part of the supply chain is the one that does not change a firm's bottom line or financial cycle easily. Customers that purchase a firm's product infrequently or suppliers that can easily be replaced are some of the types of irrelevant business partners.

Some suppliers may be fundamental to a company's operations, but they are replaceable if markets are competitive (at a cost, of course). Others may produce specialized products without substitutes. Firms should track payment terms for each category of suppliers and set up targets for DSO and DPO. Firms cannot manage what they cannot measure, after all.

Simple tables (such as Table 7.5) can contrast public and private information regarding suppliers' payment terms. In that example, supplier A is known to average 51 days in extending credit to consumers, and almost the same number of days to the company, 50 days. However, it is public knowledge that supplier B usually collects payment after 41 days but requires that the firm pays its invoice in 16 days. There seems to be an opportunity for negotiation with that supplier, all else being equal.

Table 7.5 Internal and external benchmarking of suppliers

Internal Benchmarking		External Benchmarking	
Supplier	DPO	Supplier	DPO
A	50	A	51
B	16	B	41
C	21	C	47
D	25		
E	31		
Target: 35 days			

There is no one-size-fits-all working capital management strategy, which we have repeated before, but it bears repeating. Benchmarking suppliers to approach them individually is a myriad of possibilities regarding optimizing payment terms.

7.4 Managing DIO

Direct interaction with supply chain partners can enable a company to reduce total inventory levels, reduce product obsolescence and transaction costs, react more quickly to market changes, and respond more readily to customer requests. Eventually, through trial and error, inventory management became a science. Concepts such as *just-in-time*, optimization of the production process, virtual inventory, lean start-ups, supplier rationalization, and reduction in the number of distribution places have played a prominent role in these improvements. Optimizing the warehouse location and factory picking processes reduced 'in-transit' inventories.

The company's ability to reduce DIO depends on several parameters: the sector of activity, the degree of optimization of the production process, its ability to predict the activity level correctly, and its management principles. Also, external factors such as commodity price inflation, logistics and distribution infrastructure, and rates of technological change matter.

There's a fine line between the risk of being caught off guard and the complacency of overstocking. Keeping inventory levels high reduces the risk of losing a sale because suppliers are unavailable. To avoid running out of stock, managers build safety stocks, a buffer to mitigate uncertainties in demand or supply. While it has long been recognized that reducing emergency inventories is an excellent means of reducing costs in the short term, such strategies also jeopardize operations when a catastrophe occurs. Inventory management is a *trade-off* between reducing DIO and increasing risk: the company must always focus on essential items. Generally, 80% of demand is generated by 20% of a firm's items. Spend your efforts on these "A" items, predicting the stock position and ordering frequently. The following 30% of top-selling items, the "B" items, will typically generate 10% of sales. The slowest-selling items, "C" items, are 50% of your items in stock but generate only 10% of your sales.

Companies can speculate about overstocking raw materials if they understand the opportunity costs of that decision. In many countries in the past and today, raw material could, in a way, be seen as an investment. Take

Turkey, for instance. Inflation has reached 50% in 2022. Thus, overstocking insures the company against fluctuations in raw material prices and shortages.

The lag effect of changing commodity prices (smoothed by the use of hedging policies) means that the recorded performance of inventories generally improves in the short term when prices fall and deteriorates when prices rise. The performance of large companies' inventories in prosperous economies can deteriorate due to increased investments in inventory to supply fast-growing emerging countries and commodity price inflation.

DIO depends on payment terms from suppliers and the company's ability to shorten the production cycle. Some companies focus on greater efficiency in production, supply chain, and purchasing operations. These efforts include applying leaner manufacturing and reducing complexity by simplifying the supplier base and cutting the number of stock keeping units (SKUs).

There are many advantages to moving production to low-cost countries. Increased outsourcing and global outsourcing play a significant role in driving inventory performance. Still, there are some drawbacks: containers take weeks to arrive and may suffer unexpected delays. Also, lean practices and supplier-managed.

More challenging are inventory arrangements that depend on the company's ability to predict the activity level in advance correctly. If demand begins to wane, companies reduce production to prevent inventory buildup. Uncertainties in supplies can be reduced by analyzing the delivery schedule and reliability of different suppliers or by establishing partnerships with suppliers (as is the case in the automotive industry). Organizations should collaborate with suppliers and customers if DIO is an essential metric for cash flow (for some businesses, it isn't). It is also valuable to integrate purchase forecasts into the inventory management tool. Finally, specific statistics allow companies to determine seasonality and effects from the business cycle.

Companies differ in the degree of cash management focus and the effectiveness of working capital management processes.

Supply uncertainties are problems for fashion products or industries with a lot of demand variability. Companies selling outside their regions experience longer lead times and require excess safety stocks regarding logistics and distribution infrastructure. Distribution and logistics vary widely between regions and countries, leading to significant differences in local supply chain costs, service levels, risk, and inventory performance. The World Bank periodically reports on logistical performance according to six key indicators: efficiency of customs and management of clearance at borders, quality of trade and transport infrastructure, ease of organizing shipments at competitive prices,

Table 7.6 Aggregated Logistics Performance Index, latest period

Country	LPI Rank	LPI Score	Customs	Infrastructure	International shipments	Logistics competence	Tracking & tracing	Timeliness
Germany	1	4.2	4.1	4.4	3.8	4.3	4.2	4.4
Netherlands	2	4.1	4.0	4.2	3.8	4.1	4.1	4.3
Sweden	3	4.1	4.0	4.2	3.9	4.0	4.0	4.3
Belgium	4	4.1	3.7	4.0	4.0	4.1	4.1	4.4
Singapore	5	4.1	4.0	4.1	3.7	4.1	4.1	4.3
UK	6	4.0	3.9	4.1	3.7	4.0	4.1	4.3
Japan	7	4.0	3.9	4.2	3.6	4.0	4.0	4.2
Austria	8	4.0	3.7	4.1	3.8	4.0	4.1	4.2
Hong Kong	9	4.0	3.9	4.0	3.9	3.9	4.0	4.2
United States	10	3.9	3.8	4.1	3.5	3.9	4.1	4.1

Source World Bank (2022): https://lpi.worldbank.org/international/aggregated-ranking

competence and quality of logistics services, the ability to track and track shipments, and the frequency with which shipments reach recipients within scheduled or expected delivery times.

Table 7.6 presents the latest data regarding these dimensions for the ten countries ranked highest globally.

Companies in these countries will find it easier to manage DIO than countries with low indicators. Finally, there is the risk of value loss due to some goods' obsolescence. Organizations with extensive inputs with shorter life cycles and rapid technological change risk obsolescence and economic and financial losses.

7.5 An Example of Changing Practices

This example is from a Chinese company that, like many SMEs, found itself scrambling for funds to continue growing. In 2016, the company started building reports on its customers' delays and defaults.

In each report, there is an analysis of each relevant consumer's accounts with the company, and for large consumers, their ratings with credit rating agencies are checked.

Initially, the project covered 250 consumers who purchased the company's goods and services in the previous 12 months. The company divided consumers based on sales history and risk. If a consumer bought above a specific value, considered as high level, he received a code A. The code for medium-sized consumers was B and those who bought little from the company, C.

Developing a risk profile for each consumer was more difficult. The company gathered internal information (previous delays, open invoices, etc.) and complemented it with data from credit bureaus. The numbers 1, 2, and 3 indicated low, medium, and high credit risk. Thus, companies A1 would represent customers with large orders but low credit risk, while companies B3 would be companies with medium purchases but high risk.

After segmenting customers, the firm was ready to implement new, standardized collection processes. The priority would be customers rated A3 and B3, who were either responsible for many open invoices or indicated potential default or delay risks.

The company is now proactive with these consumers. It directly contacts customers before the invoices are due. The contacts, which include calls, are made by an expert team. They are constructive and never threatening. As the CFO has explained: "We want to help our customers create new payment habits in a standardized way. It's more of a way to solve problems, not conflicts. We say: how can we help them? Is there a problem with the invoice? We have a weekly invoicing procedure. Do you prefer to go into this cycle or continue to receive sporadic invoices?".

The organization's goal is to understand the causes of late payments to prevent them from happening. The collaboration between the sales force and those responsible for the collection is essential to the project's success to establish a relationship of constructive trust between the company and its customers and reduce the DSO.

Before, sales and collection were not always in sync. The employees responsible for collection worked independently and reactively. Processes were akin to conflict resolution, with employees treating customers as potential deadbeats. The lack of standardization in the collection process sometimes caused problems, with instances of the collection staff being disrespectful to clients who missed a single payment due to clerical errors. Finance and sales were also at odds over creating minimum billing standards. With standardization, there was a change in the company's culture. The culture change was difficult at first, but today the two departments work together seamlessly.

7.6 Empowerment and the Correct Incentives

Who should be responsible for DSO, DIO, and DPO management? At first, one might think that DIO is the purview of the industrial team, while the sales team determines the payment terms for the firm's customers. However, that is not necessarily the case. To see that, assume that the industrial unit has total control over the economic cycle. Their responsibility is to establish the inventory level, the ratio between raw inputs/finished products, and more. Would the industrial director care about minimizing DIO?

For the industrial team, reducing DIO is tantamount to streamlining operations and removing redundancies that make their job easier. Not many industrial directors would voluntarily set up just-in-time processes or limit inventory buffers to use a firm's capital better. The same holds for the purchasing and the sales teams.

The salespeople would always want discretion in negotiating payment terms with customers. Of course, most sales directors try hard to have their force sell as much as possible with terms as strict as they can negotiate. However, salespeople extending payment terms for a client to close a deal is all too common.

As with many issues regarding working capital management, it is impossible to provide a blueprint that works for all types of companies. Some firms will focus on the highest possible profit margin, while others will aim for a negative cash-conversion cycle. However, three essential questions must be answered.

1. Who monitors DIO, DSO, and DPO?
2. What are the rules or principles that management teams must follow?
3. Will the processes be integrated?

To answer these questions, the CEO and the board should resolve the inherent tension between discretion vs. rules (for more, see the case study in the following subsection). They should also determine who will be responsible for creating and managing the target indicators.

In the "Sem Parar" case study, we have seen that the company made the cash-conversion cycle a target indicator for a finance executive about to be hired. But while the finance department should be tasked with building DIO, DSO, and DPO from the available financial data, they should not necessarily design it. The purely accounting version of the financial cycle components has significant shortcomings, and firms would be better served by customizing them for internal use. Working capital management works best when there is integration between the operations and the finance departments.

Companies must abandon the mechanical pursuit of ill-defined targets. Hence, the finance team cannot solely determine the production and sales teams' rules. That is due not only because of different incentives but also the stage of the company during its life cycle. Well-funded start-ups in winner-takes-all markets will necessarily have different working capital targets than when they are mature and profitable companies. Strategic consideration should inform working capital decisions.

Finally, processes should be integrated to some extent. Excessive working capital investment is an opportunity cost, as it is intangible. For many companies, especially in emerging markets, managers relate investments to fixed and tangible assets. Targets for the components of the financial cycle cannot be in the hands of the finance department or solely under the umbrella of specific executives. Examples of these choices are in the cases below.

7.6.1 Discretions vs. Rules: The Case of a Multinational Pharmaceutical Company

Cash-flow management is about tradeoffs. Extend too much credit to consumers and a company might starve for credit but require prompt payment for its products, and a firm might lose valuable customers. Such a balancing act is even more difficult for multinational companies, as they operate in business environments with distinct social norms and different negotiation rules.

The solution was simple but constraining for a multinational pharmaceutical company: worldwide payment terms for all its subsidiaries, regardless of geography or type of consumers. In an executive education class with the top executives of some of the company's subsidiaries, one of the goals was to answer why regional CEOs were not allowed any flexibility in establishing payments terms for consumers and supplies.

The rules handed over by headquarters were straightforward. Every customer must pay for the goods and services delivered by subsidiaries in 21 days, and accounting and finance departments must clear invoices 28 days upon receiving them. There are rare exceptions, such as special rules for some types of public procurement, but otherwise, the rules are the same for customers big and small and suppliers powerful or tiny.

Indeed, such an approach leads to missed opportunities. Subsidiaries flush with cash could potentially negotiate to reduce costs by paying their suppliers promptly. Those in high-interest countries could boost interest from short-term investments by limiting credit to consumers. Yet headquarters have always been resolute. For years, payment terms have been the same, and local executives should not expect any changes moving forward.

The key to answering the question came from parsing out the meaning of other corporate mandates. One example is the repeated reports about innovation risk. The board repeatedly indicated that the company should keep its focus on innovation. The directors were fine with projects not panning out as expected, as long as managers communicated about the odds that new medicines, for instance, are approved by regulators. Also, the company has a history of paying a significant portion of profits as dividends, which require cash-flows to finance it. In addition, the company centralized production in a few factories around the globe, in effect internalizing the management of days of inventory outstanding. Finally, the company maintained a policy of hedging most of its currency risk by dealing in derivatives markets to reduce the volatility of the subsidiaries' profits.

The top executives of the company's subsidiaries shared that their bonuses were related to operational performance but not cash-flow generation. Headquarters centralized most of the variables related to the cash conversion cycle effect. However, the revenue effect remained, which was the main goal for local executives. They were supposed to ensure that sales were robust and that local supply chains ran smoothly.

If allowed to change payment terms, would regional managers improve sales? Most likely, yes. Maybe Mexico's sales director could extend credit to consumers, or Egypt's CEO order that their division would start paying suppliers in seven days. Sales would rise, and costs would go down. Nevertheless, that would introduce cash-flow volatility to the organization's financial management. Of course, headquarters could manage cash flow volatility by maintaining constant lines of communication with all subsidiaries, incorporating any changes to payment terms from anywhere in the world into their expected operating working capital. But therein lies the issue: how should companies allocate their efforts?

As mentioned before, headquarters' efforts were to get the most out of research & development, ensure efficient production and distribution, and increase capacity. Managerial capabilities are limited. Coordinating information about payment terms in all subsidiaries and estimating the cash flow impacts of each decision would be costly. The company weighed the costs and benefits of allowing managerial discretion and decided on uniform global rules.

Public procurement usually has distinct rules worldwide, and subsidiaries do not have the same level of market power. Multinational companies usually do not choose a centralized model to minimize cash-flow volatility. Local conditions vary considerably, and terms of payment that seem reasonable in Japan might not cut it in Ghana. Still, there is one main advantage of centralized cash-flow management: local senior managers can concentrate on other parts of the business, leaving cash-flow administration to HQ.

7.6.2 Aligning Incentives: The C-Suite Dilemma in a Large Steel Company

Many companies face disputes between different executives regarding inventory management and liquidity measures. One such case is one of the largest steel companies in Brazil, which requested an executive education program for its top five executives, excluding the CEO. The purpose was to engage all executives for a common purpose: integrate financial metrics to complement the more familiar operational metrics.

Like most companies with a long history, which had to survive many periods of boom and bust, long-term executives wanted to please customers by delivering products on time and preferred to manage conservative inventories. What was unique about the company's situation is that operational managers considered inventories as investments. They argued that since the company had a high reliance on volatile iron ore prices, by "investing" in inventories when prices were low, they achieved two goals: flexibility and financial gains from betting on input costs.

Although fluctuating prices could harm the company if managers made the wrong bet, the main challenge with building huge inventory is strangling the company's finances. The large inventory gives the company more operational but less financial flexibility. C-suite executives were constantly at odds. While the CFO was trying to save money by stopping inventories from growing, the industrial director was looking for more inventories, especially in periods of seemingly low prices. Classic liquidity measures, especially the current liquidity ratio, would show that stock growth was not an issue. Taking cash and converting it into stocks would not change Current Assets and thus would not change the traditional liquidity ratio. In terms of liquidity for partner banks, the company was doing well. Another traditional measure, the dry liquidity ratio, would change, however. So operating managers focused on current liquidity while the CFO tried to show that dry liquidity was necessary. That is yet another example of the shortcomings of traditional liquidity measures.

In the present framework, there are no mixed signals. Inventory buildup has a substantial opportunity cost, given by the firm's weighted average cost of capital. Less liquidity is not necessarily inadequate, of course. However, there is a clear trade-off between inventories and liquidity, and the cost of holding excess stock, albeit intangible, can be pretty high.

Another source of conflict was the nature of inventories. The operations and sales team usually coordinated to maintain the highest possible stock of almost ready-to-ship stock. The operation team could optimize any downtime by redirecting production to fill up the stock, even if there were no orders for these products. They argued that having a wide selection of products ready to ship would give the company an advantage over its competitors. Of course, that resulted in the company immobilizing vast amounts of capital in building inventory and spending more on storage costs than its competitors.

To solve the conflict between Chief Operational Officer, the Chief Sales Officer, the CFO, and the other senior managers, the company ordered an executive education course for just the most senior executives. As one can imagine, it was a challenging program. Nevertheless, all trade-offs were put on the table and discussed openly. The CFO's mandate was to maintain liquidity compatible with the company's financial cycle. At the same time, other executives stressed the gains for servicing customers on time and never running out of inventory.

At the end of the course, a series of compromises were reached. When the company did not need to return cash to shareholders, executives could develop inventory strategies to generate higher returns; i.e., purchasing raw material when internal models indicated that iron ore prices were low. When cash was tight, inventory management would be more conservative. Limits for raw material purchases and the share of final goods ready to be shipped were established. The finance and operations department agreed to build specific algorithms to forecast iron ore prices. Finally, working capital management and the monitoring of the financial cycle entered the company's lexicon, with executives' compensation being redrawn to incorporate metrics linked to DIO, DSO, DPO.

The basic principle of managing DIO is straightforward: companies must have enough inventories to satisfy customer demands without overstocking. But this principle is difficult to put into practice, as operations executives may lack a sense of urgency and understanding of good cash flow management. There is no fault of them, of course. Working capital management is about opportunity costs and intangible concepts such as the weighted average cost of capital.

7.7 Adjustments to Regulatory Changes

Other country-specific characteristics impacting firms' working capital are regulatory frameworks and legal enforcement procedures. In countries with lax enforcement, customers default more frequently. Regulations can also limit the autonomy of trade credit policies. In 2014, the European Parliament published a directive to encourage prompt payment to improve the liquidity, competitiveness, and profitability, particularly small and medium-sized enterprises (Wauschkuhn et al., 2014).

> The new provisions impose new time limits for contractually agreed payment terms, the contractually agreed occurrence of default, and the duration of contractually agreed procedures of acceptance and verification. In addition, they raise the statutory interest on late payment and introduce a claim for payment of a fixed compensation in case of late payment… Agreements with consumers or public authorities may be subject to different provisions. (Wauschkuhn et al., 2014)

The directive established maximum periods for contractually agreed payment terms. DSO longer than 60 days as of the receipt of goods or the provision of services is only valid in exceptional cases, as it is otherwise considered grossly unfair to the creditor. It also describes the conditions for a late payment to be considered a default. Any express agreement according to which default occurs no earlier than 60 days after receipt of the goods or the provision of services or the receipt of the invoice is therefore valid unless it is grossly unfair. In addition, for legal transactions in a business-to-business relationship, the default interest rate on claims for payment was raised from 8 to 9 percentage points above the basic rate of interest. What is more, the creditor is entitled to claim reimbursement of the recovery costs in the event of the debtor's late payment (Wauschkuhn et al., 2014).

When the legal costs of recovery are high, companies face a difficult tradeoff. The securitization of receivables may shift the risk of late payments to other companies. Yet, the discount rate will be relatively high, significantly reducing the cash received from expected revenues (Zeidan, 2020). Figure 7.3 illustrates the differences in the strength of creditors' rights across the globe. The legal rights index created by the World Bank measures the degree to which collateral and bankruptcy laws protect the rights of borrowers and lenders and thus facilitate lending. It ranges from 0 to 12, with higher scores indicating that these laws are better designed to expand access to credit. It should be noted that the index is part of the Doing Business project, which has been discontinued. Still, the index is not among the indicators that have been accused of being manipulated.

Regulatory changes can impact the financial cycle of companies significantly. Tax authorities may change rules for invoicing or tax payments, competition authorities might restrict the discretion of large companies in negotiating payment terms, and the low quality of the legal system may

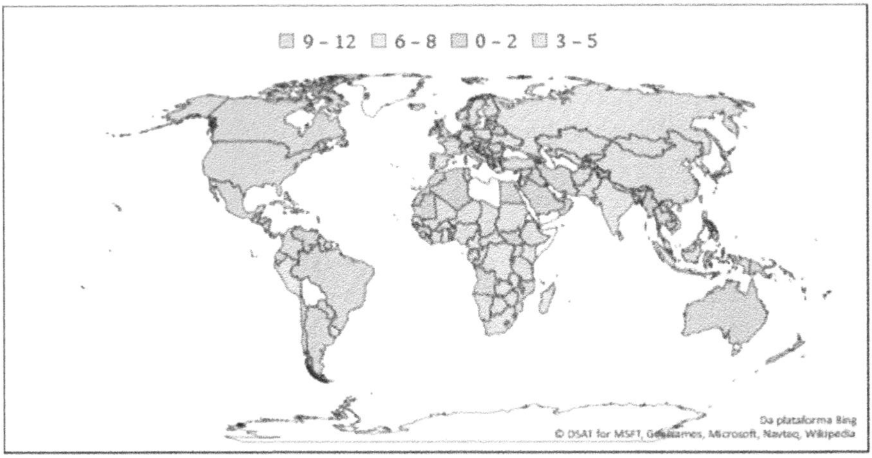

Fig. 7.3 Strength of creditors' rights across the globe (*Source* Zeidan [2020])

increase delinquency rates. The main managerial lesson is that companies should change their cash flow projections immediately after regulatory changes. When the financial cycle is not monitored, managers won't be able to forecast the cash flow variation from rules changes. And we can't manage what we don't measure.

References

Ahearn, J., & Bruce, J. (2019). *Why working capital matters: A glimpse into the shifting global environment and how working capital efficiencies can help drive change*. Treasury and Trade Solutions, Citigroup, available at: https://www.citigroup.com/tts/insights/assets/docs/articles/Why-Working-Capital-Matters.pdf

Albuquerque, R. (2014). *O caso MRV. EMBA FDC*. Mimeo.

Bulan, L., Mayer, C., & Somerville, C. T. (2009). Irreversible investment, real options, and competition: Evidence from real estate development. *Journal of Urban Economics, 65*, 237–251.

Ernst, & Young. (2019). *All tied up Working capital management report 2019*, available at: https://assets.ey.com/content/dam/ey-sites/ey-com/en_gl/topics/transaction-advisory-services/transactions-pdfs/ey-working-capital-report-2019.pdf

Gehner, E. (2008). *Knowingly taking risk: Investment decision making in real estate development*. Eburon Uitgeverij BV.

Lees, M. (2010). *A new world for accounts payable—But is it lost in transaction?* The Global Treasurer, available at: https://www.theglobaltreasurer.com/2010/08/24/a-new-world-for-accounts-payable-but-is-it-lost-in-transaction/

Qvalia. (2021). *Lost in translation, the hidden cost of invoice errors in the Nordics, 2020*, available at: https://qvalia.com/app/uploads/2021/03/Hidden-cost-of-invoice-errors-2020-report.pdf

Quiry, P., Le Fur, Y., Vernimmen, P., Salvi, A., & Dallocchio, M. (2011). *Corporate finance: Theory and practice*. Wiley.

Wauschkuhn, U., Teichmann, J., & Rojahn, A. (2014). *EU: New time limits for contractually agreed payment terms*. Global Compliance News, available at: https://www.globalcompliancenews.com/2014/09/10/eu-new-time-limits-for-contractually-agreed-payment-terms/

World Bank. (2022), *Aggregated LPI 2012–2018*, available at: https://lpi.worldbank.org/international/aggregated-ranking

Zeidan, R. (2020). Why bank credit in Brazil is the most expensive in the world? *Revista Brasileira De Finanças, 18*(4), 1–22.

Zeidan, R., & Shapir, O. M. (2017). Cash conversion cycle and value-enhancing operations: Theory and evidence for a free lunch. *Journal of Corporate Finance, 45*, 203–219.

8

Building Managerial Cash-Flow Statements for Budgeting Working Capital Investments

Working capital management is about balancing some goals: ensuring the company can grow efficiently, limiting illiquidity events, and maximizing supply-chain relationships (reducing costs or using trade credit as a financing source). Besides managing shocks such as a crash in demand or rising delinquency rates, firms must budget resources for changes in sales or the financial cycle.

Small and medium-sized companies must develop cash-flow statements adequate to their business model, especially in emerging markets. One of the significant mistakes that company founders who are not finance professionals make is relying on financial statements prepared by their firms' accountants for regulatory purposes. For instance, there is no separation between safety and operational inventories in such financial statements, a relevant distinction for establishing a company's cash-flow needs for the upcoming years.

We start with a simple cash-flow model that cannot necessarily be created from regular financial statements, given indicators such as EBITDA and the treatment of corporate income tax. The present cash-flow information is not a report of actual cash entries and disbursements but serves as the benchmark for decision-making based on the expected changes in the firm's cash balance over time. For instance, a firm may have tax credits from previous years that it can use to reduce its effective tax burden moving forward. However, for managers to decide on new investments, they should not input the reduction in payments to the government as a variable in the cash-flow projections of the company moving forward. That would inflate profits and cash flow

R. Zeidan, *The General Model of Working Capital Management*, https://doi.org/10.1007/978-981-19-3334-9_8

and could lead to companies approving projects that wouldn't be done if not for the tax credits. Of course, that also means that the cash-flow projections, in this instance, will understate the cash balances for the company moving forward, and managers should be aware of it, as executives surprised by unexpected cash surpluses tend to use the extra funds inefficiently.

As most companies are not single-product companies, we use Zeidan and Spitzeck (2015). The authors illustrate how companies can move from business as usual to more sustainable modes of production while increasing value to shareholders, using data from an actual sugar manufacturer. The company was planning to shift some of its output from regular pollution-heavy refined white sugar to organic brown sugar and reuse some of the by-products of the production process to generate energy.

The present cash-flow statement serves a two-fold purpose: a straightforward way to budget working capital investments and a valuation tool based on discounted cash flows. The company's value is equal to the present value of future cash flows, discounted by financing costs of the firm, represented by the weighted average cost of capital (WACC). Cash flows are determined by operating profits, as in net operating profits less adjusted taxes (NOPAT), less investments needs, the variation in working capital, and capital expenditures (Capex).

In the example of the sugar manufacturer, investments in sustainable practices are more extensive in the short run, increasing capital expenditures and working capital requirements. The result is a dynamic relationship between operating performance and capital expenditures in the long run—smart investments generate improved performance, even though there are periods of smaller cash flows related to increased investments.

A forward-looking cash-flow statement is built on projections. There is no manner of budgeting without some reliance on a crystal ball. Of course, managers are not fortune tellers, but a cash flow budget is a story in which the goal is to predict the most probable paths an organization can take. More important than getting every assumption behind a specific indicator right is being upfront and transparent about which beliefs are critical drivers of changes in long-term profits and which ones are of minor importance.

The simple valuation model is shown in Fig. 8.1.

The cash flow statement that integrates working capital investments into the firm valuation for a single product is represented below (Table 8.1).

The details of this cash-flow statement are in the next subsections. Feel free to ignore the following if you are familiar with this type of financial report.

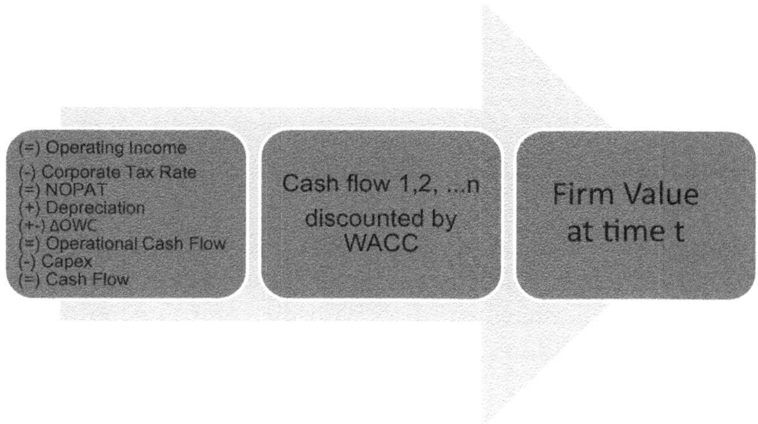

Fig. 8.1 A simple cash flow method for firm valuation

Table 8.1 One example of a managerial cash flow projection

	Year 1	Year 2	Year 3	Year 4	Year 5
Addressable market					
Market-share					
Revenue					
(-) Variable costs					
(-) Fixed costs					
(=) EBITDA					
(-) Depreciation and amortization					
(=) EBIT					
(-) Corporate income tax					
(=) NOPLAT					
(+) Depreciation and amortization					
(+-) Working capital					
(=) Operational cash flow					
(-) Capex					
(+) Terminal value					
(=) Enterprise cash flow					
Discounted by WACC					
(=) Enterprise value					

8.1 The Basics of Cash-Flow Statements

The present framework is concerned with a company's operations and the enterprise value, which ignores issues such as the worth of the firm's tangible and intangible assets (such as real estate, patents, etc.), legal liabilities, risks of fines from regulators, and others.

Table 8.2 Industry growth and the position of a firm in its market

	Year 1	Year 2	Year 3	Year 4	Year 5
Addressable market					
Market-share					
Revenue					

The framework is flexible enough to deal with multiple products, but at first, it is kept simple by focusing on a single product or service company.

The top part of the statement deals with the company's possible sales by describing the organization's addressable market and expected market share (Table 8.2).

The addressable market is usually the expected total industry output for a particular year. The concept is helpful because it clarifies possible confusion about what companies are direct competitors and the potential targets of an organization. For instance, in a valuation of Uber, Aswath Damodaran, an NYU Corporate Finance professor whose blog "Musings on Markets" provides countless valuation examples, takes issue with some of the companies' claims about its total addressable market.

He writes, in 2019: "If you believe these companies, Uber's TAM is $5.71 trillion spread across 175 countries, and obtained by adding together all passenger vehicle and public transport spending." At the time, Uber's claims about its total addressable market could have been inflated to increase share prices. WeWork, a company that at the time had an even bigger reason to misrepresent its total addressable market (TAM) as it was pursuing an IPO, steered clear of describing itself as being in real estate, framing that instead, it was a community company (Damodaran, 2019). Peloton went one up. It defined itself as a technology, media, software, product, experience, fitness, design, retail, apparel, and logistics company, naming itself Peloton Interactive for emphasis (Damodaran, 2019).

Regardless, from the most global of multinational companies to the humblest mom and pop shop, the total addressable market is where everything starts. For Apple, the iPhone's TAM may comprise half of humanity, while for a local non-gluten bakery, it may consist of wealthy consumers in a 500-m radius.

Damodaran (2019) provides a 3P Test for determining a company's addressable market, as presented in Fig. 8.2.

Once the addressable market is established, the company's market share in the foreseeable future must be projected. Not shown are the assumptions regarding prices. If a company is a price taker, prices are market-determined. For commodities, projections may come from future contracts prices. The

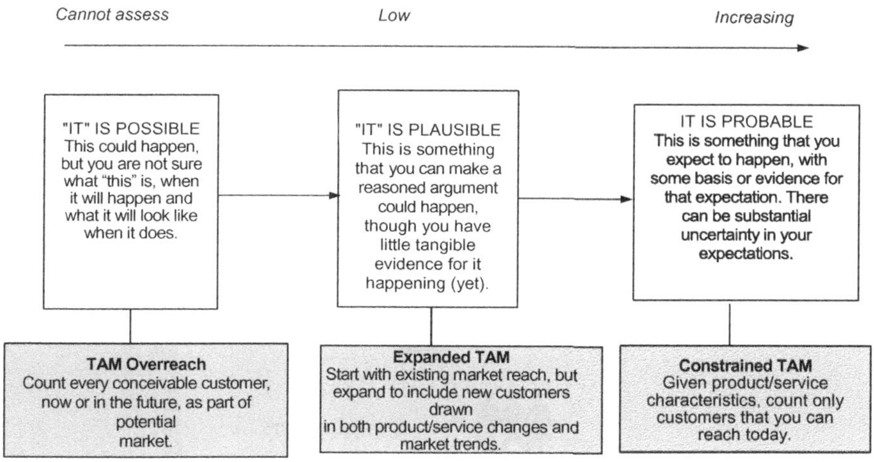

Fig. 8.2 Total addressable or accessible markets (TAM): The 3P test (*Source* Damodaran [2019])

detailed process of filling out all cells in the table and further details on the assumptions regarding prices, market share, and addressable markets is beyond this book's scope. Managers can use simple procedures for forecasting demand and prices (and thus total revenue) or design sophisticated models in which demand components are stochastic.

The second part of the cash-flow projections includes fixed and variable costs. The former depends on the production capacity that the company is aiming for the next few years and the latter on input costs. Once costs are written down, revenue minus expenses yield EBITDA, the central piece of a cash-flow statement. While some owners are concerned about revenue growth (which feeds their ego since they can tell other entrepreneurs how big their business is), EBITDA is the most crucial measure of a firm's short-term performance.

EBITDA is defined as earnings before interest, taxes, depreciation, and amortization. GAAP and IFRS do not recognize EBITDA; hence there are no formal requirements for companies to report it. However, listed companies commonly include it in financial reports. It is an accurate measure of a cash-flow generation when reported correctly, unlike EBIT, adjusted for depreciation and amortization, two non-cash indicators.

EBITDA is to a company what gross wage is to a family. Households are comfortable if their labor income is sufficient to pay off taxes, mortgages (or rent), interest from previous loans, and the remaining family expenses. Similarly, EBITDA is the cash a company generates to maintain productive

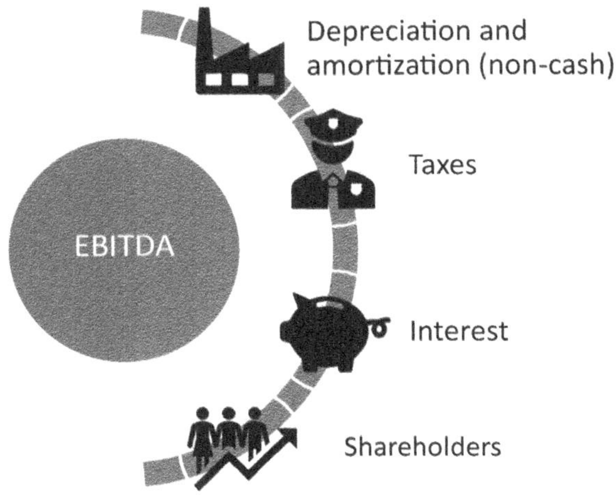

Fig. 8.3 EBITDA's flow

capacity and pay the government, banks, and shareholders (and, in addition, to support a firm's growth if required, as in Fig. 8.3).

Depreciation and amortization are used to expense the cost of property, equipment, and intellectual property, among other tangible and intangible investments. A straightforward way to interpret depreciation and amortization is the required resources for a company to maintain its productive capacity. Machines break, and properties must be renovated now and then. Suppose a machine lasts five years and must be replaced by a new one at the end. In that case, the company has two practical options: ignore the issue until the machine breaks (or is time to replace it), or put aside a certain amount (say, 20% per year) so that at the end of the five years it can seamlessly replace the equipment. Of course, there are mismatches between accounting and cash flow effects of depreciation and amortization. Assume the following situation. Accounting rules require that a piece of specific equipment bought for U$100,000 be expensed in five years, linearly. However, the organization expects it to last over ten years. Thus, for the first five years, the company will reduce its EBITDA by U$20,000 per year to account for the linear depreciation of the initial investment. Yet, the company may choose to put aside only U$10,000 per year to replace the machine, as it is expected that the equipment is going to last well over five years.

Moreover, depreciation has a cash-flow effect as it impacts how much taxes a company pays because it reduces the amount of taxable income. For instance, assume the following scenario. A company's EBITDA is U$100,000, the corporate income tax rate is 20%, and a machine that

Table 8.3 From EBIDTA to EBIT

	Year 1	Year 2	Year 3	Year 4	Year 5
(=) EBITDA					
(-) Depreciation and amortization					
(=) EBIT					

cost U$200,000 three years ago is being depreciated linearly on a five-year schedule. If there were no depreciation, the income taxes owed by the company would total U$20,000 (100,000 × 20%). However, the company expenses U$40,000 (200,000/5) as depreciation, taxable income goes down to U$160,000, and corporate income taxes are reduced to U$32,000 (U$160,000 × 20%). Thus, the company's tax bill shrinks by U$8,000, from U$40,000 to U$32,000.

Companies must report operating income (EBIT), usually the difference between EBITDA, depreciation, and amortization. Of course, some companies voluntarily report some type of "Adjusted EBITDA" that is tailored to their realities. Here, we will not detail all the accounting rules for EBIT and the following cash flow items. However, we must keep in mind that the cash generated by a company may differ from EBIT if there is still investment being depreciated and amortized (see Table 8.3).

Another crucial difference between actual cash flow and projections is the treatment of corporate taxes. The income tax due is the tax rate multiplied by the EBIT in a cash flow projection. It does not consider past tax rebates that could lower the effective tax rate or even, at this point, the debt tax shield. The reasoning behind it is that the cash flow projection we are building aims to assess if a business is viable from now on. Past debt and thus huge interest expenses may distort cash flows. It can lead us to conclude that a business is not viable when it is (if interest expenses are exceptionally high) or feasible when it is not (if today's use of past tax credits inflates a firm's cash flow temporarily).

Once we account for taxes owed, we arrive at NOPAT, defined as Net operating profit less adjusted taxes. It should also be noted that we use NOPAT instead of the common NOPLAT. NOPAT includes changes in deferred taxes, while NOPLAT is based on the actual tax paid to tax authorities. NOPLAT should be preferred when one is building precise cash-flow statements, in which the timing of disbursements are of particular importance, while NOPAT ties cash flows to the event that generates it. In simpler terms, if we want to build a projection in which we account for a payment when it is supposed to be made, instead of when it leaves a company's coffers, NOPAT can be used without loss of generality (Table 8.4).

Table 8.4 From EBIT to NOPAT

(=) EBIT
(-) Corporate income tax
(=) NOPAT

Since the NOPAT accounts for depreciation, amortization, and taxes, the remaining cash flow should be distributed to debtholders and shareholders (Fig. 8.4).

However, depreciation and amortization must be added back into the cash-flow projections before proceeding. As we have seen, these are not monetary expenses.

After that, two main stages remain, the remuneration of debtholders and shareholders and the resources required for a firm to grow.

Before, we did not set up a relationship between EBIDTA and growth. The operating profits in Table 8.3 go to the government, debtholders, shareholders, and the necessary investments to maintain the current productive capacity. For mature companies or those in the last stage of their life-cycle, claimants of NOPAT are just bondholders and shareholders. However, managers have an essential decision for companies looking to increase production and capacity: should operating profits help fund working capital investments and capital expenditures, or should the company borrow exclusively from debt markets to grow?

Suppose the company is not looking to grow its operations or productive capacity. In that case, its enterprise value is just the difference between

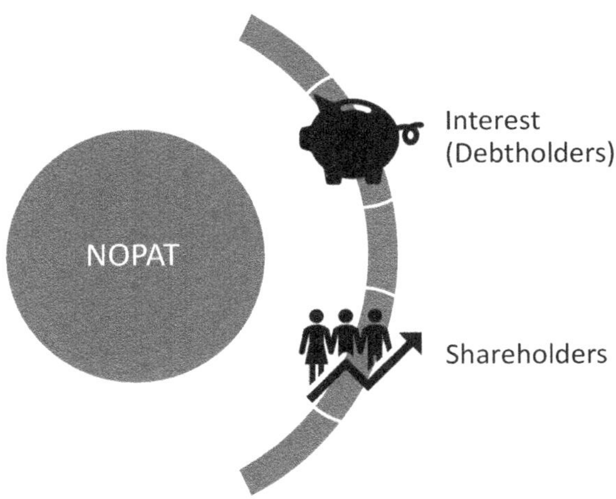

Fig. 8.4 NOPAT and the remaining claimants to a firms' cash flow

Table 8.5 NOPAT to Enterprise Value

	Year 1	Year 2	Year 3	Year 4	Year 5
(=) NOPAT					
Discounted by WACC					
(=) Enterprise value					

NOPAT and what is owed to debtholders and shareholders, represented by the organization's weighted average cost of capital. Table 8.5 represents that case.

For a company, the weighted average cost of capital is the primary opportunity cost that informs investment decisions. WACC is estimated as:

$$WACC = \left(\frac{E}{V} * R_e\right) + \left(\frac{D}{V} * R_d * (1 - T_c)\right)$$

There are two components, the costs of equity and debt. Each share depends on how relevant they are in financing the company.

The cost of equity is the share of equity (E/V) on a company's total value (usually, book value or total assets) and the rate of return required by shareholders (R_e).

The cost of debt is the share of debt (D/V) on a company's total value (usually, book value or total assets) and the interest rate paid to debt holders (R_d), adjusted for the tax shield benefit (1-T_c).

All the variables that comprise the WACC are subject to some uncertainty. For listed companies, the cost of equity follows the capital asset pricing model (CAPM). The remuneration to shareholders depends critically on beta, the indicator of systematic risk of the firm relative to the market. Beta is usually estimated through a regression using historical data. For privately-owned companies, the board of directors may decide that a specific cost of equity is the minimum return acceptable to shareholders. Or managers may use the average cost of equity of listed companies in the same industry. There are also instances in which independent business units use different capital costs to approve projects internally. The same is true for the cost of debt, although there are fewer possibilities to estimate such a number for a listed or privately-owned company. Regardless, the various possibilities show that there is no single way to arrive at the WACC for a company.

Conceptually, the company's cost of debt is the interest rate that a company pays to its lenders. However, companies don't face invariant costs of borrowing. Two projects funded at different times are likely to have used borrowed capital to varying interest rates. If companies issue bonds of different maturities, they will most likely get resources at diverse rates. In yet another example, borrowing costs change as companies mature. Thus, managers should be careful in determining the cost of borrowing to input into cash flow projections.

Even the share of debt and equity is subject to discretion. Should D/V include just interest-bearing debt or all possible claims to a company's assets from third parties? Should the equity share use the book value of equity shown in the balance sheet, or should it be adjusted somehow? There are no definite answers to these and many other questions. In the examples below, we will make stringent assumptions that result in a straightforward estimation of WACC; more sophisticated methods are beyond the book's scope.

If a company plans on expanding, NOPAT must contribute to the two components of growth: working capital and capital expenditure (Table 8.6). We have discussed the former in detail, so let's focus on the latter. A firm's capital expenditures are the investments in fixed or intangible assets that increase productive capacity. Examples include the purchase or lease of a new machine and the rights to a patent so a company can manufacture a new product.

Working capital variation is deducted from NOPAT to arrive at the operational cash flow. Then, the remaining funds are adjusted to account for capital expenditure. We proceed this way because working capital investments are the only barrier to growth if the firm does not reach its maximum production capacity. For instance, a company has a machine that can produce 1,000 units of a specific product, but right now, production is 600 units. If demand is predicted to reach 800 units, the firm must purchase inputs and invest in working capital to meet the higher demand. The company can use the cash flow from operations (NOPAT) to fund this growth if orders don't exceed 1,000 units (Table 8.6).

The final concepts that wrap up the projections for finding the enterprise value are the terminal value and the enterprise cash flow (Table 8.7). The terminal value is estimated as the present value of perpetual cash flows beyond the initial projection. The present example has detailed cash flows for the first five years. From that point on, we assume that a company's profits are stable

Table 8.6 NOPAT funding working capital investments and capital expenditure

	Year 1	Year 2	Year 3	Year 4	Year 5
(=) NOPAT					
(+-) Working capital					
(=) Operational cash flow					
(-) Capex					

Table 8.7 From NOPAT to operational cash flow

(=) NOPAT
(+) Depreciation and amortization
(+-) Working capital
(=) Operational cash flow

and perennial. Thus, the terminal value is the current value of a perpetuity in which the WACC discounts the annual free cash flows (determined as the difference between operating cash flows and CAPEX). One can assume that profits grow at a constant rate, g, but that is not required. The computation of the terminal value is straightforward:

$$TV = \frac{\text{FinalYearFCF} * (1 + g)}{\text{WACC} - g}$$

The Enterprise Value is the present value of all future cash flows. As estimated by the present method, EV is the value of a company's operations. One shouldn't confuse enterprise value with the total firm value (its equity value). For instance, EV does not consider the value of a company's assets and debt. Equity value (for listed companies, the market capitalization is the same as the equity value) is determined as:

$$\text{Equity value} = \text{Enterprise Value} -- \text{Total Debt} + \text{Cash}$$

In other words, equity value is the amount that shareholders should receive for their company if they sell it.

8.2 Setting Up an Operational Working Capital Statement

As we have discussed before, there are limits to public accounting data. Financial statements don't allow managers to track changes in operating working capital in real-time. When it comes to setting up a customized cash flow statement that allows managers to monitor DIO, DSO, and DPO, the critical step is determining the main drivers of each indicator.

This section aims twofold: to relate the economic cycle to accounting variables and classify which balance sheet information is actionable regarding working capital management. Operationally, we can divide the cash conversion cycle into systematic processes, as in Fig. 8.5.

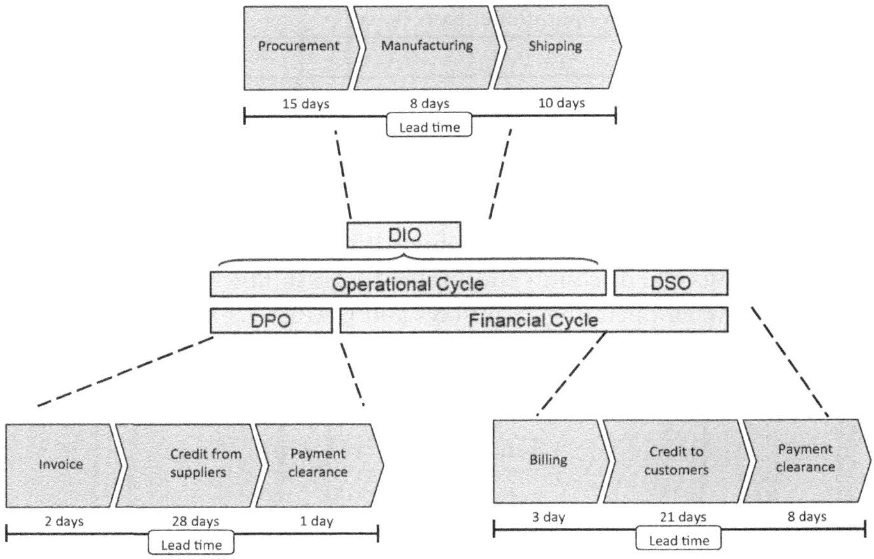

Fig. 8.5 DIO, DPO, and DSO processes

Each process can be further subdivided into activities. For instance, procurement can be divided into order preparation, input acquisition, queuing, setup time, inspection time, and put-away time or into pre-processing, processing, post-processing. There is robust managerial and scientific literature regarding inventory management. Here, we are interested in relating the systematic processes of DIO, DPO, and DSO with financial statements to improve working capital management and not in how to optimize inventory per se.

The financial cycle can be estimated from the ground up or backward from financial statements. Both methods have their pros and cons. Ground-up estimation requires considerable details about the production processes and explicit assumptions about repeated activities. Managers must track inputs through the manufacturing process till the money is collected from the sales of the final goods. More importantly, executives must indicate which processes are systematic and one-offs. For instance, assume that one machine breaks, delaying production by two days. Should that affect a firm's estimation of its DIO? There is no correct answer. If production delays happen often, managers should incorporate their estimates into DIO. The delay should be ignored if it is a one-off and DIO is estimated from regular operations.

Remember that DPO tracks the period between the input purchase decision and the disbursement of funds to pay for it. There is no single way to start counting the period for a company to pay its suppliers regarding DPO. For instance, assume that the procurement team calls a supplier and agrees to purchase 100 kgs of a specific raw material for U$10,000. It sends the invoice the following day, which the supplier receives two days later. Should the DPO "clock" start when the company purchases the item, sends the invoice, or the supplier receives it?

The standard way was to start counting when the invoice was sent in the past. However, given new regulations regarding supply chain payments in Europe and other places, it is increasingly common to start counting DPO when the invoice is received. For electronic invoices, there is no discrepancy, as the supplier receives them almost instantaneously.

Usually, the components of the financial cycle are estimated from financial data. The main concern with that approach is that it is impossible to disentangle systematic drivers of working capital changes from indicators unrelated to this type of investment. Take inventories, for instance. Safety stocks do not vary much or at all. Still, they affect the calculation of DIO if it is based on balance sheet data. More complicated are tax credits and liabilities. If a unit sale generates a tax credit, then it is a forced loan from the company to the government and should be accounted for in the estimation of the cash conversion cycle. It should be ignored if it arises from other sources, such as a writedown on previous asset purchases. Another crucial decision is the treatment of customers' delinquency. Suppose the percentage of late payments is relatively stable and the firm has solid expectations about when to expect some customers to pay. In that case, managers should build that in DSO's estimation. If delinquencies are rare or only happen with customers who represent a fraction of a firm's total sales, they can usually be ignored.

So, how should we build an operating working capital budget and estimate the financial cycle components? We recommend two estimations of DIO, DSO, and DPO: the "cave" manner and the data-driven approach.

The "cave" framework takes its inspiration from Plato's allegory of the cave. The prisoners' entire reality is the shadows they can see, even though they are not good representations of reality. Unless companies are tiny or managers have access to real-time data, it is impossible to comprehend the intricacies of its operations as it evolves. Thus, they should build a representation of the financial cycle that captures, as best as possible, their firms' recurrent operations. In Fig. 8.5, we have an example of the cave approach. DIO totals 33 days, DPO is usually 31 days, and DSO reaches 32 days. Hence, the cash conversion cycle for this company is 34 days. In this example, payment clearance takes eight days because the firm incorporates a measure of customers' delinquency into the DSO. The cave approach is best used for the senior executives to establish explicit targets for the rest of the company to pursue. Such targets should not be fixed over time and can help evaluate employees' performance, with associated bonuses if the company meets them sustainably.

The data-driven approach requires detailed data and uses financial statements for a firm to estimate its actual DIO, DPO, and DSO. Firms can automate the generation of indicators by tying the dates of invoices sent and received to cash inflows and outflows and tracking inputs throughout the production process. Unlike the cave approach, managers should settle on a methodology for calculating DIO, DPO, and DSO and update it sparingly. There are three risks with changing the process for extracting the financial cycle from the firm's internal systems data: manipulation of targets, inconsistency for strategic decisions, and managerial costs.

If executives' bonuses are tied to financial cycle targets, the calculation of these indicators should be transparent, and contingencies should be planned for in advance. It is not a great leap of logic to see why managers must be careful about setting up targets on indicators that are hard to measure consistently. Moreover, suppose the calculation of the cash conversion cycle changes constantly. In that case, managers will have a more challenging time creating budgets for the following years, and it will be more challenging to track the company's performance over time. Finally, measuring DIO, DPO, and DSO correctly is already costly, as it requires solid training to the finance professional and adaptation of the firm's information system. Updating the methodology for calculating the financial cycle often should be costly, both directly and indirectly.

Also essential is dividing which components of a firm's operations are cyclical and which ones aren't. Figure 8.6 illustrates the division in cyclical and non-cyclical current assets and liabilities from a typical balance sheet. Operating working capital is then cyclical assets minus cyclical liabilities. The non-cyclical assets comprise the firm's liquid assets, while the liabilities counterpart distinguishes between operating accounts and short-term debt.

In this book, we don't build a single approach to estimating the financial cycle but present the foundations of working capital management so firms can adapt their systems to customize their own solutions. This comprehensive framework is not enough to build strong financial cycle statements; managers should know which indicators can be managed and which should be left alone.

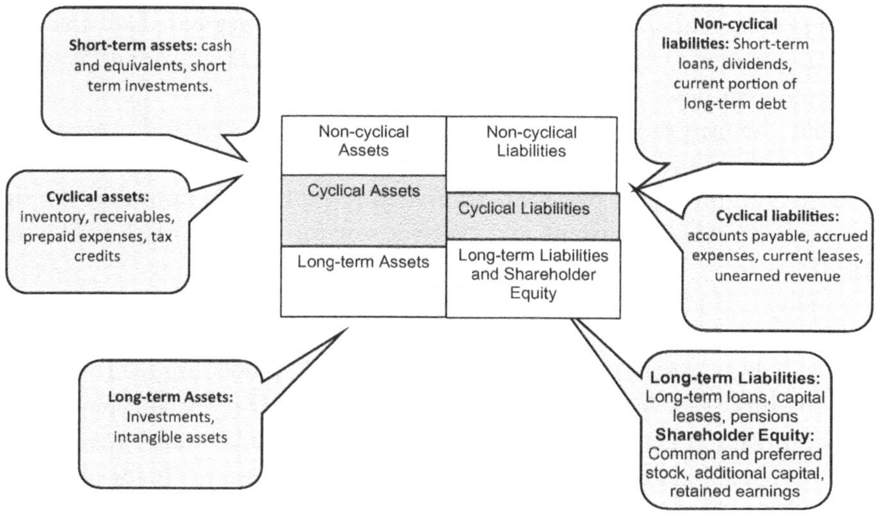

Fig. 8.6 Cyclical and non-cyclical components of the Balance Sheet

8.3 The Working of Working Capital Requirements

This section provides an example of producing cash flow projections according to the tenets detailed previously.

We use the example of a sugar manufacturer to integrate working capital investments in our standard valuation model. By choosing this particular sugar manufacturer (following Zeidan & Spitzeck, 2015), we also incorporate some sustainability-related issues in the chapter on greening supply chains.

Thus, this process gives us the benefit of illustrating how to incorporate working capital management into the rest of a company's cash-flow projections and, in addition, provides an inkling on how sustainability-related projects can increase firm value.

The case is based on actual data (with some approximations for simplicity) from Zeidan and Spitzeck (2015). The firm's valuation is based on the following assumptions:

The company produces mainly white sugar. It has 7-year contracts with farmers that supply sugar cane in close vicinity. It is located in a frontier region in which the industry is expanding. Firms in that region have lower productivity than in the central producing areas of the country. The firm's productivity is supposed to grow by 1% per year for the foreseeable future.

The initial valuation period is five years, starting in 2015. We assume that the values for the last will be constant from then on, arriving at a terminal value equal to the present value of a perpetuity based on free cash flows discounted by the company's weighted average cost of capital (WACC). Perpetual cash flows are assumed constant.

Today the firm produces 400,000 pounds of sugar a year and is expanding towards 700,000 tons in 5 years; its production is growing at approximately 15% per annum. Sugar prices are estimated to be U$15 a pound in the first year and should be constant at US$16 a ton for the rest of the valuation period.

Variable costs are US$ 10 per pound in the first year and grow by 3% a year until the last year. Fixed costs are US$ 800,000 and grow at 10% a year. Initially, capital expenditures are U$500,000, increasing by 10% a year until the fifth year. Since the company is not assumed to expand beyond the fifth year, capital expenditures don't impact the terminal value. Investments in working capital are initially U$100,000, with a constant financial cycle at 40 days.

The capital structure is 40% debt and 60% equity. The cost of capital is assumed constant at 7% a year for debt (due to some subsidized credit) and 14% a year for equity. There is no expected change in operating profits.

To estimate the additional working capital investments for the next five years, we follow:

$$\Delta \text{OWC} = \text{CCC} * \Delta \text{Revenue}$$

As the financial cycle is assumed constant, sales growth is the only driver of working capital investments. Table 8.8 brings the revenue estimates for the period.

Thus, given the financial cycle of 40 days (and considering 365 days per year), the additional working capital required to support the company's growth is shown in Table 8.9.

The initial working capital investments stood at over U$600,000. For the following five years, the company must invest over U$100,000 to fund its sales growth. At the end of the initial five years, its operating working

Table 8.8 The basics of a cash-flow statement. Part 1

	Year 1	Year 2	Year 3	Year 4	Year 5
Price	15	16	16	16	16
Quantity	400,000	460,000	529,000	608,350	699,603
(=) Revenue	6,000,000	7,360,000	8,464,000	9,733,600	11,193,640
Growth in sales		15.0%	15.0%	15.0%	15.0%

Table 8.9 The basics of a cash-flow statement. Part 2

	Year 1	Year 2	Year 3	Year 4	Year 5
C2C cycle (days)	*40*	*40*	*40*	*40*	*40*
Revenue per day	16,438	20,164	23,189	26,667	30,668
OWC	657,534	806,575	927,562	1,066,696	1,226,700
(+-) Working capital	(100,000)	(149,041)	(120,986)	(139,134)	(160,004)

capital was estimated to have almost doubled in nominal terms. The additional required investments are, respectively, US$151,111, US$122,667, US$141,067, and US$162,227, from 2016 to 2019.

Depreciation and amortization are, at first, deducted from EBITDA and then reintroduced. CAPEX impacts the firm's cash flow significantly in the first five years. Still, it has no impact on the terminal value. Incidentally, most of the company's value is driven by the cash flows from 2020-onwards. The firm's value mainly coming from cash flows from year five onwards may seem excessively ad hoc, but that was the company's reality at the time of its valuation. The company planned to go through a cycle of significant capital expenditures and later recover these investments.

Given all these assumptions, the detailed cash flow projections are described in Table 8.10. The firm's enterprise value was approximately US$9.6 million in the business as usual scenario.

8.4 The Sustainability Delta, or How Green Investments Can Increase Shareholder Value

Following Zeidan and Spitzeck (2015), the cash flow projections of two green investments are detailed: greener energy and eco-premium on organic sugar.

The greener energy project uses sugarcane bagasse, a by-product of the production process. Below are the assumptions for investment in bioenergy production for a small sugar producer:

- Capex of U$200,000 in the first year and U$100,000 in years 2 and 3.
- Energy savings (the firm is not large enough to sell excess energy until year 5, but this would require more investments in connecting the company to the grid, which we disregard at this point) of U$15,000 beginning in year 2.
- The company can use subsidized credit, reducing the firm's total cost of capital by 0.2% a year. We assume 70% debt financing with subsidized

Table 8.10 Base scenario (business as usual) for the sugar manufacturer's valuation. US$

	2015	2016	2017	2018	2019
(=) Revenue	6,000,000	7,360,000	8,464,000	9,733,600	11,193,640
(-) Variable costs	−4,000,000	−4,738,000	−5,612,161	−6,647,605	−7,874,088
(=) Operating margin	2,000,000	2,622,000	2,851,839	3,085,995	3,319,552
%Operating Margin	*33%*	*36%*	*34%*	*32%*	*30%*
(-) Fixed Costs	−800,000	−864,000	−933,120	−1,007,770	−1,088,391
(=) EBITDA	1,200,000	1,758,000	1,918,719	2,078,226	2,231,161
(-) Depreciation	200,000	−220,000	−242,000	−266,200	−292,820
(=) EBIT	1,000,000	1,538,000	1,676,719	1,812,026	1,938,341
(-) Income Taxes (34%)	−340,000	−522,920	−570,084	−616,089	−659,036
(=) NOPLAT	660,000	1,015,080	1,106,635	1,195,937	1,279,305
(+) Depreciation	200,000	220,000	242,000	266,200	292,820
(+-) Working Capital	−100,000	−151,111	−122,667	−141,067	−162,227
(=) Operational Cash Flow	760,000	1,083,969	1,225,968	1,321,070	1,409,898
(-) Capex	−500,000	−550,000	−605,000	−665,500	−732,050
(+) Terminal Value					12,483,461
(=) Enterprise Cash Flow	260,000	533,969	620,968	655,570	13,161,310
		Enterprise Value		9,662,930	

loans by innovation programs from the Brazilian government, which is a conservative assumption, as bioenergy projects are allowed to be fully funded by some Brazilian agencies (Finep, BNDES, and others).

As for other types of sugar, medium-sized and large producers who switch part of their products end up with 5–20% of the total capacity devoted to organic sugar manufacturing. In the present example, the firm could, with its current infrastructure, produce up to 5,000 tons of organic sugar a year with minimal investments, a coverage rate of less than 1.5%. More significant production would require investments in manufacturing, distribution, and marketing. Assuming no costs for introducing the product or additional marketing, given the distribution channels already in place, the assumptions for the organic sugar project are:

- Prices 20% higher than regular sugar.
- Sales in the local market, diversifying revenue streams (the company is mainly an exporter). This effect is not shown as cash flow.
- Production begins in year two and grows simultaneously as total production.

Results are in Table 8.11. The difference in enterprise value is 1.24% (we disregard the amount of debt, cash holdings, and land value).

The difference in enterprise value comes mainly from the lower weighted average cost of capital. The weighted average cost of capital is indirect, so firms don't pay up for overinvestments (in working capital or fixed assets). That is usually an overlooked aspect in working capital management and greener investments. Resources unnecessarily trapped in operations have one

Table 8.11 Cash flow projections from two green projects, US$

	2015	2016	2017	2018	2019
(=) Revenue	6,000,000	7,376,000	8,482,400	9,754,760	11,217,974
(-) Variable costs	−4,000,000	−4,738,000	−5,612,161	−6,647,605	−7,874,088
(=) Operating margin	2,000,000	2,638,000	2,870,239	3,107,155	3,343,886
% Operating Margin	*33%*	*36%*	*34%*	*32%*	*30%*
(-) Fixed costs	−800,000	−849,000	−918,120	−992,770	−1,073,391
(=) EBITDA	1,200,000	1,789,000	1,952,119	2,114,386	2,270,495
(i) Depreciation	−200.000	−220,000	−242,000	−266,200	−292,820
(=) EBIT	1,000,000	1,569,000	1,710,119	1,848,186	1,977,675
(-) Income taxes (34%)	−340,000	−533,460	−581,440	−628,383	−672,410
(=) NOPLAT	660,000	1,035,540	1,128,679	1,219,803	1,305,266
(+) Depreciation	200,000	220,000	242,000	266,200	292,820
(+-) Working capital	−100,000	−152,889	−122,933	−141,373	−162,579
(=) Operational cash flow	760,000	1,102,651	1,247,745	1,344,629	1,435,506
(-) Capex	−700,000	−650,000	−705,000	−665,500	−732,050
(+) Terminal value					12,990,302
(=) Enterprise cash flow	60,000	452,651	542,745	679,129	13,693,758
		Enterprise Value		9,782,791	

benefit: they facilitate business deals, e.g., limiting the probability that the firm runs out of production inputs or attracting clients due to extended payment terms. However, they make firms much less efficient than they could be otherwise. Credit-constrained firms can ill afford to overinvest but routinely do so.

Building cash flow projections may unearth opportunities to reduce over-investments or, at least, limit new instances of excessive resources to fund a company's growth.

Putting pen to paper regarding a firm's projected finances also serves other functions, such as helping managers overcome organization inertia. For instance, Whelan et al. (2017) developed a monetization methodology (freely available) that (1) analyzes the drivers of improved performance (mediated by sustainability-related factors; (2) identifies critical benefits; and (3) quantifies the benefits in financial terms. The central argument is that sustainability practices improve profitability across the value chain. Proper financial planning that considers these practices becomes a powerful tool for business decision-makers.

8.5 Amazon and Growth Through Negative Cash-Conversion Cycles

Nothing beats cold hard cash. Every company needs cash to grow. No company better illustrates this than Amazon—its business model is about cash, liquidity, growth, not profits. Much has been written about the company, but one dimension is often ignored: the role of trade credit in helping Amazon grow exponentially. Some, such as Uber, Xiaomi, Switch, and Airbnb, will tap private equity; others such as Mars, Bosch, and Koch Industries will use past profits, sometimes foregoing exponential growth for a more secure path to prominence.

The negative cash conversion cycle is the overlooked part of Amazon's plan of global domination. As sales rise, the negative cycle helps the company fund its investments for future revenue growth, in a positive feedback loop that requires Amazon to continue growing. It is a virtuous cycle but not without risk: new markets and products generate more cash (but not necessarily profits), allowing the company to expand its operations. As long as revenue increases, liquidity is not a concern, different from most companies that pursue a rapid expansion strategy.

Amazon has constantly defied expectations. It is now a behemoth, but for a long time, analysts pegged it as a bubble stock; the company does not deliver much by way of profits, buybacks, or dividends. In a world where share buybacks have been compared to corporate cocaine (*The Economist*, 2014), Amazon has continued to buck the trend. The company grows unrelentingly, but it is surprisingly unleveraged in a world flush with cheap credit.

The missing link in explaining its successful trajectory is that Amazon has had a negative cash conversion cycle since its beginning. Trade credit has allowed the company to fund all its investments with money from its supply chain until the mid-2000s; it helps explain why the company does not need to pay dividends, buy back its stock or generate profits. It also provides a compelling reason for the acquisition of Whole Foods. By integrating the retailer into its existing operations, Amazon should fund almost one-third of the acquisition with the cash trapped in the seemingly inefficient financial cycle of Whole Foods. While Amazon's financial cycle is approximately— 94 days, in the last financial statement before being acquired, Whole Foods' C2C was positive and stood at approximately four days.

Financial cycles tend to change as companies mature. Start-ups are usually starved for cash but do not have enough market power to extract credit lines from their suppliers or require cash advances from customers. As companies mature, adding new products, services, suppliers, and consumers results in C2C changes. New agreements usually require spot payments in Japan, especially from foreign companies. After a few years, as trust is built between suppliers and consumers, payment terms from large to small companies extend to months. Amazon, however, displays a strikingly constant negative C2C cycle throughout its history, even with the addition of specific services such as B2B cloud storage and content production. Its business model has always been based on exponential growth financed partly by its supply chain (Fig. 8.7 and Fig. 8.8).

Amazon's C2C has never been higher than –70 and lower than –120 days. Given this pattern, the company's growth meant that its operating working capital turned increasingly negative.

Amazon's negative operating working capital crossed the US$ 10 billion mark in the third quarter of 2017. Given that the nominal accumulated value of investments throughout the company's 20 years has been a little over US$ 100 billion, this means that its supply chain has financed roughly 10% of Amazon's total investments. Even more important, trade credit was the most important source of finance during Amazon's early days. Up until mid-2003 negative operating working capital could finance all the company's investments. Lately, capital expenditures have been soaring, and the company has been tapping other sources of capital. Still, there is little doubt that trade credit is a fundamental part of the company's growth strategy.

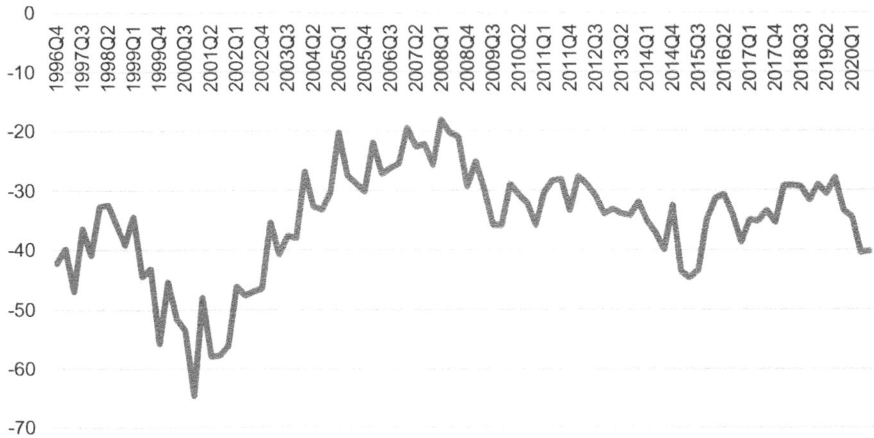

Fig. 8.7 Cash conversion cycle (days)—Amazon (*Source* Amazon's financial statements)

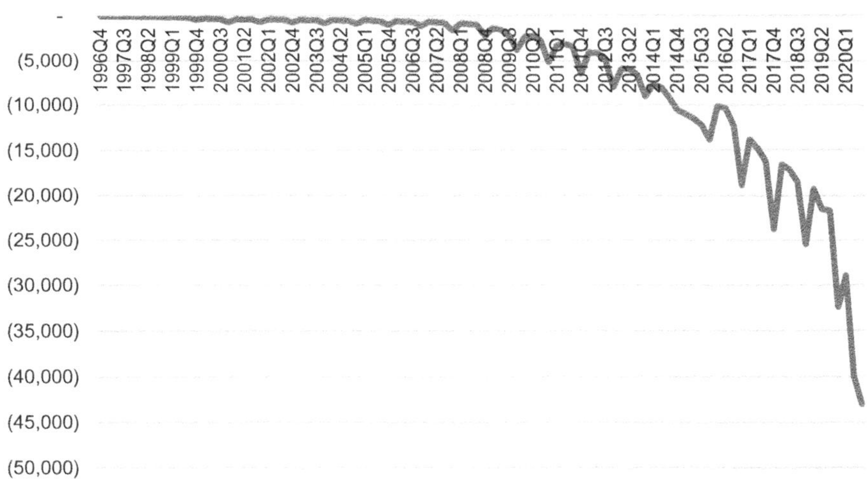

Fig. 8.8 Amazon's operating working capital (U$ million) (*Source* Amazon's financial statements)

The principle behind the cash-generation machine that is key to Amazon's growth strategy is simple: Customers pay immediately for the merchandise they order when placing an order. Amazon, in contrast, uses its market power as one of the largest retailers to extract payment terms from its suppliers that allow payment at 60 days' notice and more. For a firm that does not grow, the advantage from such 60 days of free credit is not immense, particularly in times with low-interest rates. However, if the firm is on a growth path, say its sales grow by 10 million in 60 days, the 10 million only need to be paid to suppliers with a 60-day delay. If the growth can be sustained, the 10 million can be invested in other projects. This strategy becomes even more significant once a firm experiences exponential growth. In this case, the cash generated from negative cash conversion cycles keeps increasing. If, at the same time, the firm's market power also increases, and the payment delay extracted from suppliers can be increased yet further, a firm with no profits can generate increasing amounts of cash that can be used for investment.

The crux of such a growth strategy is sustaining or accelerating growth. If growth goes to zero and a firm reaches a steady-state, the money borrowed from suppliers needs to be put into operations as working capital.

8.5.1 Amazon Prime, the Whole Foods Acquisition, and the Value of Constant Inflows

Aswath Damodaran, one of the top valuation professionals in the world, estimated that Amazon Prime, with its 85 million members, contributed around US$ 61.3 billion to the overall US$ 542 billion market capitalization of the company in 2017 (Damodaran, 2017). Prime not only enhances the company's value by locking in customers that spend almost twice as much non-Prime users, but it is also a cash-flow generator. In the US, Prime customers paid US$ 99 per year then (around U$139 now) for the privilege of future discounted shipping and access to video and music services. Prime is more than a branding, value-enhancing proposition for customers; it adds much-needed cash, allowing Amazon enough liquidity to ignore calls for buybacks and dividends.

The 96% renewal rate makes Prime a boon for a company that has been built on growth that relies on constant cash inflows to help fund it.

The Whole Foods acquisition made headlines worldwide. It illustrates another aspect of trade credit: market power and the ability to tap value unavailable to the original company.

Many large retailers have negative cash conversion cycles. Since margins are razor-thin for companies such as Walmart and Carrefour, negative financial cycles allow them to generate cash and finance growth, limiting the need for other sources of capital. The financial cycle was around -10 days for both companies, while Walmart's operating margin was significantly higher than Carrefour's (4.8 and 1.5%, respectively).

Amazon's model is distinct from other giant retailers, but there is one common aspect: all rely on trade credit to finance growth and compensate for low operating margins. And it seems that Amazon saw an opportunity in scooping up one of the few retailers with a positive financial cycle. By doing so, Amazon can use economies of scale to extract trade credit from Whole Foods' supply-chain without affecting its operating margin, freeing up cash tied in its new subsidiary's operations. The total operating working capital of Whole Foods was US$ 212 million at the time of its acquisition. If Amazon could lower Whole Foods' CCC to -94 days, it could potentially unlock US$ 4.2 billion, more than one-third of the amount it paid for the company. Even in more realistic scenarios, the financial cycle turns negative without affecting Whole Foods' operating margin due to Amazon's better supply-chain management, which unlocks that would make the retailer a cash generator as it grows.

Amazon continues to expand its empire using its supply-chain capital. Further growth likely will make it even easier to access trade credit. Bezos once said: "Your margin is my opportunity." We should add: their suppliers' cash flow is Amazon's opportunity. At the end of the day, nothing really beats cold, hard cash.

8.6 Multi-Product

How should we treat the working capital management of multi-product companies? Managerially, the best way is to treat each business unit or, at the limit, each product or service separately. It is almost impossible to do it from consolidated accounting reports, so companies must set up their internal systems to track down changes in working capital management for each relevant business category. However, tracking variations in operating working capital for each item may be challenging, even with internal data. Here, we describe some techniques for monitoring the financial cycle of specific products.

8.7 Methods For Estimating DIO For Multi-Product Firms

For a multi-product company, DIO is the most difficult to determine out of the three components of the financial cycle. That is because it is difficult to track the average time for each product to go through the production process. Monitoring production processes are even more complicated for companies with non-standardized products or services. The usual formulas for estimating

DIO, be it the accounting standard that is the ratio between average inventory and COGS or the version in this book, in which the denominator is revenue, are based on the value of the stock. COGS itself is based on the accounting for inventory:

$$\text{Cost of Goods Sold} = \text{Beginning Inventory} + \text{Purchases} - \text{Ending Inventory}$$

Thus, the typical DIO estimation requires relatively sound measures of the value of inventories. However, companies rarely keep adequate records of the value of their stock. After all, managerial incentives are geared towards transforming inputs into final products and services and selling them, not valuing remaining inventory.

A simple procedure for estimating the DIO of many different products that require little information gathering is:

$$\text{DIO} = \frac{\text{Average quantity of goods in inventory}}{\text{Daily unit sales}}$$

The reasoning behind this measure is straightforward: it provides a direct indicator of inventory turnover, or how long it takes to transform inputs into final goods. If a firm purchases lots of input for a specific product at regular intervals, then DIO is simply the time between orders. In some cases, it can be even as simple as that.

There are three main categories of inventory in increasing degrees of readiness: raw materials, work in process, and final goods. There are upsides and downsides about focusing on units sold and production rather than the value of inputs or COGS. On the one hand, tracking the amount of inventory used ignores essential considerations such as the tradeoff between keeping inputs unprocessed and ready to be sold. On the other hand, there are two main benefits. First, managers should have access to daily unit sales and the average quantity of goods in inventory, making it easier to estimate product-specific DIO than alternative arrangements. Second, safety stocks are distributed to the specific products they are related to, which makes this form of evaluating DIO more precise to cash flow variations.

Let's return to the case of L. Euler. Initially, we calculated DIO as the ratio between inventory and net revenue and not the cost of sales. Based on the daily revenue for 2021 being U$111,111.11 and average inventory U$1,000,000, we arrived at a DIO of 9 days (from 1,000,000/111,111.11). However, this process does not allow us to analyze the DIO of the firm's goods and services separately.

The firms' service revenue comes primarily from maintenance contracts. These contracts are renewed annually but billed monthly. The stock associated with services is composed chiefly of computers and other electronics. Workers are paid monthly. How does one estimate the DIO in this case? There is no unambiguous answer. If DIO were calculated as the ratio between inventory and COGS, the answer would be a relatively meaningless number, as COGS and inventory are not relevant variables in the provision of services in this example. Instead, we rely on the concepts embedded on:

$$\text{DIO} = \frac{\text{Average quantity of goods in inventory}}{\text{Daily unit sales}}$$

To inform how we estimate DIO. For L.Euler, the economic cycle of its services is approximately 30 days. Why 30 days? For two reasons. For new contracts, that is the time required for documents to be signed and the initial cycle of maintenance services to be performed. Conveniently, that is also how internal processes are set up to meet the customers' needs and how contracts are designed, as previously explained.

Our process of estimating L.Euler's DIO seems ad hoc because it is. There is no universal method for calculating the DIO of service companies, for which fixed costs are more critical than variable costs. For instance, assume that you are asked to estimate the DIO of a mobile provider. The economic cycle of a cellphone connection is instantaneous, and the DIO is zero. All costs for providing this type of service are fixed costs, and a mobile provider is the rare case of a company in which marginal costs can be considered effectively zero.

Given that it would not be extraordinary to classify all the costs to provide the company's services as fixed, we could have chosen to set L. Euler's DIO to zero. However, we prefer to be conservative in estimating the required working capital and consider that 30 days of revenue is a good indicator of the working capital necessary to keep the business running.

Regarding its goods, L. Euler sells two products, A and B. For 2021, products A and B prices were U$100 and U$50, and sales totaled U$18 million and U$9 million, respectively. Throughout the year, the company had 7,000 units of product A and 15,000 units of product B at different stages of production, on average. In addition, the company's internal accounting system indicated that the average inventory values for the two products were U$600,000 and U$800,000, respectively.

Based on the two methods described in this chapter, what is the DIO for each product? Remember that the formulas for each way to estimate DIO are:

$$DIO = \frac{\text{Inventory}}{\text{Daily revenue}} \text{and } DIO = \frac{\text{Average quantity of goods in inventory}}{\text{Daily unit sales}}$$

Thus, for product A, the variables required for the estimation of DIO are:

- Inventory: 600,000
- Daily revenue: (18,000,000/360) = 50,000
- Daily unit sales: ((18,000,000/100)/360) = 500
- Average quantity of goods in inventory: 7,000

Hence, the two DIO for product A are:

$$DIO = \frac{600,000}{50,000} = 12 \text{ and } DIO = \frac{7,000}{500} = 14$$

For product B, the variables required for the estimation of DIO are:

- Inventory: 800,000
- Daily revenue: (9,000,000/360) = 25,000
- Daily unit sales: ((9,000,000/50)/360) = 500
- Average quantity of goods in inventory: 15,000

Therefore, the two DIO for product B are:

$$DIO = \frac{800,000}{25,000} = 32\text{and } DIO = \frac{15,000}{500} = 30$$

In Table 8.12 Methods for estimating DIO, we summarize the results.

For product A, DIO from method 1 is lower than method 2, while the reverse is true for product B. However, these differences are slight, and in real

Table 8.12 Methods for estimating DIO

DIO	Method 1	Method 2
	Inventory/Daily revenue	Average quantity of goods in inventory/ Daily unit sales
Product A	12 days	14 days
Product B	32 days	30 days

life, we can potentially encounter significant disparities in DIO depending on which method we choose to use.

The two methods rely on distinct sources of information. Method 1 uses the traditional accounting measures from balance sheets. The inventory value depends on the issues mentioned above, such as safety stocks or the values used to determine the unprocessed products' value. Method 2 is invariant to a company's costs, as it is based on the number of inputs and unfinished goods and the price of the finished products. Method 1 is preferable if the goal is to determine the amount of working capital that a company has already invested. However, for the variation in working capital, Method 2 offers a better path for managers. Of course, method 1 is always available as it is based on accounting measures that must be reported on companies' balance sheets and income statements. The only caveat is that the value of the stock related to each product is registered and reported.

More importantly, the two methods allow managers to distinguish between the financial cycles of particular products. The economic cycle of product B is twice that of product A, regardless of the method used to estimate DIO.

8.7.1 Optimal Inventory Turnover, Does it Exist?

For retailers with dozens or hundreds of products, estimating product-specific DIO by the ratio between the average quantity of goods in inventory to daily unit sales may be more feasible than standard methods. For supermarkets, inventory turnover has long been an important measure to determine which brands and products stores will carry.

Lean inventory practices reduce working capital investments but may reduce firms' abilities to service their customers. There can be no general optimal inventory turnover metric because there can't be a single procedure to optimize a firm's cash-conversion cycle.

Eroglu and Hofer (2011) revisited the link between lean inventory management and performance. Usually, the inventory turnover ratio is calculated as:

$$\text{Inventory Turnover Ratio} = \frac{\text{Cost of Goods Sold}}{\text{Average Inventory}}$$

Earlier, most studies that aimed to measure productivity regarding inventory management compared firms' inventory turnover across industries. If a firm had a lower inventory turnover than the median or average of its sector, it would be deemed to manage its inventory poorly.

Previous studies also considered inventory turnover as invariant to the level of sales, resulting in absolute inventory leanness measures. However, Eroglu and Hofer (2011) argued that there might be economies or diseconomies of scale regarding inventory holdings. But the economic benefit of increased inventory leanness should depend on industry-specific inventory management characteristics. Absolute measures ignore economies of scale in inventory management. For instance, if a firm's sales double, its inventories are generally less than double due to economies of scale.

Hence, the authors propose the Empirical Leanness Indicator (ELI), which evaluates a firm's inventory leanness relative to firms of comparable size within a narrowly defined industry. Figure 8.9 presents a graphic illustration of the ELI based on a non-linear relationship between the required inventory level and sales.

The authors' approach to taking their new measure to data is fascinating, as it shows under which conditions there could be an optimal inventory turnover measure. Instead of just creating an indicator of leanness and plugging it into a regression, their measure enters the regressions in first- and second-degree polynomial forms; the relationship between inventory holdings and sales is non-linear. Significantly, if the second-degree term has a negative parameter estimate, there is an optimal level of leanness. That also means that if the parameter estimate of the quadratic term is not significant, the regression reduces to a linear model. The non-linear relationship also means that firms could have too much and too little inventory.

Figure 8.10 illustrates nine possible non-linear relationships between ELI and performance, depending on the signs of the coefficient of the first and second-polynomial terms.

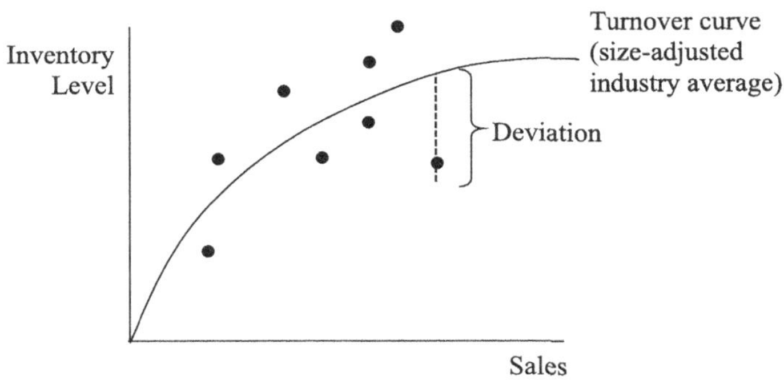

Fig. 8.9 The Empirical Leanness Indicator (*Source* Eroglu and Hofer [2011])

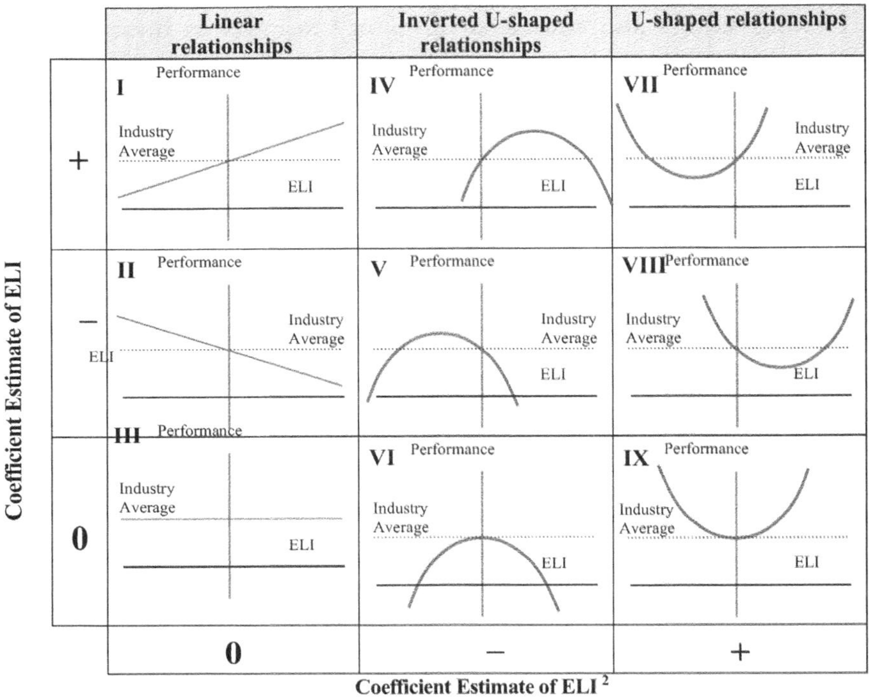

Fig. 8.10 Non-linear relationships between ELI and performance (*Source* Eroglu and Hofer [2011])

In their empirical analysis of an extensive panel data set of U.S. manufacturing companies, Eroglu and Hofer (2011) find that the significance and shape of the inventory–performance relationship vary substantially across industries. Out of 54 sectors, leanness and performance are related in 36 and unrelated in 18. Moreover, their results indicate that for most industries for which leanness affects performance, the relationship is concave, suggesting an optimum level of inventory leanness beyond which firm performance deteriorates.

The relationship between inventory turnover and firm performance has also been investigated by Hofer et al. (2012), Negrão et al. (2017), Bellisario and Pavlov (2018), and Marodin et al. (2018), alongside dozens of other scientific articles.

8.7.2 Is It Possible for DIO to Be a Negative Number?

Firms with extended payment terms to suppliers and short credit periods to consumers must take risks to achieve negative financial cycles. However, it is not uncommon to find business models in which sales to consumers happen before companies must produce their wares or perform their services.

There is no better example to illustrate this than considering pension funds, even if working capital management is not necessarily applicable to analyze this type of company. Pension fund administrators collect periodic amounts from members (and sponsors), invest the proceeds, and then pay out benefits governed by the plan's rules, sometimes decades later.

The goal of a pension fund is to accumulate enough assets to pay beneficiaries; pension funds are usually designed with a finite period. Moreover, we can use pension funds as a benchmark for the life-cycle analysis we summarized in Sect. 3.7. Figure 8.11 illustrates how pension funds are structured.

Pension funds are not the only type of business with an inverted economic cycle. Many artisans work on-demand, as do many other service companies. Manufacturing companies may also work by first selling their wares and only then producing them.

Many comic book artists complement their income by opening commission lists to their fans. That allows artists to make better estimates of their future income, as commissions are ordered before the art is produced. Some moral hazard may occur when artists are paid in full beforehand. The hobby is full of examples of artists who take years or never complete commissions

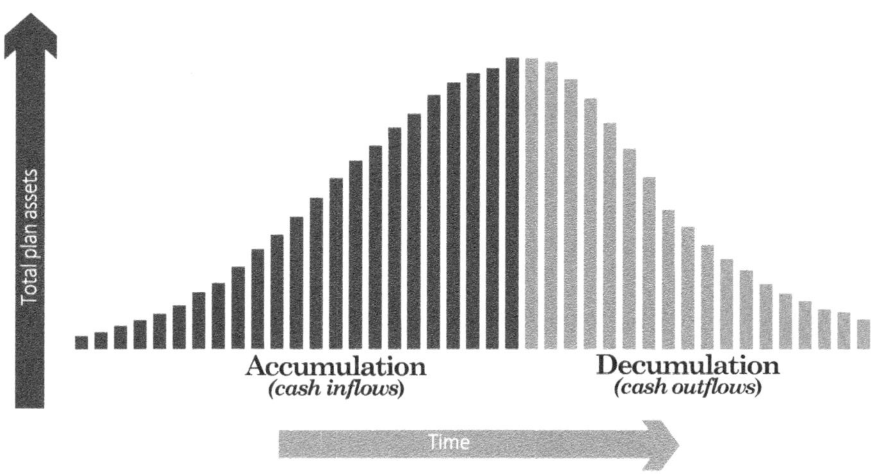

Fig. 8.11 Pension plan investment lifecycle (*Source* Boyce [2020])

because there is no financial incentive to produce the work after it has been paid.

There is nothing extraordinary about goods and services with inverted economic cycles. The impact on a firm's cash conversion cycle is no different than that of a short DSO or a lengthy DPO; companies with an inverted economic cycle will tend to have shorter financial cycles than those with long production processes.

8.8 Methods For Estimating DPO and DSO For Multi-Product Firms

Like DIO, DPO and DSO can be estimated using two approaches: one based on regularly reported financial statements and another on internal metrics. However, calculating DPO and DSO is easier than DIO.

For a company, determining its DPO could be as simple as using the payment terms for its suppliers. For instance, if the finance department pays every bill 30 days after invoices arrive and all inputs are purchased at the beginning of the economic cycle, DPO is 30 days.

However, if there are separate payment terms from suppliers, a straightforward approach is to estimate DPO for each product as:

$$DPO_i = \sum s_{ji} PT_{ji}$$

In which:

s_{ij} = share of input *j* on the value of product *i*; and
PT_{ij} = payment terms for the supplier of input *j* for the product *i*.

For example, let's assume there are two inputs for A production and three inputs for B production. For product A, s_{ij} are 40% and 60%, respectively, and PT_{ij} are 30 days and 45 days. Thus, DPO for product A is:

$$DPO_A = 0.4*30 + 0.6*45 = 39 \text{ days}$$

If for product B, s_{ij} are 10%, 40%, and 50%, and PT_{ij} are 20, 30, and 120 days, the DPO for product B is

$$DPO_B = 0.1*20 + 0.4*30 + 0.5*120 = 74 \text{ days}$$

One note: it does not matter if inputs are necessary for manufacturing both goods. In this example, the raw material with payment terms of 30 days could be the same for both goods. That wouldn't impact the interpretation of the results.

In this example, the company takes much longer to pay for the material for manufacturing product B than product A. It may be that the firm can lengthen the payment terms of other inputs for A while renegotiating terms for the most crucial material for B, offering the supplier to pay it sooner in exchange for a discount. That may reveal opportunities for the improvement of cash flow or profit margins.

Product-specific DPO provides crucial information for the improvement of cash flow management. Administrators can track which products are helping free up capital (those with longer DPO) and contribute to lower cash conversion cycles.

DSO can be estimated similarly.

$$\text{DSO} = \frac{\text{Accounts Receivable}}{\text{Daily revenue}} \text{ and } \text{DSO}_{\text{i}} = \sum s_{ji}\text{ST}_{ji}$$

In which ST is the terms of sales. We note that we include just accounts receivable in the aggregate estimation of DSO. Other charges related to credit to customers or the government, such as tax credits, may be included, depending on firms' characteristics.

The estimation of DPO and DSO in this manner requires the determination of the share of inputs or sales related to production and sales, respectively. There are two principal ways of estimating the percentage of inputs and finished goods and services in the firms' total working capital requirements: historical and target-based. The historical method uses past data to inform the budgeting of the required trade credit. The target-based process simply uses the percentages determined by management as the standard for the firms' operations.

Assume, for instance, that the firm's sales in the last four quarters are represented in Table 8.13 below.

As we can see, the share of each product in the firms' revenue changes during the year. At the end of the year, sales for product A account for 19% of the firm's sales, while the percentages are 22, 23, and 35% for products B, C, and D, respectively.

There are tradeoffs about estimating working capital requirements from annual data. In the example, sales for D represent 40% of the firms' sales in the second quarter but fall to 32% in the following trimester. Using the historical share of 35% will underestimate the impact of product's D on the

Table 8.13 Hypothetical annual sales, U$ '000

Product		Quarter 1	Quarter 2	Quarter 3	Quarter 4	Total
A	Sales	50,000	40,000	45,000	60,000	195,000
	Share	21%	18%	18%	20%	19%
B	Sales	45,000	45,000	70,000	65,000	225,000
	Share	19%	20%	28%	22%	22%
C	Sales	60,000	50,000	55,000	70,000	235,000
	Share	26%	22%	22%	24%	23%
D	Sales	80,000	90,000	80,000	100,000	350,000
	Share	34%	40%	32%	34%	35%
Total	Sales	235,000	225,000	250,000	295,000	1,005,000

company's working capital in the second quarter and will overestimate it for the following. Table 8.13 allows us to distinguish the impact of each product on the firm's working capital changes due to the revenue effect. Things get even more complicated if sales terms also vary over time.

The alternative method to historical data is to relate the weights of each product to the firms' strategy. For instance, in the current year, product D represents, on average, 35% of the firm's sales, but the goal may be to grow the other parts of the business, reducing this good's share on the firm's revenue to 30%. In this instance, managers could just set up the allotment of this product in the firm's working capital for the following year as 30%. Remember that working capital projections cannot be perfect, as there will always be uncertainty about the level of sales, the production process, and the payment terms. Setting up ad hoc contributions from each product to the firm's total revenue brings one significant advantage: it is straightforward and informs managers on the targets for the sales team.

Of course, if managers want to track working capital daily, historical data allows for even more precise cash flow estimates.

References

Bellisario, A., & Pavlov, A. (2018). Performance management practices in lean manufacturing organizations: A systematic review of research evidence. *Production Planning & Control, 29*(5), 367–385.

Boyce, J. (2020). *We need to talk about the armadillo in the room.* Treasury & Risk. https://www.treasuryandrisk.com/2020/07/07/we-need-to-talk-about-the-armadillo-in-the-room/?slreturn=20220003011858

Damodaran, A. (2017). Deconstructing amazon prime: Loss leader or value creator? *Musings on Markets*. https://aswathdamodaran.blogspot.com/2017/10/loss-leader-or-value-creator.html.

Damodaran. (2019). Insights on VC pricing: lessons from Uber, WeWork, and Peloton! *Musings on Markets*. https://aswathdamodaran.blogspot.com/2019/09/insights-on-vc-pricing-lessons-from.html.

The Economist. (2014). Corporate cocaine, September 13 edition. https://www.economist.com/leaders/2014/09/13/corporate-cocaine.

Eroglu, C., & Hofer, C. (2011). Lean, leaner, too lean? The inventory-performance link revisited. *Journal of Operations Management, 29*(4), 356–369.

Hofer, C., Eroglu, C., & Hofer, A. R. (2012). The effect of lean production on financial performance: The mediating role of inventory leanness. *International Journal of Production Economics, 138*(2), 242–253.

Marodin, G., Frank, A. G., Tortorella, G. L., & Netland, T. (2018). Lean product development and lean manufacturing: Testing moderation effects. *International Journal of Production Economics, 203*, 301–310.

Negrão, L. L. L., Godinho Filho, M., & Marodin, G. (2017). Lean practices and their effect on performance: A literature review. *Production Planning & Control, 28*(1), 33–56.

Whelan, T., Zappa, B., Zeidan, R., & Fishbein, G. (2017). How to quantify sustainability's impact on your bottom line. *Harvard Business Review, 23*.

Zeidan, R., & Spitzeck, H. (2015). The sustainability delta: Considering sustainability opportunities in firm valuation. *Sustainable Development, 23*(6), 329–342.

9

Greening Supply Chains and the Role of Working Capital Management

Companies can extract resources from their supply chain or act as trade credit lenders, increasing the liquidity of their suppliers and customers. As such, they have a crucial role in mitigating climate change.

A complete framework for climate-related action should have five dimensions: the mechanism of intervention, the scope of impact, the degree of replaceability between these two, the operational details of the intervention, and the mapping of direct and indirect effects. Table 9.1 establishes the direct costs and benefits for static mechanisms of intervention.

Mechanisms can have local, industry, or global effects. Each mechanism refers to the enforcement of behavioral change: self-governing supply-chains, government-enforced regulation, and changes in consumer behavior. Inside lag refers to the time it takes to reach a decision; outside lag is the time it takes for actions to influence environmental and social outcomes. The relative paralysis of many governments in the face of the Covid-19 pandemic illustrates how the reliance on regulation alone cannot provide the necessary incentives for local and global action. Some paradigmatic examples of international mechanisms are the Kyoto Protocol, the Montreal Protocol, and the divestment movement. The Kyoto Protocol created a market for carbon permits; it works (albeit imperfectly) by companies internalizing the costs related to environmental degradation. The Montreal Protocol established clear regulations to limit the production of chlorine- and bromine-containing ozone-depleting substances (ODSs). The divestment movement from fossil fuels acts through changes in consumer (and investors) behavior.

R. Zeidan, *The General Model of Working Capital Management*, https://doi.org/10.1007/978-981-19-3334-9_9

Table 9.1 Types of intervention to mitigate climate change

	Type of Intervention		
	Supply-side/Market	Regulation	Demand-side/Ideological
Benefits	Efficient economically; Self-reinforcing mechanism	Outside lag; Customized to local, industry, and global threats	Efficient economically; Self-reinforcing mechanism
Costs	Coordination costly; Outside lag	Inside lag; Inefficient economically	Coordination costly; Outside lag

The success of the Paris climate deal hinges on the specific designs for improving environmental outcomes. As it stands, it is unclear how countries will move towards reaching their ambitious goals. Details matter. What does that have to do with working capital management? Everything. Supply-side/market mechanisms are essential to mitigating climate change and improving social outcomes. Supply chains propagate innovation and can allocate resources to less polluting firms. Such allocation is not centrally planned but the result of companies responding to pressure from stakeholders. We turn to a case study of the beef industry in Brazil before presenting some formal models of the relationship between trade credit and the greening of supply chains.

9.1 With Great Profits Comes Great Responsibility

Many companies have made public commitments to reduce deforestation or lower greenhouse gas emissions. There shouldn't be a significant relationship between working capital management and non-financial dimensions, such as a firm's environmental impact. However, three mechanisms link trade credit decisions and firms' non-financial performance: relationships with a focal company, reputation with supply chain partners, and access to capital.

Focal companies are usually the largest organizations in a supply chain, establish the rules that other companies and usually have direct contact with customers. Apple, Unilever, Pfizer, and Ford are examples of focal companies (note that Ford and Pfizer do not sell directly to consumers, but they are still responsible for designing and marketing products to buyers). These large companies, usually publicly-listed, can dictate payment terms for suppliers and consumers. At the same time, these visible companies tend to suffer from more pressure from stakeholders than small and medium-sized companies.

Suppose that a focal company signs a deforestation-free agreement but cannot monitor all its supply-chain effectively. Limiting or extending payment terms is a tool large companies have to synchronize supply chain actions. Of course, that use of market power is not necessarily related to the impact of supply chain members on the environment, but it can be.

The relationship between trade credit and the greening of supply chains is easier to visualize when focusing on SMEs' reputations. Firms with better management practices should negotiate better terms with other supply chain members and financial institutions. Conceptually, non-financial performance can be classified in different ways. Here, we are primarily concerned with the greening of supply chains but also mention the more general relationship between trade credit and corporate social responsibility (CSR).

We have evidence that non-financial performance helps firms access trade credit. Xu et al. (2020) use a sample of 2455 individual firms over the 1996–2016 period to investigate the relationship between CSR and trade credit. They find that higher overall CSR scores are related to more trade credit. There are positive associations between trade credit and the environment, employee relations, community, and diversity, the individual components of CSR as operationalized by the authors. The authors highlight that CSR plays a role in increasing the suppliers' willingness to extend trade credit.

Climate change mitigation requires cooperation between members of the supply chain. Embedding non-financial performance as criteria for trade credit arrangements is already part of the relationship between large companies and their suppliers. For instance, over ten years ago, Plambeck (2012) already observed that limiting the bullwhip effect (for more, see Sect. 5.4.3) should also reduce greenhouse gases emissions, and incentives are aligned between suppliers and consumers to do so. There is also an indication [e.g., Inman and Green (2018), Lartey et al. (2020), and Singh et al. (2021)] that lean management and green combine to impact environmental and operational performance.

More importantly, we can expect a positive feedback loop between optimizing working capital management, operational performance, and environmental outcomes. Henao and Sarache (2022) distinguish between two models of the relationship between these factors. The cumulative model has operational performance at the base and environmental and social at the top. The "trade-off" model suggests that improvements in one dimension come at the expense of another. The authors support the cumulative model using data from Colombian manufacturers. We turn to a case study about the poultry industry to explore these ideas further.

9.1.1 The Poultry Industry

What is the role of focus companies? Pohlmann et al. (2020) study the poultry industry in Brazil and the role of focal companies in improving the environmental outcomes of the industry.

Figure 9.1 illustrates the poultry supply chain. The focal companies are in these parts of the supply chain: feed mill suppliers, live poultry transport companies, poultry processors, rendering plants, and distributors.

The authors summarize the relationships of a specific focal company with other institutions in Table 9.2. The company is a poultry processor founded in 1971. It has 1000 employees and slaughters approximately 75,000 poultry/day.

Based on the Global Supply Chain Forum, the authors categorized the relationship between supply chain members in three types of business process links: managed, monitored, and not-managed. The focal company integrates

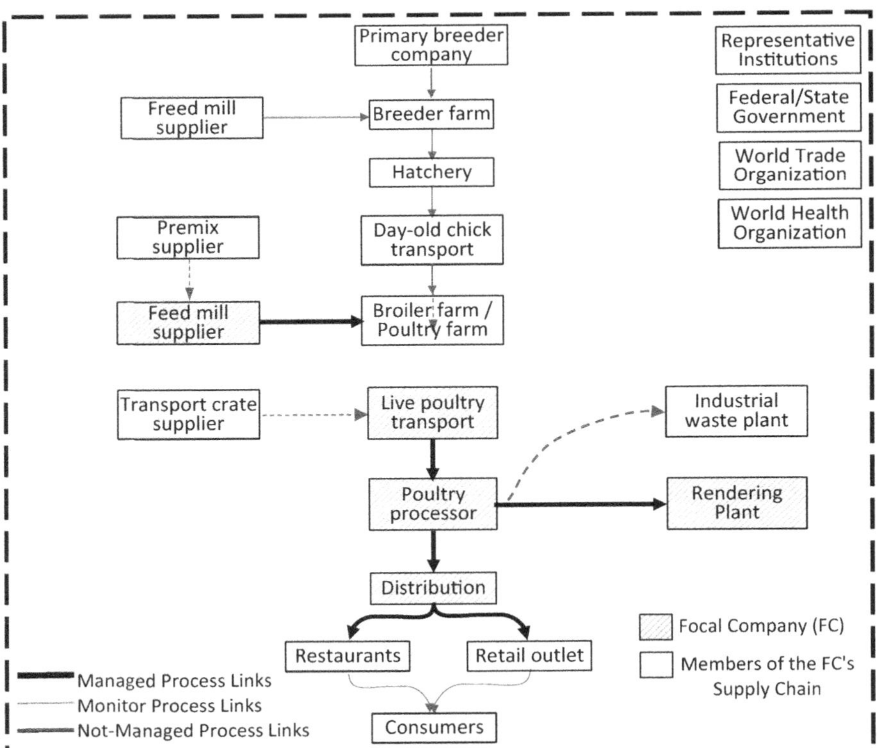

Fig. 9.1 Poultry supply chain and business process links (*Source* Pohlmann et al. [2020])

Table 9.2 Relationships between focal companies and other institutions

Institution	Business process	Focal firm
Federal Government	Animal transport guide, live poultry sanitation inspection (before and after slaughter) and products certification (official veterinarian within the poultry processor), feed mill and rendering plant sanitation inspection	Monitor
State Government	Sanitation inspection in the broiler farm	Monitor
WTO	Regulation of international marketing	Monitor
WHO	Criteria for food safety	Monitor
Primary breeder company	Breeding birds whose offspring are used as breeding birds. These include pedigree (elite/foundation), great-grandparent, and grandparent flocks	Not-managed
Feed mill supplier to Breeder farm	Supplies feed	Not-managed
Breeder farm	Produces eggs for hatching	Not-managed
Hatchery	Obtaining chicks from fertile eggs	Not-managed
DOC transport	Preparation for transportation	Not-managed
Premix supplier	Premixes and blends formulations	Monitor
Feed mill supplier to broiler farm	Mixing of soybean and corn bran with the premix	Managed
Broiler farm	Raising process until reaching the target market weight	Monitor
Poultry transport crate supplier	Poultry crate manufacturing	Monitor
Live poultry transport	Preparation for transportation	Managed
Poultry processor	DOC buying process, reception, slaughter, scalding, de-feathering, washing (evisceration and giblet processing), chilling, cutting, packing, freezing, storage and dispatch	Managed
Integrated rendering plant	Byproduct processing	Managed

(continued)

Table 9.2 (continued)

Institution	Business process	Focal firm
Industrial waste plant	Inorganic residues processing: plastic packaging waste and the PPE	Monitor
Distributor	Products distribution	Managed
Retail outlet	Traditional products sale	Not-managed
Consumers	Products consumption	Not-managed
Restaurants	Traditional products sale	Not-managed

Source Pohlmann et al. (2020)

the managed process links. The monitored process links are not as critical, but the focal company audits these processes managed between the other member companies. The focal company is not involved in the not-managed process links, or the links are not critical enough to warrant the use of resources for monitoring.

These complex relationships are intrinsically related to environmental issues and trade credit. For instance, according to Pohlmann et al. (2020), topics such as organic waste, water consumption, and energy consumption that are common among most supply chain members are not monitored by the focal company. The principal firm manages the energy consumption and industrial waste related to the connection from feed mill suppliers to broiler farms, the poultry processor, and the integrated rendering plant. The focal company also generates guarantees for the securitization of receivables by some supply chain members.

Society would benefit if firms commit to a rapid greening of supply chains, but that is unlikely. Organization inertia by itself is a formidable obstacle. Still, the case of the poultry industry illustrates the many avenues that focal companies can take to improve the social and environmental outcomes of their entire supply chains. There are often no real trade-offs between profitability and ecological effects; markets are merely stuck in low-value equilibria (Zeidan et al., 2020). Moreover, institutional pressures positively influence suppliers, like the case of the Brazilian automotive supply chain. Vanalle et al. (2017) investigated that industry and found that institutional pressure impacted companies to pursue green supply chain management practices. Specifically, they discovered that suppliers' advances in developing environmentally friendly goods and environmental partnerships with them, supplier's advances in developing environmentally-friendly packages, and the cost of environmentally friendly packaging are the central pressures influencing green supply chain management practices.

Trade credit policies can be used for good. We have seen in earlier sections that companies with market power can abuse their position by extracting most surplus from a supply chain. However, here we describe the possibilities that trade credit policies can directly or indirectly foster behavioral change in the members of the focal companies' supply chains. We turn to the commitment towards green standards now.

9.2 Standards as Commitment Devices

Later published in the Harvard Business Review (Whelan et al., 2017), the research project summarized in this section started as a commission by Carrefour and McDonald's, two of the largest global beef retailers (directly or indirectly). These companies made public commitments to reduce or eliminate deforestation from their supply chain. In 2010, Carrefour pledged to zero deforestation by 2020 as part of the Consumer Goods Forum (CGF). McDonald's states it is accelerating its efforts and remains committed to eliminating deforestation from its global supply chains by 2030.

These companies faced severe obstacles to keeping their promises. For instance, Carrefour found that geo-monitoring was more challenging than first thought. The main reason is that the Brazilian beef industry is fragmented, and hundreds of thousands of small ranches are in remote areas. At one point, the company was hiring satellites to scan the regions where their suppliers were located. Another issue is that grazing is common in Brazil; hence herds wander around large areas.

Because of the difficulties in pursuing their goals, both companies helped sponsor a project to improve the environmental outcomes of the supply chain members of the beef industry in Brazil. The project was led by the Center for Sustainable Business at NYU Stern. Partners included AT Kearney, who led the piloting of the methodology; retailers McDonald's and Carrefour; slaughterhouses JBS (the largest beef producer in Brazil) and Mafrig; Brazilian cattle ranchers, Antea Group, and the NGOs The Nature Conservancy, Instituto Centro de Vida (ICV) and Imaflora. The Betty and Gordon Moore Foundation provided partial funding for the research (Whelan et al., 2017).

The authors develop tools specific to the beef industry in Brazil that supply chain members can use to monetize the benefits of sustainability actions. More importantly, the research generated a publicly available valuation tool for ranchers, slaughterhouses, and retailers: https://www.stern.nyu.edu/sites/default/files/assets/documents/Methodology_20170526_v1_TNC_0.xlsx.

Figure 9.2 shows the public tool's cover and some of the inputs required

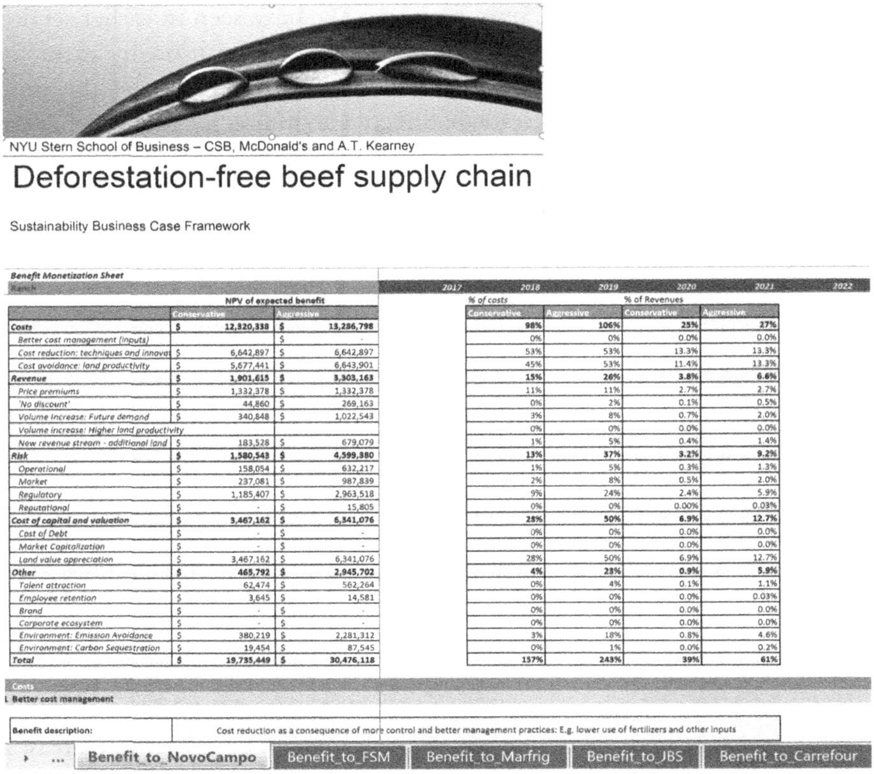

	NPV of expected benefit		% of costs		% of Revenues	
	Conservative	Aggressive	Conservative	Aggressive	Conservative	Aggressive
Costs	**$ 12,320,338**	**$ 13,286,798**	**98%**	**106%**	**25%**	**27%**
Better cost management (inputs)		$ -	0%	0%	0.0%	0.0%
Cost reduction: techniques and innovat	$ 6,642,897	$ 6,642,897	53%	53%	13.3%	13.3%
Cost avoidance: land productivity	$ 5,677,441	$ 6,643,901	45%	53%	11.4%	13.3%
Revenue	**$ 1,901,615**	**$ 3,303,163**	**15%**	**26%**	**3.8%**	**6.6%**
Price premiums	$ 1,332,378	$ 1,332,378	11%	11%	2.7%	2.7%
'No discount'	$ 44,860	$ 269,163	0%	2%	0.1%	0.5%
Volume increase: Future demand	$ 340,848	$ 1,022,543	3%	8%	0.7%	2.0%
Volume increase: Higher land productivity			0%	0%	0.0%	0.0%
New revenue stream - additional land	$ 183,528	$ 679,079	1%	5%	0.4%	1.4%
Risk	**$ 1,580,543**	**$ 4,599,380**	**13%**	**37%**	**3.2%**	**9.2%**
Operational	$ 158,054	$ 632,217	1%	5%	0.3%	1.3%
Market	$ 237,081	$ 987,839	2%	8%	0.5%	2.0%
Regulatory	$ 1,185,407	$ 2,963,518	9%	24%	2.4%	5.9%
Reputational	$ -	$ 15,805	0%	0%	0.00%	0.03%
Cost of capital and valuation	**$ 3,467,162**	**$ 6,341,076**	**28%**	**50%**	**6.9%**	**12.7%**
Cost of Debt	$ -	$ -	0%	0%	0.0%	0.0%
Market Capitalization	$ -	$ -	0%	0%	0.0%	0.0%
Land value appreciation	$ 3,467,162	$ 6,341,076	28%	50%	6.9%	12.7%
Other	**$ 465,792**	**$ 2,945,702**	**4%**	**23%**	**0.9%**	**5.9%**
Talent attraction	$ 62,474	$ 562,264	0%	4%	0.1%	1.1%
Employee retention	$ 3,645	$ 14,581	0%	0%	0.0%	0.03%
Brand	$ -	$ -	0%	0%	0.0%	0.0%
Corporate ecosystem	$ -	$ -	0%	0%	0.0%	0.0%
Environment: Emission Avoidance	$ 380,219	$ 2,281,312	3%	18%	0.8%	4.6%
Environment: Carbon Sequestration	$ 19,454	$ 87,545	0%	1%	0.0%	0.2%
Total	**$ 19,735,449**	**$ 30,476,118**	**157%**	**243%**	**39%**	**61%**

Fig. 9.2 Monetization tool – Center for Sustainable Business, NYU Stern (*Source* Whelan et al. [2017])

to monetize the effects of a rancher's sustainability practices.

An example comes from Novo Campo. As Whelan et al. (2017) describe: "cost-wise, the ranchers are: (1) reducing the costs of inputs such as fertilizers through better management; (2) reducing the cost per kg produced through better agricultural techniques such as pasture recuperation, water distribution, fencing and rotation of pasture; and (3) eliminating the need to lease additional land for production through sustainable intensification (more cattle per hectare). For example, the total cost per head produced in Novo Campo was 39% lower than on conventional ranches: $283 per head versus $460.

These changes led to significant gains for ranchers, who experienced an increase in productivity of 2.3 × per kg of beef per hectare. Profitability was up by 6.8x. GHG emissions were reduced up to 20%. Morale also improved, as ranchers saw these improvements in quality and productivity as a source of pride, stability, and competitive advantage."

The authors find that deforestation-free commitments reduce risk, and sustainable agriculture practices create financial opportunities for all value chain actors. They also conclude that it seems investments in deforestation-free traceability and other legal requirements can be paid for with the economic gains from adopting sustainable agriculture practices. Finally, Whelan et al. (2017) argue that the methodology can be adapted for any industry or value chain by (1) analyzing the drivers of improved performance (using the mediating factors in our model); (2) identifying key benefits; and (3) quantifying the benefits in financial terms.

Regarding the behavior of the focal companies in the supply chains, both McDonalds and Carrefour reduced the number of suppliers significantly to achieve their deforestation pledges. There was an extensive impact on fresh, frozen, processed meat, retailers, and warehouses suppliers. Carrefour managed to have 100% of Brazilian beef suppliers geo-monitored by 2020, complying with the country's forestry policy. Both companies have more ambitious policies to combat deforestation by 2025 and 2030.

We now turn to formal studies on the relationship between corporate best practices and trade credit.

9.3 Trade Credit and Climate Change

There are few empirical studies about the relationship between trade credit and climate change, but their results align with the framework developed in previous sections. There are two primary strands of the scientific literature that examine the relationship between trade credit and non-financial performance. The first looks at how climate and non-economic risks affect firms' demand and supply for trade credit. The second studies the companies' response regarding non-economic investments such as CSR. Does spending on climate change mitigation and other socially responsible investments help firms access trade credit?

Islam and Wheatley (2021) is an instance of the former. They examine the association between climate risk and trade credit. Their central hypothesis is that firms exposed to climate risk-driven liquidity shocks prefer to use less trade credit. They use the Global Climat Risk Index of 86 countries, concluding that firms in countries characterized by severe weather events prefer to use less trade credit. In addition, there is a negative association between trade credit and climate risk that is more pronounced for firms with more volatile cash flow and less collateral.

The study by Zhang et al. (2020) exemplifies the latter. They investigate whether suppliers value customer firms' socially responsible activities by examining the relationship between corporate social responsibility (CSR) and firms' access to trade credit. Firms with better social performance should be more likely to receive trade credit because suppliers view customers' CSR activities as a signal of trustworthiness and capacity to meet financial obligations. Interestingly, they describe other channels: (a) trade credit opens the possibility for suppliers to secure a share of their customers' future business opportunities, which are expected to be higher for socially responsible firms, and (b) the risk associated with the diffusion of adverse shocks through the supply chain due to trade credit is lower for socially responsible firms, making them more attractive partners for suppliers. Their results indicate that socially responsible customers receive more trade credit from suppliers.

Shou et al. (2020) complement these results with a sample of Chinese firms. They look at small and medium-sized manufacturing companies with a selection of 1020 listed firms. Instead of a simple connection, the authors posit a non-linear relationship between CSR and trade credit. Figure 9.3 and Fig. 9.4 summarize the authors' framework and main results.

The non-linear relationship between CSR and trade credit emerges from signaling theory. The negative signal is due to CSR performance signaling that the firm has a large pool of financial resources, and their supply chain members behave as if the company has sufficient cash flows and hence less need for trade credit. The positive signal is more straightforward: better CSR performance enhances a firm's reputation, and more trustworthy organizations are more likely to get access to trade credit from their partners. In a study that also uses data for Chinese companies, Nguyen and Nguyen (2022) corroborate this non-linear relationship. Their results confirm their hypotheses.

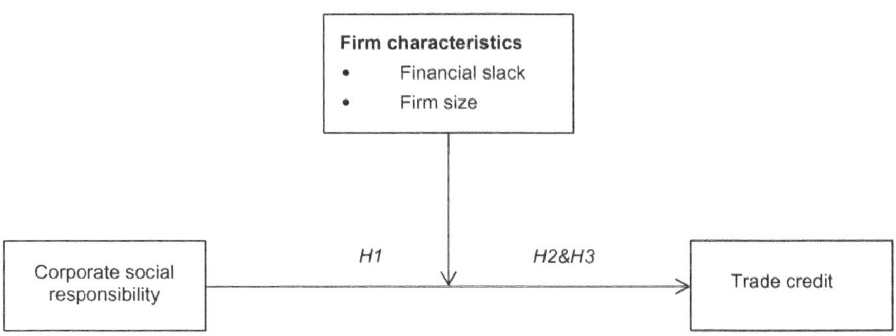

Fig. 9.3 The antecedents of the conceptual model of Shou et al. (2020) (*Source* Shou et al. [2020])

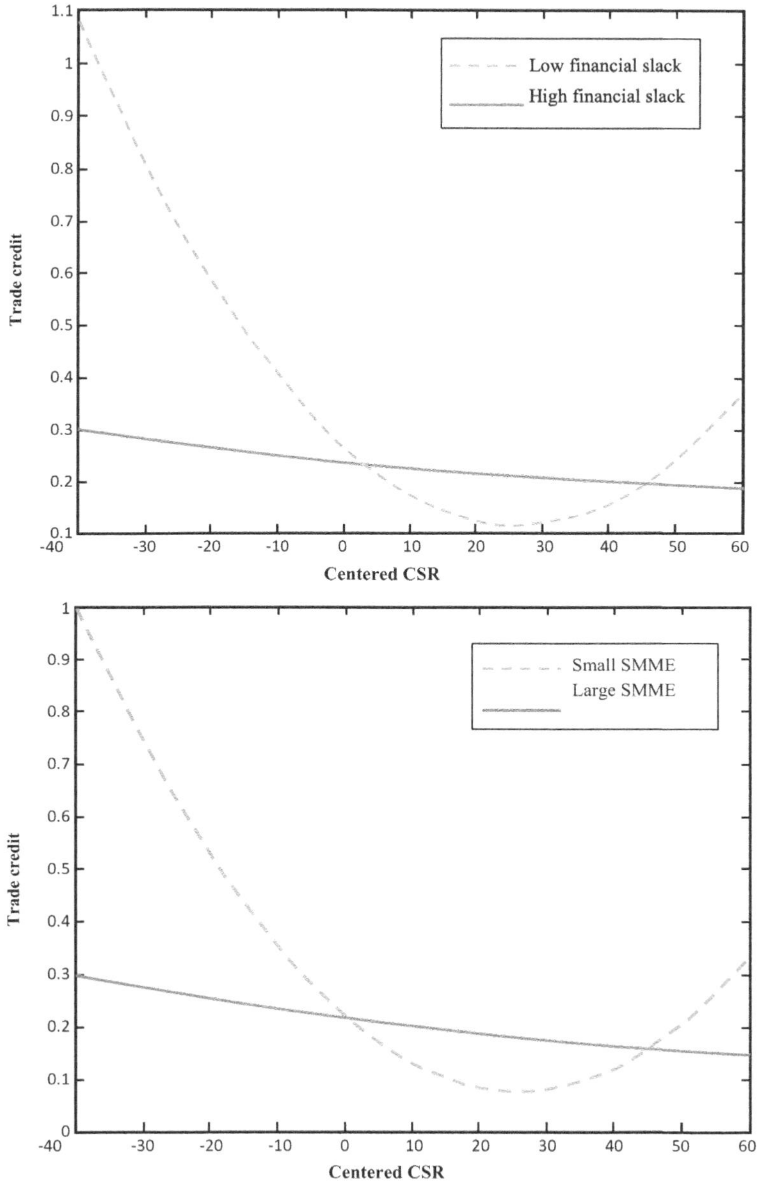

Fig. 9.4 Two dimensions of the non-linear relationship between CSR and trade credit (*Source* Shou et al. [2020])

9.4 Low-Value Equilibrium in Supply Chains

Zeidan et al. (2020) expand on Whelan et al. (2017) by showing under which conditions supply chain coordination can improve environmental outcomes while making companies more profitable. The main result from their work is to explain the emergence of low-value equilibrium that slow down the greening of supply chains.

A low-value equilibrium is a suboptimal result of a technology choice—in this case, sustainability actions—by companies in the supply chain. A stable competitive market equilibrium maximizes all firms' profits in a supply chain but falls short of maximizing the social welfare function of environmental sustainability. Low-value equilibrium relates to the part of the production system for which technologies for cleaner production exist and are economically feasible but are still underutilized. The intuition behind the concept is simple: markets may be caught in a competitive equilibrium that maximizes a narrowly defined definition of economic and social welfare, but not a more comprehensive social welfare function that perpends environmental sustainability. Thus, the concept of low-equilibrium allows us to investigate the mechanisms by which we should move from a purely economic market equilibrium to a more sustainable future; in this scenario, the competitive market equilibrium would not be Pareto optimal. Companies would increase their profit while improving environmental outcomes, or to put it simply, cleaner production would come at a profit. Such a win–win scenario would be in line with calls for sustainable production. Companies can increase their profits and reduce GHG emissions (or improve animal welfare and reach other sustainable environmental goals) to a degree, ascribing to the business scenario of sustainability or the eco-imperative.

We know that for an n-player game, $G = \{A1, \ldots, An; \pi 1, \ldots \pi n\}$ of the chosen technology space $A1, \ldots, An$ and related profits $\pi 1, \ldots \pi n$, there is always a Nash equilibrium (in mixed strategies). The strategies $A * 1, \ldots A * n$ are at a Nash equilibrium if, for each player i, $A * i$ is at least tied for player i"s best response to the other players' strategies (Gibbons, 1997). Nevertheless, such Nash equilibrium might not maximize social welfare, including environmental sustainability $w1, \ldots wn$ related to the choice of technology. This static version of a technology selection guarantees a unique equilibrium; however, nothing relates profits π to environmental sustainability. To address this, we include a Shapley value (Shapley, 1953), specifying that the differences in marginal benefits and costs for green investments contribute to the low-value equilibrium of the Brazilian beef industry.

The surplus value (θ) is the source of the Shapley value distributed throughout the supply chain. The innovation lies in relating this surplus-value to the cost of creating it, complementing models such as that of Dai et al. (2017), and creating a bridge between green supply chain coordination literature and companies' praxis.

If we assume a cost (C) for the creation of surplus value (sv), separable in firm (c_i) and part ρ of industry cost (C_j), and $\vartheta_i(\pi)$ represents the Shapley value of firm i, then, the surplus value for firm i is the discount cash-flow at the cost of capital (k). This formula is as follows:

$$\theta = \sum_{i=0} \frac{(\vartheta(\pi)_t - c_{it} - \rho C_{jt})}{(1+k)^t}$$

Sustainable investments happen whenever E(θ) > 0. However, there is a catch: if there is asymmetric information regarding other companies incurring (C_j), the profit function of firm i is:

$$\begin{cases} \sum_{i=0} \frac{(\vartheta(\pi)_t - c_{it} - \rho C_{jt})}{(1+k)^t} \text{if enough companies incur in } C_j \text{, and} \\ -(c_i + pC_j)\text{otherwise} \end{cases}$$

The equation above illustrates the coordination failure of green investments. Companies benefit from sustainable investments only if there is coordination, meaning that most companies in the supply chain commit to green investments. In this framework, this commitment is simultaneous, but it does not need to be. If we relax simultaneity, companies can observe obligations by other companies, enhancing the probability that the surplus-value θ is going to be created.

Even though the Shapley value is challenging to compute, this formal definition allows us to establish important insights to consider. Sustainability-related investments depend on the entire supply chain rather than any one firm.

Uncertainty about marginal benefits may impede green investment, even when companies are willing to invest, with such expenditures potentially increasing the aggregate output-reducing negative externalities. The concept of the Shapley value—which incorporates marginal contributions and benefits into coordinated supply chain efforts for improving environmental outcomes—can describe the efficiency, symmetry, and monotonicity of green investments.

If private and social marginal costs differ, pure competitive markets fail to yield socially efficient outcomes. In most markets, either regulation or private coordination mechanisms are necessary to combine competitive incentives with social benefits. Therefore, it is essential to highlight how the specific appropriation of benefits related to green investments keeps companies from pursuing such investments fully, if at all.

These insights complement Albert (2019), Chen et al. (2020), and Hestad et al. (2020), especially showing that transformations towards more sustainable production cannot necessarily be achieved through existing management rationales and practices. They require changes in supply-chain behavior.

Sustainability actions may bring value to supply chains through tangible and intangible benefits. Benefits include access to trade credit, greater customer loyalty, better employee relations, improved innovation, better media coverage, higher operational efficiency, better risk management, improved sales and marketing, improved supplier relations, and more value-added stakeholder engagement (Ortiz-de-Mandojana & Bansal, 2016).

Some surplus-value may come from higher prices for sustainable products than common goods and services (Lubin & Esty, 2010). Greener supply chain investments may also mediate factors that would make it more beneficial to society than altogether blocklisting noncompliant suppliers (Wilhelm et al., 2016).

The pressure on the interviewed companies for sustainable actions must come from somewhere. Ayuso et al. (2013) show that large businesses are the most demanding in the requirements imposed on their suppliers, which follows naturally from a centralized supply chain, where the supply chain leader (coordinator) is usually the most prominent company. Similarly, larger and listed companies have been shown to invest more in sustainability (Martínez-Ferrero & Frías-Aceituno, 2015).

There are, of course, challenges that need to be overcome for a strategic-partnership approach toward supply chain management, a practice that moves away from the commodity approach toward sourcing resources. First-tier suppliers follow the leading firms in supply chains and act as a bridge between the buying company and upstream suppliers in disseminating sustainability standards along multi-tier supply chains (Wilhelm et al., 2016). The empirical results for the case study in Zeidan et al. (2020) point toward coordination failures that result in low-value equilibrium supply chains, even though the potential financial benefits for all industry stakeholders may be largely positive. Such failures cannot quickly be resolved, although we know that revenue-sharing contracts can Pareto-dominate buyback contracts under financial constraints (Kouvelis & Zhao, 2016). In the specific case of the beef industry in Brazil, no formal contracting exists, and stakeholders indicate that industry associations or other non-firm stakeholders may act as coordination hubs.

The case study of their work is about the beef industry in Brazil. The coordination problem in that industry, in which benefits (if they exist) are unevenly distributed across complex commodity supply chains (Ford & Despeisse, 2016), may be overcome by public and private institutions. For example, NGOs may play a significant role, acting as focal points to make costs and benefits transparent to all supply chain participants. Industry-based associations could also take action, although it is not easy to predict whether they would prioritize green investment over sources of profits from lobbying, expanding capacity, and marketing. One such example is organizations within the Brazilian beef supply chain successfully promoting Angus cattle and creating price premia. There are many cattle breeds in Brazil, such as Brahman, Nelore, Indubrasil, and Sindi. Yet, slaughterhouses and retailers only pay a premium for certified Angus cattle. The Brazilian Association of Angus developed a national certification procedure in 2003 and advertised it throughout the country. It also coordinated better access to trade credit terms for small companies. Due to this campaign, the price differential between Angus and other cattle is approximately 7.5%. The certification process relies on the coordination between producers, the association, and slaughterhouses. One of the reasons for the certification's success has been the association that functioned as the foremost institution and coordinated supply chain efforts. In this sense, the process works, as Wilhelm (2011) argued, especially competition management through horizontal supply chain relations, the emergence of informal supplier learning groups, and the social cohesion among an inner group of suppliers within the network.

9.5 Trade Credit, the Covid Pandemic, and Company Survival

There are numerous effects of the covid pandemic on businesses, from a sudden stop in sales for lockdown places to surges in delinquency from corporate customers. The relationship between the covid pandemic and trade credit may seem like a poor fit on a chapter about greening supply chains, but that is not necessarily the case.

The greening of supply chains is not only a moral imperative; it also makes sense from a risk management perspective. And, like the covid pandemic, there may be surprising shocks to businesses' operations. The covid pandemic was the first time in living memory that economies voluntarily locked down, even if not entirely.

One of the main consequences of the covid pandemic was a reshuffle of trade credit relationships. In previous chapters, we have seen that trade credit has one primary advantage over bank credit concerning supply chain efficiency: partners can better observe other supply chain members than financial institutions. But the covid pandemic has brought forward new sources of risk. Especially at the beginning of the pandemic, there was significant uncertainty about which companies would be able to survive the lockdowns.

Srivastava and Gopalakrishnan (2021) use a cross-country quarterly firm-level dataset to study the impact of the COVID-19 pandemic on the trade credit channel of firms. They find that firms with poor credit quality obtain lower amounts of trade credit from their supplier firms during the quarters following the COVID-19 outbreak. In contrast to the credit substitution documented between formal financial institutions and suppliers, less creditworthy firms are credit rationed by their suppliers during a credit market crisis. Furthermore, they document that firms with better growth prospects and firms with better stakeholder relationships are able to obtain trade credit in the post-pandemic period, despite their poor creditworthiness.

As the authors write: "our empirical analysis supports the view that supplier financing is conditional on the product market conditions and is not always a great substitute for bank credit."

Environmental risks may not be entirely dissimilar to the covid outbreak. Of course, many effects of climate change are slow-burning. However, extreme climate events should become more common, disrupting production and consumption in similar ways to the pandemic.

Trade credit is an important vehicle to supply chain efficiency. Environmental risks can limit that transmission mechanism, though. The greening of supply chains is more than a moral imperative; it also makes business sense.

References

Albert, M. (2019). Sustainable frugal innovation—The connection between frugal innovation and sustainability. *Journal of Cleaner Production, 237*, 117747.

Ayuso, S., Roca, M., & Colomé, R. (2013). SMEs as "transmitters" of CSR requirements in the supply chain. *Supply Chain Management: An International Journal, 18*(5), 497–508.

Chen, Y., Ma, J., Miao, C., & Ruan, X. (2020). Occurrence and environmental impact of industrial agglomeration on regional soil heavy metalloid accumulation: A case study of the Zhengzhou Economic and Technological Development Zone (ZETZ), China. *Journal of Cleaner Production, 245*, 118676.

Dai, R., Zhang, J., & Tang, W. (2017). Cartelization or cost-sharing? Comparison of cooperation modes in a green supply chain. *Journal of Cleaner Production, 156*, 159–173.

Ford, S., & Despeisse, M. (2016). Additive manufacturing and sustainability: An exploratory study of the advantages and challenges. *Journal of Cleaner Production, 137*, 1573–1587.

Henao, R., & Sarache, W. (2022). Sustainable performance in manufacturing operations: The cumulative approach vs. trade-offs approach. *International Journal of Production Economics*, 244, 108385.

Hestad, D., Tàbara, J. D., & Thornton, T. F. (2020). Transcending unsustainable dichotomies in management: Lessons from sustainability-oriented hybrid organisations in Barcelona. *Journal of Cleaner Production, 244*, 118766.

Inman, R. A., & Green, K. W. (2018). Lean and green combine to impact environmental and operational performance. *International Journal of Production Research, 56*(14), 4802–4818.

Islam, M. N., & Wheatley, C. M. (2021). Impact of climate risk on firms' use of trade credit: International evidence. *The International Trade Journal, 35*(1), 40–59.

Kouvelis, P., & Zhao, W. (2016). Supply chain contract design under financial constraints and bankruptcy costs. *Management Science, 62*(8), 2341–2357.

Lartey, T., Yirenkyi, D. O., Adomako, S., Danso, A., Amankwah-Amoah, J., & Alam, A. (2020). Going green, going clean: Lean-green sustainability strategy and firm growth. *Business Strategy and the Environment, 29*(1), 118–139.

Lubin, D. A., & Esty, D. C. (2010). The sustainability imperative. *Harvard Business Review, 88*(5), 42–50.

Martínez-Ferrero, J., & Frias-Aceituno, J. V. (2015). Relationship between sustainable development and financial performance: International empirical research. *Business Strategy and the Environment, 24*(1), 20–39.

Nguyen, L., & Nguyen, K. (2022). Corporate social responsibility, trade credit provision and doubtful accounts receivable: The case in China. *Social Responsibility Journal*, forthcoming.

Ortiz-de-Mandojana, N., & Bansal, P. (2016). The long-term benefits of organizational resilience through sustainable business practices. *Strategic Management Journal, 37*(8), 1615–1631.

Plambeck, E. L. (2012). Reducing greenhouse gas emissions through operations and supply chain management. *Energy Economics, 34*, S64–S74.

Pohlmann, C. R., Scavarda, A. J., Alves, M. B., & Korzenowski, A. L. (2020). The role of the focal company in sustainable development goals: A Brazilian food poultry supply chain case study. *Journal of Cleaner Production, 245*, 118798.

Shou, Y., Shao, J., Wang, W., & Lai, K. H. (2020). The impact of corporate social responsibility on trade credit: Evidence from Chinese small and medium-sized manufacturing enterprises. *International Journal of Production Economics, 230*, 107809.

Singh, R. K., Kumar Mangla, S., Bhatia, M. S., & Luthra, S. (2021). Integration of green and lean practices for sustainable business management. Business Strategy and the Environment.

Srivastava, J., & Gopalakrishnan, B. (2021). In-kind financing during a pandemic: Trade credit and COVID-19, MPRA Paper No. 111433, posted 12 January 2022, https://mpra.ub.uni-muenchen.de/111433/8/MPRA_paper_110965.pdf.

Vanalle, R. M., Ganga, G. M. D., Godinho Filho, M., & Lucato, W. C. (2017). Green supply chain management: An investigation of pressures, practices, and performance within the Brazilian automotive supply chain. *Journal of Cleaner Production, 151*, 250–259.

Whelan, T., Zappa, B., Zeidan, R., & Fishbein, G. (2017). How to quantify sustainability's impact on your bottom line. *Harvard Business Review*, 23.

Wilhelm, M. M. (2011). Managing coopetition through horizontal supply chain relations: Linking dyadic and network levels of analysis. *Journal of Operations Management, 29*(7–8), 663–676.

Wilhelm, M., Blome, C., Wieck, E., & Xiao, C. Y. (2016). Implementing sustainability in multi-tier supply chains: Strategies and contingencies in managing sub-suppliers. *International Journal of Production Economics, 182*, 196–212.

Xu, H., Pham, T. H., & Dao, M. (2020). Annual report readability and trade credit. Review of Accounting and Finance.

Zeidan, R., Van Holt, T., & Whelan, T. (2020). Existence inductive theory building to study coordination failures in sustainable beef production. *Journal of Cleaner Production, 267*, 122137.

Zhang, Y., Lara, J. M. G., & Tribó, J. A. (2020). Unpacking the black box of trade credit to socially responsible customers. *Journal of Banking & Finance, 119*, 105908.

10

Formal Models on Trade Credit

10.1 Trade Credit Contracts

This section summarizes Fabbri and Menichini (2010) and Yang and Birge (2018). Both models are concerned with the design of trade credit contracts and how risk is shared by the supply chain and the banks that offer trade credit.

In Fabbri and Menichini's (2010) model, firms' suppliers can better extract value from the liquidation of assets in default and have an information advantage over other creditors.

As the authors write, the model allows them to derive six predictions on trade credit use: (1) Financially unconstrained firms (with unused bank credit lines) take trade credit to exploit the supplier's liquidation advantage; (2) If inputs purchased on account are sufficiently liquid, the reliance on trade credit does not depend on credit rationing; (3) Firms buying goods make more purchases on account than those buying services, while suppliers of services offer more trade credit than those of standardized goods; (4) Suppliers lend inputs to their customers but not cash; (5) Greater reliance on trade credit is associated with more intensive use of tangible inputs; (6) Better creditor protection decreases both the use of trade credit and input tangibility.

Like the in-kind finance model in Sect. 3.9, the present starts with a risk-neutral entrepreneur with an investment project. Her firm's production uses a tangible and an intangible input, which can be interpreted as raw material or physical capital for the former and as skilled labor for the latter. The firm is a price-taker in both the input and output markets.

R. Zeidan, *The General Model of Working Capital Management*,
https://doi.org/10.1007/978-981-19-3334-9_10

The purchase of inputs is observed only by their suppliers. Outsiders cannot observe the amount invested but can verify how much is produced. The company produces many units with probability p, or few units.

When demand is high, the increasing and strictly concave production function is $f^H(I_t,I_{nt})$, where I_t and I_{nt} are the amount of tangible and intangible inputs purchased, respectively. When demand is low, the company produces nothing.

As the authors note: "To carry out the project, the entrepreneur uses observable internal wealth (A) as well as external funding from competitive banks (L_B) or suppliers (L_S) or both. Banks and suppliers play different roles. Banks lend cash. The supplier of intangibles provides the input, which is fully paid for in cash. The supplier of tangibles sells the input but can also act as a financier, lending both inputs and cash."

As in the in-kind model, because the entrepreneur can divert funds borrowed from banks, this leads to moral hazard. Suppliers don't face the same issue, as they can observe inputs invested. Unlike the in-kind model, diversion is related to just tangible inputs, as it is impossible to extract resources from investments in the intangible inputs.

The sequence of events is summarized in Fig. 10.1.

Banks and suppliers make contract offers that specify loan size, repayment obligations, collateral, and the number of inputs purchased. The entrepreneur chooses among contract offers; the investment or diversion decisions are taken, uncertainty resolves, and repayments are made.

Figure 10.1 summarizes the sequence of events. Here, we note that the sequence in Yang and Birge (2018) differs by the entrepreneur deciding if she will accept the supplier offer and only in the middle of the production process may decide to take out a bank loan (Fig. 10.2). Their model focuses mainly on supplier-customer relationships, as there is no direct competition between suppliers and banks for lending to the entrepreneur.

The main goal is to determine the optimal trade credit contract. Firms maximize profits, which can be split into two components: the return from

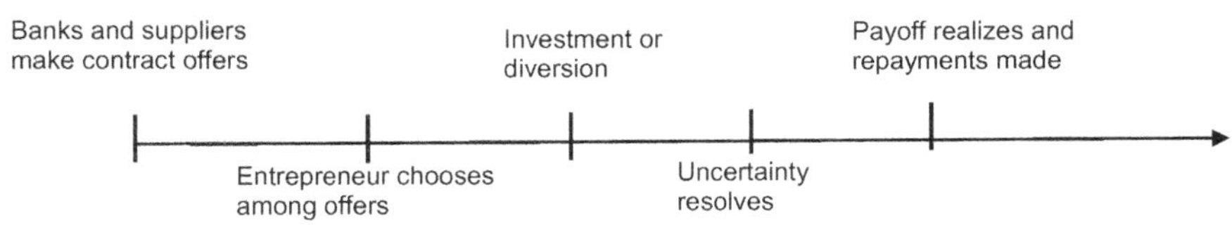

Fig. 10.1 Sequence of events (Fabbri & Menichini, 2010)

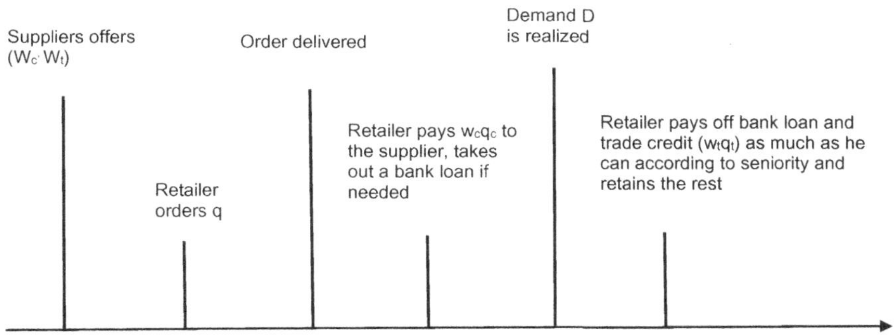

Fig. 10.2 Sequence of events (Yang & Birge, 2018)

production (EP) and diversion (D). The expected return from production is:

$$EP = p\left[f^H(I_t, I_{nt}) - R_B^H - R_S^H\right] + (1-p)\left[f^L(I_t, I_{nt}) - R_B^L - R_S^L\right]$$

Because the output is zero in the bad state, limited liability implies that the repayments to banks and suppliers in this state are both zero. The return from diversion is:

$$D = \phi\{\beta_t(q_t - I_t) + [A + L_B + L_S - q_t]\}$$

The term in round brackets denotes the return from tangible input diversion, net of the amount invested in production. The square brackets show the residual cash diversion return (the amount of cash not spent on the input purchase). An opportunistic entrepreneur purchases only tangibles and never intangibles for diversion. In the model, partial diversion is never optimal.

One of the main results of the model is a lower bound on trade credit equal to the collateral value of the inputs pledged to the supplier:

$$L_S \geq (1-\gamma)\frac{\beta_S}{r_S} I_t$$

As the authors put it: "the supplier's finance is profitable ($L_S > 0$) only if his opportunity cost of funds r_S, discounted for the saving in repayment obtained by pledging the collateral to the supplier instead of to the bank, is lower than the opportunity cost of funds of the bank r_B. In equilibrium, the right to repossess and liquidate the collateral goes to the supplier".

The main consequence of this equilibrium is that suppliers are more willing to provide credit than banks because suppliers are less vulnerable to diversion; the supplier's informational advantage reduces moral hazard.

The primary implication of the model is to divide trade credit supply in the liquidation and incentive motives. The authors claim that their theory reconciles an apparent conflict between the theoretical literature and the empirical evidence. On the one hand, in arguing that trade credit mitigates bank credit rationing, the academic literature (Biais & Gollier, 1997; Burkart & Ellingsen, 2004) established a positive relationship between trade credit and borrowing constraints. On the other hand, some empirical results point out that reliance on trade credit is practically unaffected by the degree of credit rationing (Marotta, 2005; Petersen & Rajan, 1997).

The motivation for trade credit demand (incentive or liquidation) affects the properties of the financial contract between the entrepreneur and the financiers. Thus, the supplier gets an increasing repayment contract, with an extra return for any unit of trade credit taken above the collateral value. The bank always designs a contract with repayment increasing in cash flows, as the bank gets a positive return only in the good state.

The final propositions of the model are as follows:

- Financially unconstrained firms take trade credit to exploit their suppliers' liquidation advantage.
- Firms buying services make more purchases because of tighter credit constraints, while firms buying goods (both standardized and differentiated) finance the same share of their purchases independently of credit rationing.
- Firms buying goods (both standardized and differentiated) make more purchases than firms buying services.
- Suppliers of services offer more trade credit than suppliers of standardized goods.
- Credit-constrained firms have higher trade credit intensity and use technologies more intensive in tangible assets than unconstrained ones.
- When located in countries with weaker creditor protection, credit-constrained firms have higher trade credit intensity and a technological bias toward tangibles. Unconstrained firms have the same trade-credit intensity and input tangibility across countries with different degrees of creditor protection.
- The liquidation motive is more critical when the good is durable when it has not been transformed into finished products and when bankruptcy codes protect contractual rights in general and supplier debt claims in particular.

The model by Yang and Birge (2018) complements these propositions by including the conditions by which firms will use trade credit as risk-sharing and those in which a company may extract surplus value from another. In their model, a company may extract value by offering trade credit at a higher cost if the other firm has low cash levels.

Regarding the supply contracts, suppliers can offer two prices: a unit cash price, paid by the buyer (the retailer) on delivery, and a unit credit price, paid after demand is realized. This contract allows the authors to capture the two types of trade credit terms most commonly used in practice: net terms if the cash price equals the credit price and two-part terms if not.

The retailer decides its order in response to the contract and how to finance inventory. As the authors note: "the supplier's payoff depends on the buyer's realized demand through the (partial) contingency of the buyer's trade credit payment to the supplier. Such a contingency effectively lowers the buyer's marginal cost, allowing the buyer to stock at a higher inventory level and, hence, boosts sales for the supplier."

The retailer must decide the total order quantity and how to allocate q between the units financed via cash and bank loans. Notably, if the retailer borrows from banks to immediately pay the supplier, it can enjoy an early payment discount.

One of the central results is a pecking order of inventory financing. The retailer's first option is to use its cash reserves. However, as its cash position decreases, the retailer borrows from the banks to take advantage of the early payment discount and, finally, borrows from suppliers when bank credit is exhausted.

Cash is preferred to bank credit because it brings about distress costs (more about it in Sect. 6.3). Bank credit is chosen to trade credit as long as the marginal discount factor of the bank loan exceeds the early-payment discount. After that, the retailer finances inventory using credit extended by its suppliers.

Another significant result is the emergence of risk-sharing, summarized in the following proposition: "under the optimal trade credit contract, the retailer orders strictly more than under the optimal price-only contract with only a bank loan."

Comparing price-only contracts is essential because (for instance, Lariviere & Porteus, 2001) price-only agreements are insufficient to ensure supply-chains coordination.

Risk-sharing emerges because the repayment partly depends on the realized demand, which means that the supplier essentially bears part of the downside.

Under price-only contracts, retailers carry this risk alone. A relevant implication from their model is that "under the optimal trade credit contract, when the retailer uses external sources to finance inventory, trade credit is always used."

When the cash level is not too low, moderate risk-sharing generates a win–win situation for the supply chain members. Interestingly, "the retailer may not necessarily benefit when the supplier becomes more efficient at collecting defaulted trade credit (lower α_t) as smaller α_t not only lowers deadweight loss but also enables the supplier to extract profit from the retailer more efficiently."

Figure 10.3 illustrates the impact of the optimal trade credit contract on the two supply chain members and the efficiency of the supply chain.

Finally, if cash levels are, trade credit hurts the retailer, as the supplier can better extract surplus. In addition, unlike the supplier, the retailer may

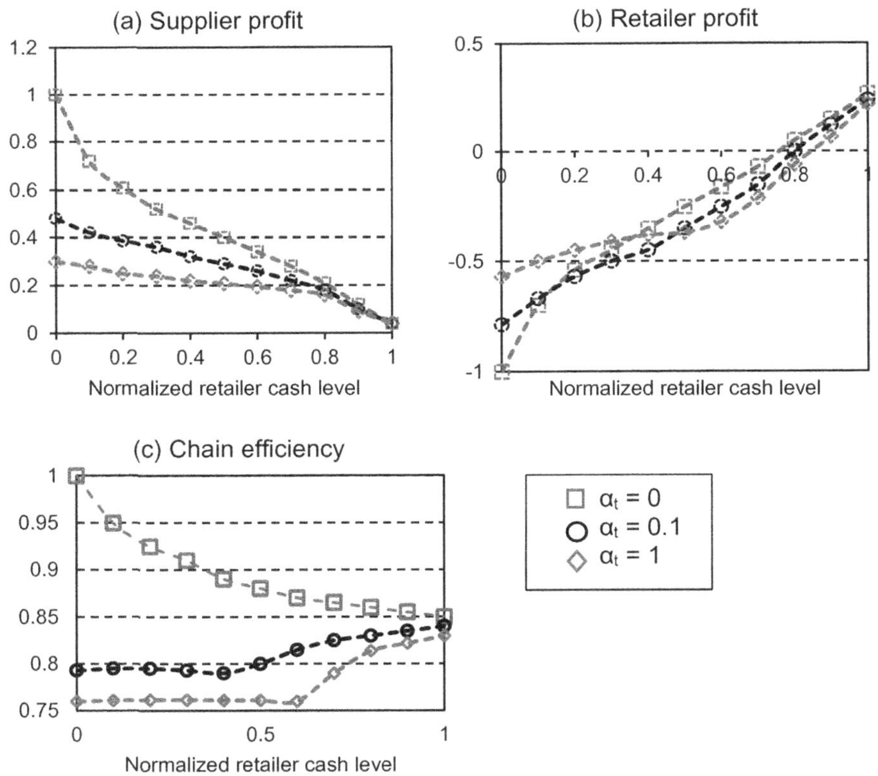

Fig. 10.3 Supply chain performance under the optional trade credit contract

not necessarily benefit when the supplier becomes more efficient at collecting defaulted trade credit.

We can tie the propositions from Yang and Birge (2018) to the types of behavior investigated earlier in the book. The main lessons from the model come from the interplay between supply-chain members being anything but complex. Risk-sharing increases supply chain efficiency but depending on the bargaining power of companies other members may lose out. Trade credit can benefit the entire supply chain, but that is not a given. One company's optimal working capital management may trigger a credit crisis in other supply chain members. How can companies reduce free rider and moral hazard behavior? We turn to a case study about the subject next.

10.1.1 Trust and Supply-Chain Finance: How a Japanese Retailer Limits Moral Hazard

This case illustrates some of the propositions from Fabbri and Menichini (2010) and Yang and Birge (2018). In particular, the example below is about how supply-chain relationships may be built with the end goal of win–win situations, but not without failsafe against opportunistic behavior.

The main propositions from Fabbri and Menichini (2010) are built upon the idea that suppliers have an informational advantage over financial companies in extending trade credit.

The essential benefit of long-term business relationships is predictability. Companies know that inputs will arrive on time, that the goods' quality is acceptable, and that contractual terms are respected. More importantly, long-term suppliers and customers can provide credit under challenging circumstances while helping to keep competitors at bay.

There is no single avenue for managers to build long-term relationships. The road was long for entrepreneurs who wanted to bring a Japanese company's discount retail model to Latin America. But the original question remains: how can one trust their suppliers and customers?

The entrepreneurs were descendants of Japanese immigrants and owned retail stores in Peru. The business model they wanted to import was similar to the Dollar Store in the United States and 1 Euro Store in Europe. Unlike the deep discount retailers in the rest of the world, the Japanese retail chain offered better quality products for slightly higher prices. Most products would come from China, but the Japanese managers developed strong quality controls, inventory models, and demand projections to determine the ideal mix of products for specific neighborhoods. For the Peruvian entrepreneurs, bringing this model to their country meant bypassing the trial and error of developing all the moving pieces required for a business model with slim margins to thrive.

The Japanese managers were open to partnering with the Peruvian entrepreneurs, but there was one condition: every order would have to be prepaid for a long time. The East Asians argued that they were not interested in a short-term relationship. They were ready to extend long payment terms to their customers, but only if they came to trust them. That confidence would come from the sacrifices of their clients for the first few years of their business arrangement. Once the Peruvian managers showed a commitment to their partnership by agreeing to terms that were initially worse than they could get elsewhere, the Japanese chain would flip the script and extend payment terms to over 180 days after the merchandise reached Peruvian shores.

The South Americans accepted the deal. After eight years of pre-paying every shipment, the Japanese announced that they were ready for the second phase of their long-term relationship. Today, the managers of the Peruvian chain count on at least 180-days to pay for their imported goods and enjoy an excellent business relationship with their Japanese suppliers.

Of course, the arrangement between these parties is unusual. We rarely see a shift from pre-payment to over half a year payment terms. What was the reasoning for both parties to enter this type of relationship?

I interviewed the Peruvian interviews and worked with them on other projects. From their point of view, they believe that they would not have the ability to develop the business model of a retail chain that combines affordable and high-quality goods by themselves. Supply-chain management remains the purview of the Japanese retail chain. Even today, with over ten stores, the operations in Peru would not have enough scale for managers to negotiate low prices with all the suppliers of the Japanese chain. They also do not have to bear the transaction costs of dealing with multiple suppliers to get the goods into the country. More importantly, the trust built between organizations means that both companies can operate under the assumption that they can concentrate on market risks instead of counterparty risks. The managers from Peru have expressed confidence that their exclusivity agreement holds. Thus, they do not fear being blindsided by the Japanese firm supplying competitors.

The case highlights how companies in different cultures can build trust to increase trade credit. For instance, Fisman and Love (2003) show that private firms in higher social trust regions use more trade credit from suppliers, extend more trade credit to customers, and collect receivables and pay payables more quickly. These results are even more robust in areas with weak protection of property rights.

From the perspective of Japanese organizations, companies in South America present macroeconomic risks unrelated to the behavior of individual companies. Even if their clients are trustworthy, property rights in Peru are not as strong as in Japan, and social trust is also weaker. Social trust helps private firms overcome institutional difficulties in financing their activities (Wu et al., 2019). Strategies that require stringent short-term commitments, such as pre-payment of initial shipments with the promise of future benefits, reduce information asymmetry.

This type of arrangement is also consistent with other evidence by Fisman and Love (2003). The authors show that "industries with higher dependence on trade credit financing exhibit higher growth rates in countries with weaker financial institutions. Furthermore, consistent with barriers to trade credit access among young firms, most effects come from growth in preexisting firms' size."

Trade credit relationships can be win–win relationships. Companies with worse credit ratings but trustworthy can tap into the capital from larger companies in their supply chains. New companies can tap into the established relationships of perennial firms, and foreign firms can bypass the learning curve of local markets.

10.2 A Trade Credit Model with Asymmetric Competing Retailers

What happens when we make the business environment more complex? Trade credit emerges from strategic interactions. Companies usually have numerous business partners, some with hundreds of suppliers and millions of consumers.

Trade credit strategies must be generalized from models with few companies, though; models with thousands of agents are untractable. Frameworks that consider companies with different degrees of bargaining power can lead to interesting insights. In this subsection, we summarize Wu et al. (2019), who model a supply chain of a manufacturer selling to two asymmetric retailers engaged in inventory (order quantity) competition in the presence of demand uncertainty and an exogenously given retail price. That leads to a Stackelberg–Nash game solved by backward induction.

Each retailer's demand incorporates its primary demand and reallocated demand from its competitor. This asymmetry emerges from: (i) the weak retailer being capital-constrained and (ii) the bargaining power of the dominant retailer, implying it enjoys a lower wholesale price.

The main feature of the model is that the trade credit offered by the manufacturer to the weak, capital-constrained retailer can be used by the manufacturer as a strategic response to the bargaining power of its dominant retailer.

The authors aim to answer the following questions:

- How do operational decisions and performance change when the supply chain parameters change?
- What is the role of capital constraint under trade credit with inventory competition?
- Which credit will the various parties prefer when bank and trade credit with an endogenous wholesale price (TCW) are available?
- Which trade credit contract will the various parties prefer when both a TCW and a trade credit with an endogenous interest rate (TCR) are available?

Figure 10.4 illustrates the model structure.

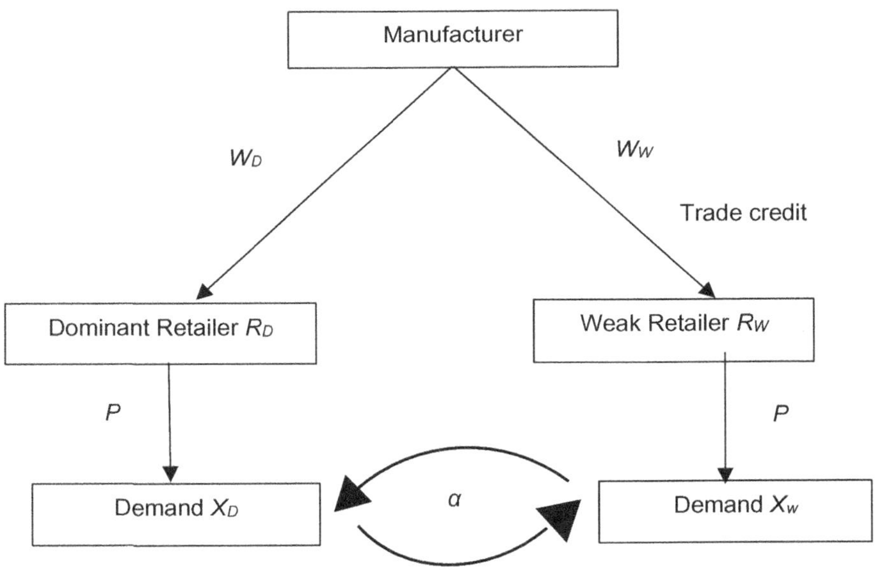

Fig. 10.4 Model structure with asymmetric retailers (*Source* Wu et al. [2019])

Assume a manufacturer and two competitive retailers R_i, in which ($i = \{D, W\}$). The manufacturer sells the same product to both retailers at wholesale prices w_i. Demand is uncertain, but both retailers sell the same fixed retail price p to the final consumers. Salvaged products have a value s per unit at the end of the sales season. Consumers have a preferred retailer—customers who prefer a retailer form the *primary demand* (X_i). If a retailer runs out of inventory, its unmet demand is reallocated to the other retailer; this is called *cross-demand*.

The primary demand follows a cumulative distribution function (CDF) $F_i(X_i)$, and a probability density function (PDF) $f_i(X_i)$, on $[0, +\infty)$. The total demand for each retailer is:

$$\overline{X}_i = X_i + \alpha\left(X_j - Q_j\right)^+$$

where $(a)^+ = \max(a, 0)$.

The weak retailer has a limited budget, B, for procurement. Due to its bargaining power, the manufacturer cannot influence the wholesale price offered to the dominant retailer, w_D. Another interpretation is that w_D is based on a long-term contract. In contrast, the manufacturer offers a take-it-or-leave-it wholesale price, w_W, to the weak retailer. Thus, the manufacturer has an incentive to provide trade credit to the weak retailer, allowing a higher wholesale price than in the absence of extended payment terms. Furthermore, the manufacturer can determine an interest rate charged on trade credit, enabling it to earn extra profit for the risk without breaking anti-price discrimination laws.

The sequence of events is as follows. First, the manufacturer offers a trade credit contract at w_W to the weak retailer and a warranty at price w_D to the dominant retailer; the former is a decision variable, and the latter is exogenously given. Second, both retailers order (Q_D; Q_W) simultaneously. The weak retailer pays the manufacturer as much of its $w_W Q_W$ wholesale cost as possible out of initial capital B and receives trade credit for the rest of the order. The dominant retailer pays in full. Third, demands are realized, and both retailers immediately receive total payments from end customers. Finally, the weak retailer repays the manufacturer the remainder owing.

The model assumes no private information, unique risk preferences, default first (strategic or otherwise), transaction costs, or taxes. The authors partition the retailers' demand into eight areas to determine the game's equilibrium. Four of these regions, Ω1,..., Ω4, correspond to low orders, and the remaining four, Ω5,..., Ω8 correspond to high realized demand. Figure 10.5 illustrates the demand state regions with capital constraints.

Table 10.1 describes these regions.

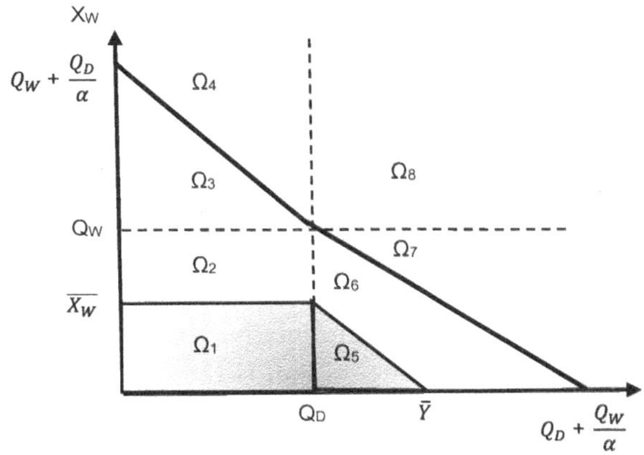

Fig. 10.5 Demands state regions with capital constraints (*Source* Wu et al. [2019])

Table 10.1 Demands state regions

Event	Definition	Demand Region
Ω_1	No reallocated demand with bankruptcy	$X_D < Q_D$, $X_W < \overline{X}_W$
Ω_2	No reallocated demand without bankruptcy	$X_D < Q_D$, $\overline{X}_W \le X_W < Q_W$
Ω_3	Reallocated demand to R_D with salvage	$X_D < Q_D$, $X_D + \alpha X_W < Q_D + \alpha Q_W$
Ω_4	Reallocated demand to R_D without salvage	$X_D < Q_D$, $X_D + \alpha X_W \ge Q_D + \alpha Q_W$
Ω_5	Reallocated demand to R_W with bankruptcy	$X_D \ge Q_D$, $X_W < Q_W$, $\alpha X_D + X_W \le Y$
Ω_6	Reallocated demand to R_W without	$X_D \ge Q_D$, $X_W < Q_W$, $Y < \alpha X_D + X_W \le \alpha Q_D + Q_W$
Ω_7	Reallocated demand to R_W without salvage	$X_D \ge Q_D$, $X_W < Q_W$, $\alpha X_D + X_W \ge \alpha Q_D + Q_W$
Ω_8	No reallocated demand without salvage	$X_D \ge Q_D$, $X_W \ge Q_W$

Source Wu et al. (2019)

Notably, in the case of Ω_1 to Ω_5, the weak retailer would go bankrupt. The primary bankruptcy threshold is

$$\overline{X}_W = \frac{(W_W - s)Q_W - B}{p - s}$$

Solving for the Nash Equilibrium of the retailers for given wholesale prices and demand substitution rates requires determining the weak retailer's bankruptcy probability (BP), the inventory substitution rate (ISR), and the budget threshold that makes trade credit helpful.

If there is no trade credit, the non-credit constrained firm orders just a little over the minimum amount, a prudent strategy that hurts its performance. Trade credit leads to the weak retailer ordering more and the strong retailer ordering less. Altogether, the supply chain's efficiency and inventory level increase; trade credit mitigates the strong retailer's bargaining power, and competition weakens the coordination role of trade credit (Kouvelis & Zhao, 2012). As Wu et al. (2019) note: "this mitigation partially motivates the manufacturer to offer trade credit to the weak retailer. Indeed, as documented in empirical work (Fabbri & Klapper, 2016), suppliers often offer trade credit to their small downstream buyers."

The supply chain equilibrium when the weak retailer doesn't have a sufficient budget, but there is no trade credit available is:

$$Q_W^* = \frac{B}{W_W^*}$$
$$G_W(W_W^*, Q_D^*, Q_W^*) = 0$$
$$G_D(W_W^*, Q_D^*, Q_W^*) = 0$$

As the authors note, the implication is that the retailers should build the loyalty of their customers and increase the fraction of customers switching to them from other channels.

There is nothing simple about the model, which is one of the reasons that no book can contain all possible knowledge associated with working capital management. Given the expected reaction functions for the retailers, the manufacturer sets the optimal wholesale price to the weak retailer under trade credit as the solution to:

$$W_W^* = \arg\max\left\{W_D Q_D^* + \mathrm{B} + \mathrm{E} + [REV_W] - c\left(Q_D^* + Q_W^*\right)\right\}$$

$$W_D \leq W_W \leq p$$

Thus, the wholesale price depends on the manufacturer's marginal revenue from the dominant retailer, the weak retailer's initial capital, and the substitution rate.

Finally, the authors extend their model to a market with n competing retailers, but we skip the presentation for brevity, as the results are qualitatively similar.

10.3 The Price of Reverse Factoring

This section summarizes Kouvelis and Xu (2021), who study a two-firm supply chain where a sizeable downstream retailer determines the wholesale price. Then, the SME supplier decides how much inventory to produce and stock at the retailer's location. That is a classic pull supply chain setting in which the supplier owns inventory before sales.

The authors argue that retailers are stepping up to help alleviate suppliers' cash flow stress due to rising financing costs for SME suppliers. Their model's interest stems from the description and drivers of reverse factoring (often referred to as a supply chain finance program). As they write, under this new scheme, the retailer essentially acts as an underwriter of the suppliers' accounts receivable risk and works with a third-party bank to ensure the lending of money to their suppliers with a relatively lower interest rate.

The authors motivate their study as similar to the practices of Jingdong, Procter & Gamble, and Walmart. They describe the example of Jingdong, China's second-largest e-commerce company. Starting in October 2013, Jingdong has cooperated with banks to streamline procedures for its suppliers to get loans. They write that Jingdong has the wholesale pricing power, and the suppliers decide how to produce to meet the drop shipping demands by the e-commerce site customers. A Jingdong supplier could ask the company to verify its accounts receivable and use this to borrow from a cooperating bank much more quickly and at a lower rate than usual.

Similarly, Procter & Gamble's decision in April 2013 to extend its payment terms for all suppliers by 30 days was complemented by the firm's reverse factoring program helping suppliers finance their increased working capital requirements. Walmart uses vendor-managed inventory programs with key suppliers, with suppliers assuming the responsibility of replenishing inventory as needed at prenegotiated wholesale price schedules. After the global financial crisis, Walmart's Supplier Alliance Program was offered to more than 1,000 apparel suppliers.

Regarding the model details the decision variables are the retailer's wholesale price w, the supplier's production quantity q, and the bank's/factor's interest rate r. Exogenous parameters are r_f, the risk-free interest rate; p, the retail price; c, the unit production cost for supplier at time 0; t_1, the supplier's production lead time; and t_2,

the retailer's payment term). The cash conversion cycle is thus $ccc = t_1 + t_2$.

The supplier is capital-constrained and must access bank financing to produce what is needed to support the retail demand. The supplier's effective unit production cost c_B consists of the original and financing costs. As in previous models, if the credit rating of either firm increases or the supplier's liquidity risk decreases, the equilibrium wholesale price decreases. In addition, the production quantity and both firms' profits increase. Supply-chain efficiency increases when firms are less constrained, as expected.

We concentrate on the part of the model with factoring. As the authors note, factoring is a short-term (post-shipment) financing scheme for suppliers. Factoring can be done either on a "non-recourse" or "recourse" basis. If the receivable is sold without recourse, then the supplier is not liable for any delinquency in the payment of the underlying receivable. The supplier is accountable for the uncollected amount if the receivable is sold with recourse.

The timing of events in the model is in Fig. 10.6.

Events follow a game-theoretical setup similar to a Stackelberg game, in which players make decisions sequentially.

One of the main results of the model is that there are feasibility conditions for recourse and non-recourse factoring. For the former, the condition is $C_s > C_F$; recourse factoring is only feasible for those suppliers with relatively high credit ratings and low liquidity risk, as in Fig. 10.7. The cash advance for the supplier is:

$$L_F = (1 - \rho_s) w S(q)$$

In non-recourse factoring, the feasibility condition is $C_s > C_N$. In addition, the supplier's cash advance is the expected value of the accounts receivable discounted by the interest rate:

$$L_N = e^{-\eta_r t_2}(1 - \rho_r) w S(q)$$

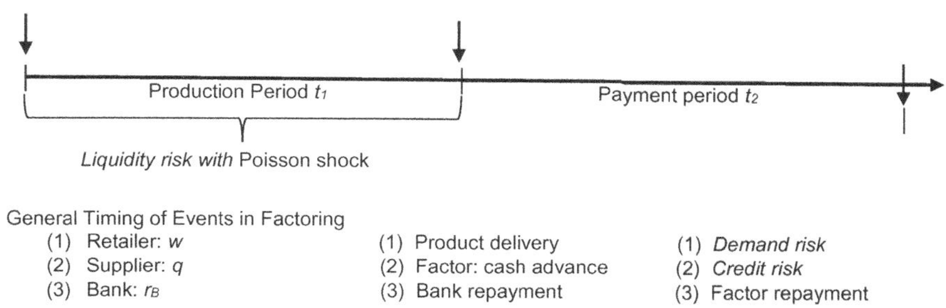

Fig. 10.6 Timing of events regarding reverse factoring (*Source* Kouvelis & Xu [2021])

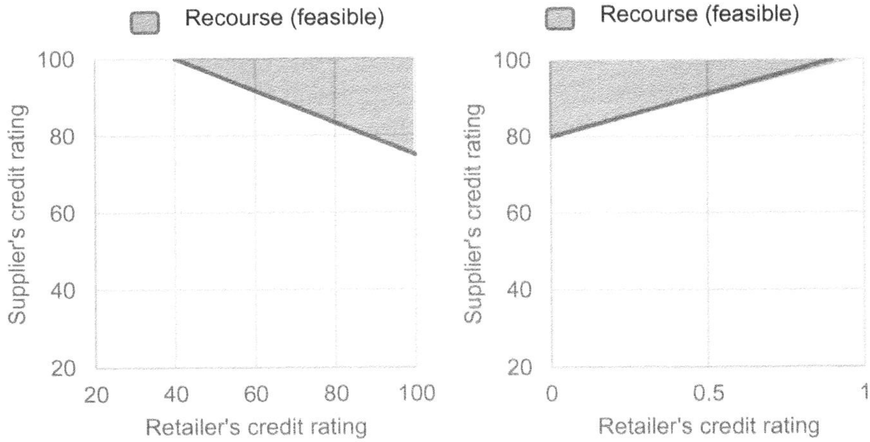

Fig. 10.7 Feasible region for recourse factoring (*Notes* Parameters: $p = 3$, $c = 1$, $t_1 = t_2$; left: $\lambda_s = 0.2$; right: $C_r = 80$ (*Source* Kouvelis & Xu [2021])

As the authors observe, two main differences stand out. First, L_F depends on the supplier's credit rating, whereas L_N is based on the retailer's credit rating. Such distinction is driven by the fact that the supplier (respectively, retailer) is obligated to the factor in recourse (respectively, non-recourse) factoring, leading to the different interest rate premiums charged by the factor. Second, there is also an implicit difference in the timing of the factor's interest collection. In recourse factoring, the supplier repays the interest (along with principle) at time t_c. However,

in non-recourse, the interest is charged at time t_1, and the value of L_N reflects such interest deduction.

Another central result is comparing recourse and non-recourse factoring when both are feasible. It turns out that the comparison is straightforward.

$$\underbrace{\Lambda_N(C_r) - \Lambda_F(C_s, C_r)}_{\text{value of non - recourse}} = \underbrace{\Lambda_F(C_r, C_r) - \Lambda_F(C_s, C_r)}_{\text{value of credit rating differential}} + \underbrace{\Lambda_N(C_r) - \Lambda_F(C_r, C_r)}_{\text{value of risk reallocation } >0}$$

The value of the credit rating differential is positive if the retailer's credit rating is higher than the supplier. The value of risk reallocation is always positive. It quantifies the benefit of transferring the demand risk inherent in accounts receivable from the supplier (in recourse) to the factor (in non-recourse) when both share the same credit rating. Thus, there is a tradeoff for the supplier. For those with reasonably high credit ratings, the value of the credit rating differential may be negative, dominating the positive value of risk reallocation and indicating that nonrecourse destroys value to the company. It should be noted that the retailer's preference over the two factoring schemes is aligned with the supplier's.

Finally, the authors analyze reverse factoring, also deemed approved payables finance. In that scheme, the buyer authorizes the invoice, and finance is raised separately against the accounts payable by the supplier from a financial institution. The bank relies on the buyer's creditworthiness without recourse to the supplier. Such programs are buyer-initiated and typically implemented with the help of web-based platforms. Reverse factoring has two main differences. First, after receiving the goods, the buyer approves the invoice, which allows the supplier to receive funds at a more favorable borrowing rate. Second, in return for offering the reverse factoring program, the buyer has an extension to the payment delay to the supplier. As the authors also note: it is often argued that the associated benefit of extended payment terms motivate large retailers to initiate the reverse factoring program.

The framework in the previous chapters can easily explain the rationale for reverse factoring programs. As we have noted before, SMEs would most likely be better served by improved planning of the financial cycle to avoid factoring, if possible. Still, even if factoring is more expensive, there are situations in which its availability matters significantly: sales volatility, asset-specific public procurement, and growth bottlenecks. Suppliers get access to finance, buyers get extended payment terms, and banks collect interest (see Sect. 6.4 for more on the subject).

References

Biais, B., & Gollier, C. (1997). Trade credit and credit rationing. *The Review of Financial Studies, 10*(4), 903–937.

Burkart, M., & Ellingsen, T. (2004). In-kind finance: A theory of trade credit. *American Economic Review, 94*(3), 569–590.

Fabbri, D., & Menichini, A. M. C. (2010). Trade credit, collateral liquidation, and borrowing constraints. *Journal of Financial Economics, 96*(3), 413–432.

Fabbri, D., & Klapper, L. F. (2016). Bargaining power and trade credit. *Journal of Corporate Finance, 41*, 66–80.

Fisman, R., & Love, I. (2003). Trade credit, financial intermediary development, and industry growth. *The Journal of Finance, 58*(1), 353–374.

Kouvelis, P., & Xu, F. (2021). A supply chain theory of factoring and reverse factoring. *Management Science, 67*(10), 6071–6088.

Kouvelis, P., & Zhao, W. (2012). Financing the newsvendor: Supplier vs. bank, and the structure of optimal trade credit contracts. *Operations research, 60*(3), 566–580.

Lariviere, M. A., & Porteus, E. L. (2001). Selling to the newsvendor: An analysis of price-only contracts. *Manufacturing & Service Operations Management, 3*(4), 293–305.

Marotta, G. (2005). When do trade credit discounts matter? Evidence from Italian firm-level data. *Applied Economics, 37*(4), 403–416.

Petersen, M. A., & Rajan, R. G. (1997). Trade credit: Theories and evidence. *The Review of Financial Studies, 10*(3), 661–691.

Wu, D., Zhang, B., & Baron, O. (2019). A trade credit model with asymmetric competing retailers. *Production and Operations Management, 28*(1), 206–231.

Yang, S. A., & Birge, J. R. (2018). Trade credit, risk sharing, and inventory financing portfolios. *Management Science, 64*(8), 3667–3689.

Index

R. Zeidan, *The General Model of Working Capital Management*, https://doi.org/10.1007/978-981-19-3334-9